Powell, Bacon and Hough

Formation of Coast Lines Limited

NICK ROBINS

MALCOLM McRONALD

The passenger steamer *Samuel Hough* (1905) operated by Samuel Hough Limited in collaboration with F H Powell & Company on the Liverpool to London service.

FOREWORD

Coast Lines was for a time one of the great success stories of British shipping. Focussing on the coastal liner trades, the group dominated its chosen sector of business more successfully than almost any other shipping company in the United Kingdom. Its portfolio of acquisitions spread tentacles around the country like an octopus. But it is also one of the great untold stories of the shipping industry. Accounts of its rise, and almost equally precipitate decline, have been at best superficial. For instance, one can search in vain for detailed histories of the pioneering nineteenth century operators of coastal liner services who combined to form Powell, Bacon and Hough Lines in 1917, and morphed into Coast Lines Ltd in 1919.

Coast Lines' story has long fascinated me, and many years ago I contributed one of the brief, superficial, published histories which I lamented earlier. It has also been a largely unfulfilled ambition of mine to chart the prehistory of the company, and especially the three players which came together in 1917. Although I amassed details of many of their ships, the idea of writing a history was abandoned on realising how little archival material had survived. So little regard did Coast Lines pay to its history that much historical documentation was allowed to rot away in damp warehouses.

But Nick Robins and his collaborators have proven their mettle in being able to reconstruct the prehistory of Coast Lines, and to compile a superb collection of photographs of the ships involved. This was apparent in Nick's book on constituent Tyne-Tees, and was again evident in his collaboration with Colin Tucker on M. Langlands and Sons. In choosing to work with Malcolm McRonald he has a partner who is an acknowledged expert on Irish Sea shipping and a meticulous ship historian.

The story of Coast Lines' major ancestors told in this book has three strands. Each of these has threads of its own, tying together Liverpool, Bristol and Wexford, amongst other ports whence came the various (and changing) partners. The two authors seem to have left few stones unturned, and indeed few stones undiscovered, in researching these stories. The variety of their sources is impressive, including as they do many regional and long-lost newspapers, together with more recent books plus technical and enthusiast journals. Alongside this has been painstaking work in the registration papers which are by far the best source for those wishing to uncover the histories of individual British ships.

'Powell, Bacon and Hough; Formation of Coast Lines Ltd' makes a significant contribution to our knowledge of an important, but often forgotten, sector of British shipping history. I can only look forward to the largely untold stories of other important coastal liner companies who eventually came under Coast Lines' control.

Roy Fenton, Wimbledon.

First published 2017 by
Bernard McCall, 400 Nore Road, Portishead, Bristol, BS20 8EZ, England.
Tel: +44 (0)1275 846178
email: bernard@coastalshipping.co.uk. website: www.coastalshipping.co.uk
ISBN 978-1-902953-81-6
Copyright © Nick Robins and Malcolm McRonald

Printed by   : Gomer Press, Llandysul Enterprise Park, Llandysul, Ceredigion, Wales, SA44 4JL
Telephone   : +44 (0) 1559 362371   Fax: +44 (0) 1559 363758
Email   : sales@gomer.co.uk   website: www.gomerprinting.co.uk

Front cover: *Masterful* (1905), from a contemporary promotional image captioned: 'S.S.MASTERFUL, one of Great Britain's largest coasting steamers belonging to the Powell Line, Liverpool.'

Back cover: Cover of a souvenir brochure sold to visitors to the Q Ship HMS *Suffolk Coast* during her post-war tour of Britain as a show ship.

CONTENTS

PREFACE

Powell, Bacon & Hough Lines was renamed Coast Lines Limited in 1917. Powell, Bacon & Hough Lines Limited was incorporated in 1913 from three separate threads that can be traced back to the early nineteenth century. However, unlike the history of Coast Lines Limited, this early history is largely unrecorded and relatively little known. It is nevertheless an exciting story of services slowly being developed from Liverpool, principally in the coastal liner trades to Bristol and London and the emigrant and livestock trade from Wexford to Liverpool.

The history includes the formation of three companies, F H Powell & Company, John Bacon Limited and Samuel Hough Limited, and their predecessors, along with the background and business prospects that promoted their inception. In the 1880s, Powell, Bacon and Hough companies started to collaborate and pool resources against an ever increasing threat of competition from the railways and other coastal shipping companies. That they should become one in 1913, as Powell, Bacon & Hough Lines Limited, under the charismatic manager Alfred H Read, was a logical development.

Unravelling the history of these ancestors of Coast Lines Limited has relied heavily on a number of data sources. These include shipping registers held by the Merseyside Maritime Museum, the National Archives and other local Record Offices, the Customs Bills of Entry for Liverpool and Bristol, held by the Merseyside Maritime Museum and the Bristol Record Office, British Newspaper Archive, Mercantile Navy List, and Lloyd's Register.

The authors are indebted to David Whiteside for sourcing a number of photographic images for the book. These have come both from his own collection and from that of the World Ship Society Photo Archive, for which David is curator. Help in identifying sources of data and in finding images has come from a variety of individuals, and everybody that has helped, including the many museum and archive staff who have helped with searches, are thanked gratefully. As usual we are indebted to Bernard McCall and his staff for producing yet another beautifully presented book.

Nick Robins, Crowmarsh, and Malcolm McRonald, Heswall.
(December 2016)

OTHER TITLES BY NICK ROBINS

TYNE TEES SHIPPING COMPANY AND ITS ASSOCIATES
BIRDS OF THE SEA - 150 YEARS OF THE GENERAL STEAM NAVIGATION COMPANY
COAST LINES KEY ANCESTORS - M LANGLANDS & SONS
MANCHESTER LINERS - AN EXTRAORDINARY STORY
PASSENGER TUGS AND TENDERS
THE SHIPS THAT CAME TO MANCHESTER

All available from www.coastalshipping.co.uk

Chapter 1

THE FOUNDATIONS OF COAST LINES

The merger of F H Powell & Company, John Bacon Limited and Samuel Hough Limited to form Powell, Bacon & Hough Lines Limited took place on 1 October 1913. John Bacon Limited had already become a subsidiary of F H Powell & Company in 1912 and the three Liverpool-based companies had collaborated over services and operations for some years prior to that. The new merged company was a logical pooling of resources and saving on over-capacity that was driven by ever-increasing pressure on freight tariffs from the railways. The new company was taken over by the Royal Mail Group (Elder Dempster & Company) in April 1917 and was rebranded as Coast Lines Limited on 7 June 1917. It had already traded under the banner 'The Coast Line' during the Great War.

The story of how Coast Lines Limited became the greatest British coastal shipping enterprise under its charismatic chairman Sir Alfred H Read is well known. His tussle with parent Royal Mail Group to separate it financially, as Royal Mail began to founder under its disgraced leader Lord Kylsant in 1931, is also widely understood. But best remembered are the ships of the Coast Lines' empire, especially the engines-aft motor ships with up to twelve passenger berths, such as the iconic pair *British Coast* and *Atlantic Coast* and the later *Ocean Coast* and *Pacific Coast* all dating from the 1930s. Others will remember the magnificent cross-channel passenger motor ships *Irish Coast* and *Scottish Coast* which were built in the 1950s.

The *Scottish Coast* (1957) about to lock in at Liverpool – a magnificent ship that perhaps should never have been ordered.
[Nick Robins]

In hindsight the **Scottish Coast**, magnificent though she was, had been ordered on the basis of a flimsy business plan, emergency relief duties and a barely profitable summer service between Glasgow and Dublin, by an incoming Chairman determined to have his way.

By the late 1950s the company was at its zenith. In 1960 George Chandler wrote in his book *Liverpool Shipping*:

> The principal shipping line operating on the oldest of the sea routes from Liverpool – the coastal – is Coast Lines Limited, stated to be, with its associates, the world's largest coastal shipping line, with a fleet in 1958 of 173 steamers, totalling 114,737 tons, excluding five vessels totalling 5,373 tons under construction. Coast Lines carries close on a million passengers and transports over half a million head of cattle each year to various parts of the United Kingdom…

> Founded in 1917, the history of Coast Lines spans the third of three natural periods into which the history of Liverpool's coastal shipping may be divided. From 1207 to 1830, Liverpool's coastal trade was conducted in the main by individual ships which were sponsored by an individual or by a number of individuals in association, each of whom took a share. From 1830 to 1917, Liverpool's coastal shipping to English ports was organized into several main lines, which absorbed many of their rivals, but managed to maintain their own existence. From 1917, when a number of lines fused themselves into Coast Lines, Liverpool's coastal shipping and, indeed, that of many ports in the United Kingdom, has been increasingly dominated by Coast Lines, which has taken over a considerable number of hitherto independent shipping lines.

The year 1917 was indeed a very significant year for Liverpool, despite the ongoing Great War. The fiftieth anniversary of the Mersey Docks and Harbour Board in 1907 had been celebrated by the building of a new head office at Pier Head. In 1911, the Royal Liver Insurance Company had moved into its impressive Royal Liver Building, and finally the Cunard Steamship Company occupied its new headquarters building in 1917 – collectively changing the face of the Liverpool waterfront in a statement that said to the world 'Look at us, isn't Liverpool doing well!'. All three companies were world leaders in their respective fields. It is against this background of success and celebration that Coast Lines Limited set out on its iconic journey, under the Managing Directorship of Alfred H Read, towards becoming the premier shipowner in the British domestic coastal shipping trades.

The story of Coast Lines Limited goes back far beyond its incorporation in 1917. However, unlike the history of Coast Lines Limited itself, the prehistory is largely unrecorded and is relatively little known. It is nevertheless an exciting story of services being developed from Liverpool, principally in the coastal liner trades to Bristol and London and the emigrant and livestock trade from Wexford. The history goes back to the formation of three companies, F H Powell & Company, John Bacon Limited and Samuel Hough Limited, and beyond to their predecessors and the background and business prospects that promoted their creation; all this in the nineteenth century, some of it in the early nineteenth century.

The story starts very much in the sailing ship era before the steam engine had achieved economic parity with sail. However, the steamship soon began to acquire year-round reliability so that it could maintain schedules even in the winter months, reliability against which the traditional sailing ships could no longer compete. Throughout the evolution of all three strands of what one day would lead to Coast Lines Limited are colourful and dedicated seafarers, and clear-headed managers who were determined to see their businesses thrive, particularly against the increasing threat of competition from the railways on the core Bristol and London routes.

The Powell Line's wharf at Bristol in the 1900s.

Of the three constituent companies, F H Powell & Company essentially traded from Liverpool to Bristol, and to London via south coast ports. John Bacon Limited traded from Liverpool and Preston to the Bristol Channel and to Wexford, and Samuel Hough Limited from Liverpool to London via south coast ports. Each company also had other interests: Powell, for example, had colliers dedicated to supplying the crack transatlantic liners lying in the Mersey with quality high calorific Welsh coal for their bunkers, as well as deep sea tramp ships. Hough also had tramp ship interests and Bacon developed trade to and from the near continent. The steamer *Augusta* was, in 1862, the first ship to carry the famous black funnel and white chevron adopted by the Powell ships and later, of course, by its successors, Powell, Bacon & Hough Lines Limited and Coast Lines Limited. The *Amelia* had the black funnel but no chevron.

F H Powell & Company was a partnership whose members and their shares varied periodically. The actual ownership of the vessels was complicated. In accordance with normal practice, the ships were registered in the names of the individual shareholders, not all of whom were involved with the operation of the ship. The shareholders varied between different ships, with a holding of four shares being the norm for the small shareholders, with frequent transactions and changes. The names of many of the small shareholders appear repeatedly for different ships, suggesting that the partners had a pool of willing investors, some of whom were clearly family members. The shipping registers, including Lloyd's, usually recorded ownership under the name of the managing owner, who was at various times John Swainston (died 1837), George Cram, Frederick H Powell (died 8 October 1874), John Ellis (a partner in the firm, but also one of F H Powell's executors), Colonel Alfred Read and his son Alfred H. Read. From the 1890s, there was a close association with Samuel Hough and his successors, with some of F H Powell's ships being partly owned by Samuel Hough Limited.

John Bacon Limited can be traced back to John Edward Redmond, of Wexford, who entered the Wexford-Liverpool trade in 1837. John Redmond was a Wexford banker, who later became the Member of Parliament for Wexford from 1859 until his death in 1865. At Liverpool, John Redmond's first agent was Thomas Richards. At a date between 1837 and 1839, Thomas Richards was replaced by Thomas McTear, who had been the agent for the 'opposition' ship *Antelope*, and was also the agent for the Cork Steam Ship Company. It seems possible that the change of agency occurred at the same time as the withdrawal of *Antelope*. Thomas McTear went out of business in June 1846, and was replaced as agent by William Fitzsimons and William Daunt Applebee, who traded as Fitzsimons & Applebee (Thomas McTear's agency for the Cork Steam Ship Company passed at the same time to W. Wilson & Son). William Fitzsimons had been trading as an agent for sailing ships operating between Wexford and Liverpool since before 1830. William Applebee had been John Redmond's agent at Bristol. In late 1850, the partnership's name was changed to Fitzsimons, Applebee & Company, implying the admission of at least one more partner. Although this is speculative, it may well be that this was the occasion when John Bacon was admitted to the partnership.

The partnership was renamed John Bacon & Company in 1860, implying that Messrs. Fitzsimons and Applebee had withdrawn from the business. In his early years in charge, John Bacon himself held only a minority of the shares in his ships, although later, he was often the sole owner of them. After the death of John Bacon in 1886, all his ships were registered in the name of his executor, Joseph Wright, who continued to operate the fleet for the beneficiaries. During this period, Joseph Wright took delivery of new ships, which were also registered in his name as executor. In 1889/90, the entire fleet was transferred to a limited company, John Bacon Limited.

The *Sir Walter Bacon* (1913), was built to the order of John Bacon Limited, but within months of being commissioned was renamed *Gloucester Coast* when Powell, Bacon & Hough Lines Limited took over ownership. She is seen in the experimental funnel colours of that company.

The founders of the group of owners leading to Samuel Hough's ownership were Thomas McClune and Frederick Augustus Tamplin, who traded under the name McClune & Tamplin. They became the Liverpool agents for the British & Irish Steam Packet Company (B&I) when it started a Liverpool to Waterford service during the period of great competition on the Irish Sea in 1850-1851. Following the agreement of 1851, which ended the era of competition, B&I extended its existing Dublin to London service back to Liverpool, and McClune & Tamplin were appointed agents for the service at Liverpool.

McClune & Tamplin began its own service on the Liverpool to London route in 1856 when B&I withdrew from the Liverpool to Dublin section of its service to London. In due course one of the partners' names came to the fore following the death of the older partners – this was Samuel Hough. It was under Hough's name that the Liverpool to London interests were developed.

The hazards of the coastal trades, not least the occurrence of fog or high winds, caused many an accident. The congested channel approaches to Liverpool and London and the shallow bar at Wexford also placed ships at risk. A large percentage of the ships in the early days of trading were lost by foundering after a collision or were wrecked on a windward shore. As time went on the safety records of the three companies improved, while aids to navigation also became more reliable. When the three companies merged in 1913, the next five years were committed to dealing with the additional hazards of the Great War. Despite all this, incidents of loss of life were few, with both passengers and crews telling stories of survival against seemingly hopeless odds.

An advertising image of the *Powerful* (1903) on the Liverpool to London passenger service, issued by F H Powell & Company.

Despite all the difficulties of coastal navigation, the passenger ship to London was timed to arrive alongside within a window from 15 minutes early to 15 minutes late. It was just not allowed to arrive outside that scale, as 20 minutes or 30 minutes was unacceptable. Clearly life could be quite stressful for the masters of these ships who were compelled to arrive on time, yet equally driven to navigate their ships safely in all weathers. It is these pressures that account for so many of John Bacon's ships stranding on Wexford Bar, their masters and pilots impatient to await the tide, and collisions and sinkings in the Mersey and elsewhere during periods of poor visibility.

The *Faithful* (1900), seen as the *Kyle Bute* sometime after 1934. She was renamed *Thoughtful* in 1906, and *Suffolk Coast* in 1908, and was sold for further service in 1911.

All three companies, F H Powell & Company, John Bacon Limited and Samuel Hough Limited, relied on tramping to bolster their earnings, especially the coal trade from South Wales. Each had ships designed for their core services as well as larger colliers which could be employed gainfully carrying bulk cargoes. Each at times tried to develop new services, notably to the continent, and each of the companies, to some extent or another, competed for the trade on offer. Nevertheless, there was dialogue between the management of the three companies and rate wars were never allowed to develop between, for example, the Powell interests and the Hough interests on the Liverpool to London route.

The coastal liner companies did compete aggressively with the railways for trade. As such they played a vital part in reducing the railway monopoly and maintaining sensible tariffs. All three enterprises, Powell, Bacon and Hough, assumed their part in this economic maintenance, taking the higher value, lower volume, goods for their customers on a reliable and scheduled service to their destination port ready for collection. A door-to-door service was yet a concept for the future.

The three companies traded independently until the early 1880s when collaboration first began. In 1879, Powell and Hough operated the weekly service between Liverpool and London on alternate weeks and advertised the route jointly, initially with Powell's steamer *Truthful* working with the *Mary Hough.* The so-called Great Victorian Depression then persuaded the Powell and Bacon interests also to share the trade on offer rather than compete. Collaboration developed over the next twenty years to a degree that a merger of the three companies was almost inevitable. Nobody in the shipping industry was surprised when the proposed new company was finally announced in 1913.

The *Sir Roger Bacon* (1912) was almost immediately subsumed into the merged fleet and later renamed *Pembroke Coast*; the ship was sold in 1933 to Wexford Steamships Company Limited and renamed *Wexfordian*, as seen here leaving Birkenhead.

The *Welsh Coast* (1915) was built for Powell, Bacon & Hough Lines Limited, and survived under various owners until scrapped in 1957.

The *Suffolk Coast* (1917) was the last ship to be ordered by Powell, Bacon & Hough Lines. She was requisitioned in 1918 for use as a camouflaged Q Ship but was never used in anger. She is seen here in peacetime in the Mersey.

The champion of the newly formed Powell, Bacon & Hough Lines Limited was the Managing Director of F H Powell & Company, Alfred H Read. The early years of the new company saw Read battling with the issues of running a shipping company during wartime, while licences were needed to build new ships after 1917 that would replace those lost to enemy action. He was able to take the company into the ownership of Elder Dempster & Company after the Great War and tap the resources of its parent, the Royal Mail Group, to expand his coastal liner services rapidly through acquisition of existing companies (Chapter 14). In 1919 Coast Lines Limited, as it had become, was also able to purchase two standard wartime coasters, the **British Coast** and **Western Coast**, to make up for war losses and complete them to its own requirements. Before long, Coast Lines Limited would become the dominant player in the British coastal liner trades.

The *Western Coast* (1919) was one of a series of wartime standard ships sold before completion after the Great War. *Western Coast* and sister ship *British Coast* were the first ships commissioned by the newly formed Coast Lines Limited.

Coast Lines Limited, along with its various associate companies, was the only independent operator of Irish Sea 'cross channel' passenger ferries. As such it was an important moderator for the railway-owned ferries, providing competition to what otherwise would have been a railway monopoly in the trade, as was the case in the English Channel. In time Coast Lines Limited became the only operator of the coastal liner services, although after World War II only the Liverpool to London route carried passengers as well as cargo, and then only in ships with up to twelve berths available in twin cabins.

The *Southern Coast* (1911), seen at Liverpool, carried on the traditional passenger service between Liverpool and London alone after the Great War. She was replaced by motor ships with just twelve berths in 1936.

Association with the Royal Mail Group and its Belfast shipyard Harland & Wolff inevitably led to early development of motor ships. The engines were built at Belfast under licence from Burmeister & Wain of Copenhagen, and the first of a group of thirteen similar motor ferries, the **Ulster Monarch**, was commissioned in 1929. The last ship of the series was the **Scottish Coast**, which took up service in 1957.

The company's cargo ships continued to serve the trades developed by Messrs Powell, Bacon & Hough Lines Limited. As additional companies were bought into the group, their steamers were allocated to the most suitable trade and did not necessarily stay on their former owner's routes. Some companies were allowed to retain their separate identity, B & I, Belfast Steamship Company and the merged fleets of the Laird and Burns interests, Burns & Laird Lines Limited, while others such as M Langlands & Sons disappeared rapidly into the overall corporate scheme. Ships could transfer between associate companies several times; management guidance advised that a ship not working profitably for more than three months must be submitted for re-allocation for more gainful employment within the group. It was this flexibility, coupled with the size of the overall company, that enabled Coast Lines Limited to stay abreast, if not slightly ahead, of the railway-owned fleets. A third key factor was the superb management skills of Sir Alfred H Read, a man said to know all his staff by name, quite a feat when his fleet numbered over 100 ships in the 1950s.

Sir Alfred Read, company manager and later chairman, was held in high esteem, not only by his peers but also by Government. For example, in 1927 a House of Commons Committee invited the London, Midland & Scottish and the London & North Eastern railways jointly with Coast Lines Limited to 'devise some scheme for the transport service to the West Highlands of Scotland to be taken over by one or other of these companies'. The existing provider, David MacBrayne Limited, had become grossly undercapitalised, effectively bankrupt, such that it could no longer afford to bid for the various mail contracts it had previously so cherished, let alone consider upgrading its ailing fleet of steamships. In 1928 a scheme presented jointly by Alfred Read and Sir Josiah Stamp of the London, Midland & Scottish Railway was accepted, and Read became manager of the newly formed and jointly owned David MacBrayne (1928) Limited.

The end of the Coast Lines dynasty came about through its reluctance to embrace the roll-on roll-off revolution. Too little too late, the new Liverpool to Belfast ferries, **Ulster Queen** and **Ulster Prince**, were obsolescent on delivery with low headroom garage decks that could not accommodate modern lorries. Coast Lines eventually disappeared into the P&O Group in 1971 with a history of trading going back to 1829 when Swainston & Cram began as partners.

The roll-on roll-off ferry Ulster Prince (1967) arriving at Liverpool in July 1968.   *[Nick Robins]*

Alfred Henry Read 1871-1955

Alfred Henry Read was born at 10 Georges Road, West Derby, Liverpool, on 18 July 1871, the eldest son of Colonel Alfred Read and Emily Blanche Read. Alfred's grandfather died at sea as told by Robert Sinclair in his history of the Belfast Steamship Company:

> Alfred H Read's grandfather, also named Alfred Read, was a master mariner, and died, it is said, of fever on a voyage taking stores to the armies at the Crimean War. He was buried at Genoa. Behind him he left one son, again Alfred, and a widow, Mary, whose maiden name was Davey. Now Mary had a nephew, William Davey, who became a partner of Sir Alfred Jones of the Elder Dempster Line. He had achieved this status by 1879, eleven years after the foundation of the firm, and later became sole partner after the death of Sir Alfred Jones. It was William Davey who introduced his orphaned cousin to the firm of F H Powell & Company in 1869.
>
> Young Alfred Read had business experience in London and was listed at first in the Liverpool directories as an accountant. He is then shown as a cashier with Messrs F H Powell but by 1881 was described as a shipowner, indicating that by then he had become a partner. He married and had two sons and two daughters. The eldest son was Alfred Henry Read…

Michael S Moss, in his biography of Alfred H Read wrote:

> He was educated at Liverpool College, and then in Switzerland and Paris, before being apprenticed to the Glasgow-based Anchor Line with services on the North Atlantic and to India. In 1893 at the age of twenty-two he joined the family firm, which then owned four small steamers. He gradually persuaded his partners to acquire more ships and Powell owned nine by the turn of the century. Read began to give all the ships names ending in 'Coast', and like other owners transferred some to single-ship companies to spread his risk.
>
> From the beginning of his career Read was keenly concerned to improve accommodation for crews on his ships, and also to ensure that new recruits were well trained, playing an active role in the management of the Lancashire and National Sea Training Home. He was twice married, first to Jean Charlotte (d. 1919), daughter of Hugh Frederick Macneal, on 11 April 1918, then on 25 September 1920 to Elena, daughter of Henry Fisher and widow of Charles Vincent.
>
> By the turn of the century Alfred Read was a prominent shipowner in Liverpool, and was elected to the Mersey Docks and Harbour Board, on which he served until 1920, and he was chairman of the Liverpool Steam Ship Owners' Association in 1912…
>
> Freight rates rose during the First World War, and the coastal trades experienced serious competition from the railway companies, whose rates were kept artificially low by the government. Because most coasters were too small to be requisitioned for military service, coastal shipping was not controlled until 1917, when Read was appointed Director of Home Trade Services at the Ministry of Shipping. His contribution to the organisation of coastal services during the unrestricted U-boat campaign and his commitment to training young seafarers were recognised with a knighthood in 1919.
>
> Powell, Bacon and Hough Lines was sold in 1917 to the fast-expanding Royal Mail group of Sir Owen Cosby Philipps… to form Coast Lines Ltd, with Read as managing director… By the late 1920s it was the largest coastal shipping company in the United Kingdom, and although part of the Royal Mail group it was effectively controlled by Read. An autocratic figure, he directed the greatly expanded group with paternalistic despotism, frequently visiting offices 'without warning to the staff [to see] how the work was being done'
> (*The Times*, 10 March 1955)…
>
> When the Royal Mail group collapsed in 1930, he quickly took action to save Coast Lines by taking independent advice from the distinguished accountant Sir John Mann. The complexity of restructuring the group made a Stock Market floatation impossible until 1934, and then only by the government of the Republic of Ireland agreeing to purchase all the Irish business [an agreement that was not carried through at that time]. Read was managing director of the new firm until 1946, and finally retired as chairman in 1950. He also served as a member of the Port of London Authority from 1934 to 1941. He was a founder member of the Institute of Transport in 1919, acting as vice-president (1927–30) and president (1936–7).
>
> Widely regarded as the doyen of coastal shipping, Read was a private man and typical of the new generation of managers who characterised British trade and industry in the first half of the twentieth century. One of his interests was hunting, and he served as joint master of the Avon Vale foxhounds in the West Country. Sir Alfred died on 8 March 1955 at the British Hospital, Lisbon, Portugal. He was survived by his second wife.

Chapter 2

JOHN SWAINSTON, GEORGE AND HENRY CRAM, GEORGE SMITH AND FREDERICK POWEL

Swainston & Cram 1829 - 1837
Swainston, Cram & Company 1837 - 1837
Cram & Smith 1837 - 1840
Cram, Smith & Company 1840 - 1848
Cram & Company 1848 - 1851
Cram, Powell & Company 1851 - 1859
F H Powell & Company 1859 - 1913

Britain emerged from the industrial revolution in the 1820s with a rapidly growing need for commerce and trade. There were no public railways and roads were poor and treacherous. Industrial wages were low as workers left the land to seek new prospects in the steam-driven factories. Trade with Europe was difficult, with France recovering from its political revolution, but there was an increasing appetite for domestic trade, not least from Liverpool with its burgeoning industrial hinterland.

The main west coast ports were Bristol and Liverpool. Liverpool had finally shaken off its privateering that continued throughout the Napoleonic Wars. With the advent of steam-driven industry, the port was set to grow as George Chandler described in his book *Liverpool Shipping*:

> From 1813, when the East India Company's monopoly of trade was abolished, until 1857, imports of cotton into Liverpool increased five times, while imports of sugar and West Indian rum went up fifty per cent during the same period. The greatest increase was in the import of wheat from North America, as the railway opened up the western parts of the United States and Canada. Wheat imports increased tenfold from 1813 to 1857. Salt exports from Liverpool increased three times.

Competition for trade between Liverpool and Bristol had been going on since the early eighteenth century and Liverpool was the clear winner. Nevertheless Bristol remained a vibrant and important port with a hinterland that included much of the industrial English Midlands as well as the all-important link with London.

Given the development of trade in the first half of the nineteenth century, it is not surprising that a number of new shipping enterprises should develop and succeed on the coastal domestic routes. Trade initially depended on sailing ships; fast sailing ships connected Liverpool with Glasgow twice a week, there were regular sailings to ports in North Wales and there were sailing ships that ran down to London on a disorderly and haphazard schedule. Many of the ships were owned by their master with other family members investing in a one ship business through the 64th share system. There was little co-operation between masters, so that three ships might sail for London one week and none for the next two weeks. There were, however, a number of routes that were poorly covered, and that between Liverpool and Bristol was one that would certainly welcome newcomers to the trade.

The sail-assisted wooden-hulled paddle steamer was developing fast. However, the hulls were small and consequently the engines were of limited weight and thus too weak for steamers to venture out to sea year-round. Most of the paddle steamers hibernated for the winter. This would soon change, but for the moment the sailing smacks, brigantines and schooners were firmly in charge of the coastal domestic trades.

Of the three companies that eventually came together to form Coast Lines, the Powell interests in shipowning were the oldest. They can be traced back to a partnership between John Swainston and George Cram, of Liverpool, who were in business together as shipping agents in Liverpool. Swainston & Cram had regular arrivals from London and Yarmouth; also Newcastle and Fowey. Some Bristol merchants, including William Scott, James Leau & Francis Fisher, established the Bristol and Liverpool Smack Company in 1826 to start a regular service between the two ports. Swainston and Cram were appointed as their Liverpool agents. The new company took delivery of two sailing sloops, the *Arrow* in November 1826 and the *Dart* in the following month. Both immediately entered service to Liverpool, with their first arrivals in Liverpool respectively on 8 and 30 December 1826. Initially sailings were at roughly four-weekly intervals.

The new service was clearly successful and, in December 1828, Swainston & Cram bought two further ships for the service, so becoming more than just agents. The two ships were the *Hope* and the *Swift*, which until then had been operated between Glasgow and Liverpool by the Clyde and Liverpool Shipping Company. They were re-registered at Liverpool, but the ownership of both was shared between Liverpool and Bristol interests. Messrs Swainston & Cram retained 16/64 shares of the *Hope* and only 8/64 shares of the *Swift*. The smack *Hope* had been built at Bridport in 1822 for the Clyde and Liverpool Shipping Company and was 65 feet long by 20 feet breadth with a depth of 11 feet. The sloop-rigged *Swift* came from the same builders and was originally a smack but was re-rigged in 1825. The main role was to develop the cargo service between Liverpool and Bristol by having a fleet of sailing ships such that a regular schedule could be advertised for the new service. The two ships were gainfully employed in the Liverpool and Bristol trade.

In June 1829, the same group of owners bought the *Arrow* and the *Dart* from the Bristol and Liverpool Smack Company. The four ships together were the very seed of what eventually would become Coast Lines Limited. In 1830, *Arrow* arrived at Liverpool from Bristol eight times between 18 January and 3 November; the *Dart* nine times, the first on 8 February, the last on 28 December, while the arrival on 9 August was via Newport; the *Hope*, nine arrivals plus one from Swansea; and the *Swift* ten times. It would seem that the wooden-hulled paddle steamer *Lee*, of Liverpool, operated by the Saint George Steam Packet Company, was making inroads into the Bristol traffic as she managed up to four round trips a month in the calmer part of the year and either one or two round trips in the worst weather of the winter.

One of the Bristol owners, Frederick Beeston, had earlier commissioned the brigantine *Herefordshire* in 1824, a ship that became associated with the Bristol and Liverpool route of Swainston & Cram and was eventually bought for the core service. The Bristol base was tucked away up the Redcliff Back but was suited to the trade as it was near the city centre.

In 1831, Swainston & Cram bought their next ship. This was the schooner *Carlisle* which they bought from William Dowson and others of Carlisle, for whom she had been built in 1824. They were quickly able to sell 56/64th of the share capital of the ship so that they could invest in a further purchase the following year. This was the *Lady Peel*, a schooner-rigged ship of similar dimensions to the earlier vessels, and completed in 1827 for Sir Robert Harvey of Thorpe in Norfolk. Again Swainston & Cram were able to sell shares in their new ship with each partner retaining eight shares.

Sadly on 10 October 1832, only a few months after she had joined the Liverpool to Bristol service, the *Lady Peel* was wrecked. She ran aground in thick fog on Flat Holm in the Bristol Channel on a voyage south to Bristol. By the end of the month it was reported that she was a total wreck with parts and cargo washing ashore. Early the following year Swainston & Cram were able to replace her with the schooner-rigged *Adonis* which was built in 1832 at Neyland for owners at Milford. A sixth ship, the brigantine *Confidence*, joined the fleet in 1833 when she was purchased from John Gibbs of Plymouth, for whom she had been built in 1827. Again Swainston & Cram retained 16 shares in the ship and sold the other 48. The *Confidence* was an altogether more substantial vessel than her predecessors being some 71 feet long by 20 feet breadth. A similar brigantine, the *Ann*, was also purchased in 1833, an older ship dating from 1815 when she had been completed for owners in North Wales. Swainston & Cram retained 18 shares in her, presumably reflecting improvements in their bank balances as well as reluctance on the part of others to invest in such an old ship. In 1833, they also bought the smack *Greyhound*, dating from 1820, and retained 16 shares in her.

The nine ship fleet not only maintained the core weekly Liverpool to Bristol service but was also able to satisfy occasional demand for shipments north to Cumbria and intermediate calls also to North and South Wales. The next purchase by Swainston & Cram was a rather more substantial vessel, the *Manchester*, which had been completed in 1826 for owners in Liverpool. Bought in 1834, she was retained by the partners on a 24/64th basis with the remaining 40 shares sold mainly to merchants in Bristol. On 21 November 1835 the *Carlisle* was wrecked near Parton, Whitehaven on a passage from Liverpool; her crew was saved. Next to join the fleet was the *Jane* in 1835, then a five year old brig, followed in 1837 by the seven year old schooner *Arethusa*.

John Swainston died in 1837 and George Cram, as executor, became the majority owner of the previously jointly owned ships and managing company. The company was then redesignated Cram & Smith and later Cram, Smith & Company. George Adam Cole Smith was a wealthy businessman who dealt in a variety of broking and agenting activities. At the end of February 1848 the title changed to Cram & Company. George Cram had obviously become a wealthy man at this stage in his life as he is recorded in 1845 as the tenant at Harbreck House, a property within the Leyland family estate at Fazakerley. He eventually moved to Chester (in 1851) to pursue his interest in shipbuilding.

The *Adonis* sailed from Newport on 9 March 1838 on a northbound voyage and was later reported missing, her fate unknown. Less than a year later, the *Confidence* went missing after she sailed from Bristol on 4 January 1839; one of her lifeboats was washed ashore on the Pembrokeshire coast 41 days later. George Cram also bought a half share in the 75 feet long brigantine *Pearl*, built at Yarmouth in 1826. Ownership passed to Cram, Smith & Company in 1841. On 7 November 1842 the sloop *Arrow* was wrecked near Cemlyn Bay on a voyage from Bristol to Liverpool; all the crew survived. Two weeks later it was recorded that 'The *Arrow*, ashore near Cemlyn, has gone to pieces'.

The *Swift*, sloop-rigged, was run down and sunk by an unidentified steamer on 13 February 1841 off the Skerries, Anglesey. She had been on passage from Bristol to Liverpool. Her crew was picked up by the *Rival*, of Keswick, and landed at Liverpool.

A trading brigantine off the River Avon.

[from an oil painting by Joseph Walter dated 1838]

It was announced in a notice in the *London Gazette* that George Adam Coles Smith had been declared insolvent and that he would appear before the judge on 8 December 1848 to secure the confiscation of his effects:

> George Adam Coles Smith, formerly residing in Breck Road, Everton, and carrying on business in South Castle Street, both in Liverpool, Lancashire, in co-partnership with George Cram and Henry Cram as Ship-Brokers and Commission Agents under the firm of Cram, Smith & Company, afterwards residing in Pleasant Street, Kirkdale, Liverpool, aforesaid, a part of the time carrying on business with James Brough Pow, as Ship-Brokers and Commission Agents, under the firm of Smith, Pow & Company, afterward occupying an office in Strand Street, Liverpool, aforesaid, Ship-Broker and Commission Agent on his separate account under the firm of George Smith & Company, and later a lodger in Rodney Street, Toxteth Park, Liverpool, aforesaid Ship-Broker.

It is likely that Smith had fallen foul of the ship broker's nightmare, having bought a ship for onward sale when no purchaser was forthcoming. The consequence of his bankruptcy was that Cram, Smith & Company became just Cram & Company in late December 1848.

The schooner-rigged sailing ship *Hope* was lost on 26 December 1848. The *Hope* (Captain Softley) was on passage from Liverpool to Bristol, but collided with the *Eugenia*, which had sailed from Liverpool for Mobile on 21 December. The collision occurred about 30 miles off Holyhead. The *Hope* sank but her crew were saved and taken aboard the *Eugenia*.

The first appearance of Frederick H Powell's name in the Liverpool Register was on 28 October 1833 when he bought 2/64th shares in *Confidence*. Later he also bought a few shares in *Manchester, Ann, Greyhound, Jane, Swift, Hope, Arethusa* and *Pearl*. In 1839 the brigantine *Monkton* was purchased by Frederick Powell from Canadian owners shortly after she had been completed at St John, New Brunswick. In 1841, Frederick Powell bought a half share in the schooner *Latimer*, completed only two years earlier at Holyhead for local owners. Then, on 2 January 1847, Liverpool ship builder John Dawson & Company launched the 68 feet long wooden schooner *Ann Powell* for Frederick Powell (40 shares) and others. She was named after Frederick Powell's wife. The last sailing ship was Ferdinand Beeston's *Herefordshire* which had been re-rigged as a schooner when she was lengthened in 1831. She was bought in 1852 by Cram, Powell & Company.

But just how had the outsider Frederick Powell managed to muscle in to the established Cram & Company so that it was rebranded Cram, Powell & Company in 1851? Dr Ernest Reader, then Public Relations Officer for Coast Lines, explained in an article in *Sea Breezes*, February 1949 (although his reported dates are woefully incorrect, the gist of the merger is seemingly correct):

> …Mr Frederick Hillman Powell, a Bristol merchant who shipped general cargo from that port to Liverpool, became financially interested in the company [Cram & Company], and with the Swainson [sic] interest dropping out of the partnership adopted the name Cram, Powell & Company. When Mr Powell joined the line he brought to it a considerable tonnage from his previous interest, including the brig *Locomotive* (Capt. Softley) originally built to convey railway engines and material to the River Plate…

Frederick Powell was indeed a respected merchant in Bristol. He not only shipped goods to Liverpool, but he also shipped goods to any port, near or far, that inducement allowed. He had close links with industry in the Midlands bringing goods to Bristol for export, rather than letting them go through Liverpool. Frederick Powell also owned several ships on general trading duties as well as the *Locomotive*, the brigantine *Queen of Avon*, and the barques *Chrystaline* and *Eliza Ann*, for example, were all engaged on foreign trade. The *Eliza Ann* had been built at St John, New Brunswick, and Powell had acted as broker for her purchase in Liverpool in 1857, retaining half the shares in her. The merging of the Cram and Powell interests was, therefore, seemingly in the best interests of both partners as it enabled Cram to widen his trading horizons and Powell to focus on the Bristol and Liverpool link. Nevertheless, the foreign trade and foreign-going ships were kept largely separate from the Bristol to Liverpool interests, almost to the extent that they were two separate companies [note that the foreign-going ships are not listed in the Fleet List, Appendix 1, as they have little bearing on the development of the coastal trades].

Cram, Powell & Company was now a substantial shipowner. Normally the company owned only a portion of a ship (often 16 or 24 shares out of 64). Other part-owners were regular investors, with the same names appearing against various different ships. However, a noticeable feature was that the ships operating regularly on the Liverpool to Bristol service had several Bristol residents among their shareholders. Such names included Ferdinand Beeston, Thomas Bryant Pollard and Richard Rowe (trading as Pollard & Company), Henry Taylor, John Burge Plummer, Thomas Etheridge, William Townley, Michael Hinton Castle, Henry Taylor and John Middleton Halsall (trading as Taylor & Halsall), Samuel Brown, Robert Leonard, Thomas Drake, the elder, Thomas Drake, the younger and John Drake (trading as Thomas Drake & Sons), Danvers Hill Ward, Henry Pritchard, and Charles Olive, Henry Olive and Thomas Gadd Matthews (trading as Olive and Matthews). Ships which were employed predominantly in other trades lacked these Bristol shareholders, and had a much greater proportion of Liverpool shareholders.

The new partnership lost the brigantine *Jane* on 31 July 1851 when she was abandoned off the Skerries after striking rocks. She was on a passage from Bristol to Liverpool; all the crew survived. Other ships were sold, the *Monkton* in 1845, the *Ann* in 1847, and the *Arethusa* in 1853.

Frederick Powell brought with him an appetite for the steamship. He recognised the regularity of schedules that could be achieved if the company began to invest in steamships, while keeping some of its sailing ships on the Bristol to Liverpool route as support. In 1852 an order was placed with George Cram, now of Chester and a shipbuilder, for an iron-hulled sail-assisted screw steamer. She was launched into the Dee on Saturday 19 March 1853 and christened *Amelia* after a family friend, Amelia Cornish, who lived in the south of England, and could not be present at the launch. Like other steamships built by Cram, she was towed round to the Mersey where her engine was installed. She was a small ship, just 146 feet long with a breadth of 21 feet and of 300 tons gross. The *Amelia* was registered at Liverpool and required a crew of 15 men; her master was Captain Atkin. The *Chester Chronicle*, Saturday 19 March 1852, noted:

> First iron ship launch at Chester: At 25 minutes past one, the stays being all unloosed, Miss Elsee, niece of Mr Cram, who was standing on the platform under the vessel, hurled a decanter of wine at the bow and named her *Amelia*. She immediately glided down the incline gradually and majestically into the waters of the Dee, amidst the plaudits of the crowd, her temporary crew, and the firing of a canon… The impetus with which the *Amelia* moved off the stays carried her to a greater distance in the river than the ropes from her to the shore would allow. The ropes broke, and immediately she made use for the first time of one of her nautical appliances – the anchor. Another rope was shortly attached to her, the anchor was raised and she soon afterwards hove to at the Quay… She is of 350 tons

burthen, will be rigged out in Chester, whence she will proceed to Liverpool where she will receive her engines, and make ready for her first voyage. She is intended to ply between Liverpool and Bristol…

In 1851, George Cram had sold some of his interests in shipowning leaving Henry Cram in charge of his investment at Cram Powell & Company. He and Thomas Cram bought into the Sandycroft shipbuilding yard near Hawarden on the Dee and eventually George became its owner in 1853. However, he immediately got into financial difficulties and in August 1854 his creditors began legal proceeding to take possession of all his business and personal assets. They included his bankers, Williams & Company of Chester; John Williams and Sir Stephen Glynne owners of the land, Septimus Ledward, iron merchant, and Roberts Roberts of Chester, slate merchant. The shipbuilding company was repossessed by the bank and George Cram was declared bankrupt. The trading name Cram & Company was retained for ship broking and agenting at Liverpool.

The *Amelia* was clearly a success, as a similar slightly beamier vessel was commissioned by associates Rowe & Powell of Bristol in 1855. This was the *Athlete*, built at Bristol and registered there. She carried a crew of 17 men. While the *Amelia* stayed on Bristol duties the new *Athlete* was used on a new Liverpool to London service, although London sailings were discontinued briefly at the start of the following year. During 1855 the *Amelia* is recorded as arriving at Liverpool from Bristol 41 times, normally on a weekly round trip. The *Athlete* did seven Bristol trips.

The *Amelia* was wrecked in the morning of 29 March 1857 when she ran ashore in fog in calm weather at the extreme tip of St Govan's Head, Pembrokeshire. All passengers and crew were saved. The *Amelia* was on a passage from Bristol north to Liverpool. The *Morning Post*, Saturday 4 April 1857, recorded:

> A serious loss has been sustained in the wreck of the *Amelia*, iron screw steamer, plying between Bristol and Liverpool, which struck on the point of land jutting out to the north of St Govan's Head whilst on a voyage to the latter port. She was laden with a general, but valuable, cargo, and with her crew of 16 men and 19 passengers had on board 35 individuals. The crew immediately took to the boats and landed the passengers in safety – the steamer filling so rapidly that in a short time she went down, and in close proximity to the cliffs, her masts being visible above the water. The cause of this disaster seems to lie in the fact that the *Amelia* hugged the land too closely in rounding the high promontory known as St Govan's Head to the north east of which she now lies.

Later that same year Charles Castle and Frederick Powell of Bristol took delivery of the *Augusta*, also built and registered locally. She was slightly smaller than the *Athlete*. The *Augusta* completed her maiden voyage to Liverpool in November and assumed the duties of the *Athlete* on the Liverpool to London service. This allowed the *Athlete* to move to the Liverpool to Bristol route, although the following year the *Athlete* is noted running to London more than to Bristol.

The success of the steamships is reflected in the sale of three of the sailing ships in 1856: the *Pearl*, *Greyhound* and *Dart*. The *Dart* went on to have a very long subsequent career until she was wrecked on 16 September 1907. The schooner *Herefordshire*, Captain Hutchinson, on passage Liverpool to Bristol, became a total wreck at Cemlyn after running ashore on 25 October 1858. The crew were safely landed and then helped to bring materials ashore.

Henry Cram remained with the business until 1859. George Cram had by then withdrawn all his money from the partnership and Cram, Powell & Company inevitably fell to the majority ownership of Frederick H Powell as reported in the *London Gazette*, dated 1 July 1859:

> Take notice, that the partnership heretofore between us and the undersigned, Henry Cram and Frederick Hillman Powell, carrying on business of Ship-Brokers, at Liverpool in the County of Lancaster, under the style of firm of Cram, Powell, and Company, was this day dissolved by mutual consent; and that all debts owing from or to the said concern will be paid and received by the said Frederick Hillman Powell, who will occupy the offices in South John Street, lately occupied by the said firm. Witness our hands this 30th day of June, 1859: Henry Cram, Frederick H Powell.

But for the dream of George Cram to become a major innovative shipbuilder, albeit one without an engine building capacity, Powell may never have become a major shipowner, but so it was. It was not long before Cram, Powell & Company was rebranded F H Powell & Company, and a new era began.

Chapter 3

F H POWELL & COMPANY – 1859 TO 1885

When Henry Cram left Cram, Powell & Company in 1859, the ships engaged on the domestic routes comprised the steamers *Athlete* and *Augusta* while the sailing ships *Manchester* and *Ann Powell* worked elsewhere. Had it not been for the bankruptcy of George Smith in 1848 and George Cram some eight years later, the ascendency of Frederick Powell would not have been so rapid. As it was, Powell became head of the company which now bore his name rather than the name of Smith or Cram.

The newly formed F H Powell & Company, maintained its core Liverpool to Bristol service, and its newly developed secondary Liverpool to London service, with the two steamers. The *Manchester* was not used on the domestic trades after September 1857 and was sold during 1859. The *Athlete* was used exclusively on the Bristol service and inaugurated the regular sailings from Liverpool on Tuesdays and back from Bristol on Saturdays. The *Augusta* worked on the London service in 1859, although the *Augusta* was retrenched to the Bristol service in February 1860 replacing the *Athlete* which was employed elsewhere later in the year. Roles were reversed in 1861 when the *Augusta* took up nomadic duties to a range of ports while the *Athlete* remained on Liverpool to Bristol duties.

Captain Laver, master of the *Athlete*, had an excellent reputation as described by Ernest Reader:

> The ship was very popular with merchants, and so great was their confidence in Capt. Laver that they did not insure their cargoes sent by her. This fine old seaman retained command of his ship until 1875, when he retired after 30 years service with the company. During half that period he had been in command of the *Athlete* and his many hundreds of voyages between Liverpool and Bristol were entirely without accident of any kind.

The *Ann Powell*, under the command of Captain Hughes, was lost on 14 February 1861, at about 8 am, when she was wrecked on the Scarweathers in the Bristol Channel. All her crew were taken off by the *Peri* and landed at Neath. The *Ann Powell* had been on passage from Liverpool bound for Bristol. The storms that weekend created havoc in Kingstown Harbour and numerous vessels were wrecked or foundered both in the Irish and North seas and along the south coast. F H Powell & Company was now the owner of steamships only.

The great storm of February 1861 – devastation in Kingstown Harbour.

[Illustrated London News]

The trading name Cram & Company was retained in parallel with F H Powell & Company. Cram & Company/F H Powell & Company acted as agents and ship brokers at Liverpool looking after timber imports from northern Europe and hosting Frederick Powell's overseas traders, as excerpts from the 1860 Liverpool Customs Bills of Entry and Liverpool Dock Registers illustrate:

LIVERPOOL – F H POWELL & COMPANY:

Athlete Arrived from Bristol Jan 3, 10, 18, 27; Feb 4, 11, 22; Mar 13, 19, 27; Apr 3, 10, 16, 17, 23; May 1, 8, 16, 22, 30; Jun 7.

Emerald (187 tons, of Liverpool). Arrived from Bristol Mar 10.

Augusta Arrived from Bristol June 26; July 4, 11, 17, 23, 31; Aug 7, 14, 22, 28; Sept 4, 10, 18, 24; Oct 1, 9, 17, 27; Nov 1, 8, 15, 22, 29; Dec 6, 13, 20, 28.

Augusta Arrived from London Jan 10; Feb 16.

Cleator Arrived from London Jan 21.

William France Arrived from London Apr 16.

William France Cleared to Constantinople (in ballast) June 9.

Madge Wildfire (sailing vessel) Arrived from London Jun 12.

Empire (409 tons, of London, 20 men). Arrived from London July 4.

Flying Eagle (409 tons, of London, 17 men). Arrived from London Aug 6.

Cleator Arrived from London Jan 21.

Crystaline Cleared to Rio de Janeiro Feb 3.

Ann Powell Cleared to Galway Feb 22.

Locomotive Cleared to Marseilles Feb 28.

Eliza Ann Cleared to Demerara Apr 5.

Edmiston Cleared to Danzig Aug 14.

Edith Cleared to Dordt Aug 15.

Confidence Cleared to Dordt Sep 27.

LIVERPOOL – CRAM & COMPANY (Clarence Dock):

Cleator (290 tons) Arrived from London Jan 21. Departed to Cardiff.

De Brus (177 tons) arrived from London Mar 29. To Canada Dock.

William France Arrived from London Dec 10.

In 1861, the London to Liverpool route was reinstated when the *Augusta* commenced on the service. The new company spent its first two years consolidating what trade it had before it sought more new tonnage. In 1862, it bought the six year old iron screw steamer *William France* of 379 tons gross. The registered owners were Frederick Powell and six others, but her tenure under Powell's management was short. The *William France* started a new service from Liverpool to Dunkirk in October 1862. However, on 5 December 1862, she collided about five miles off the Nore with the French steamer *Albert*, of Dunkirk, after which the *William France* sank quickly. Her crew was able to get safely aboard the *Albert* which put back to Gravesend for repairs. The *William France* had been on passage from Liverpool to London and all that could be seen at the point where she sank was the top of her masts. Some of her rigging and spars and a small quantity of the cargo were later recovered.

The *William France* was replaced in the following year by the purchase of the larger iron screw steamer *Marley Hill*, which had been built in 1854 for the General Iron Screw Collier Company of London. The *Marley Hill* ran alongside the *Augusta* from October 1863 onwards, so that a weekly departure could be scheduled from both Liverpool and London. Intermediate calls were made on some trips at Plymouth and Southampton. In October 1863 the *Clyde* was bought from the Carron Company; she dated from 1851 and was a similar sized vessel to the *Marley Hill*. The *Clyde* had three masts with a tall funnel abaft the mainmast and a fiddle bow. The *Clyde* and her sister the *Carron* introduced steam on the Carron Company's London to Grangemouth service; while the *Carron* was lost in 1859 the *Clyde* had become too small and too slow for the Carron Company but was ideally suited to Powell's mode of business.

In 1864, another ship was bought from the General Iron Screw Collier Company of London. This was the *Northumberland*, built in 1853 by Palmer Brothers at Jarrow. She had a gross tonnage of 363. Both the *Marley Hill* and the *Northumberland* were employed for a time importing Welsh coal to the Mersey for bunkers for the *Great Eastern* and the crack Cunard Line ships.

On 25 June 1865, the *Clyde* went ashore while entering Dunkirk on a voyage from Liverpool. Captain Murphy failed to make the entrance into the harbour and the ship went onto the beach. The *Clyde* sustained damage to her bowsprit and much of the forepart of the vessel but she was successfully towed off the shore and into the dock by a tug. The master stated that she did not make any water.

Excerpts from the 1865 Liverpool Customs Bills of Entry illustrate the services that were operated that year:

> *Athlete* Cleared to Bristol Jan 3; May 16, 23, 30; Jun 6, 13, 27; Jul 4, 11, 18, 25; Aug 1, 29; Sept 5, 12, 19, 26; Oct 10, 17; Nov 1, 7, 14, 21, 28; Dec 12, 19, 26.
> *Augusta* Cleared to London Jan 2; Feb 14; Apr 1, 27; May 13; Jun 1, 21; Jul 6, 22; Aug 14, 26; Sep 16, 30; Oct 25; Nov 16; Dec 5, 22.
> *Augusta* Cleared to Bristol Jan 24; Feb 22. (Also shown Oct 24, but corrected to London on Oct 25.)
> *Clyde* Cleared to London Jan 16; May 27.
> *Clyde* Cleared to Bristol Feb 7, 14, 22, 28; Mar 14, 21, 28; Apr 4, 11, 18; May 2, 9.
> *Clyde* Cleared to Dunkirk July 17.
> *Marley Hill* Cleared to London Feb 9, 25; Mar 24; Apr 13; May 1; Jun 10, 29; Jul 15; Aug 3, 25; Sep 9, 28; Oct 13; Nov 4; Dec 8, 29.
> *Northumberland* Cleared to Bristol Jan 11; Mar 13, 29; May 6; Oct 27; Nov 9; Dec 2.
> *Northumberland* Cleared to London Jan 30; Apr 20.
> *Northumberland* Arrived from London Feb 15; May 3, 25.
> *Northumberland* No consignee. Arrived from Cardiff (coal) Jan 2, 26; Mar 8, 25; Apr 11; Oct 23; Nov 4, 18.
> *Crystalline* Cleared to Galveston Dec 5.
> *Locomotive* Cleared to Lagos Dec 6.
> *Oscar* (197 tons) Cleared to Bristol Aug 8, 15.
> *Oscar* Arrived from Bristol Aug 21.
> *Oscar* Cleared to Honfleur Nov 23.
> *Blanche* (174 tons) Cleared to Nantes via Ardrossan Oct 17.

The first purpose-built steamship to be ordered by F H Powell & Company was the *Mersey*. She was built by T R Oswald's Pallion Shipyard in 1867. The *Mersey* was a large ship of 608 tons gross, with a length of 199 feet 6 inches and a breadth of 27 feet 5 inches. The *Clyde* was sold to T R Oswald in 1867 for further service, seemingly as a trade-in for the newly-built *Mersey*. The *Clyde* later foundered off Jutland, Denmark, in January 1870.

In April 1868, F H Powell & Company bought the four year old steamer *Edith Owen* from Ford & Company in London. She was a smaller ship than the *Mersey* of 497 tons gross but nevertheless a valuable addition to the fleet which now numbered six ships. Both the new ships offered some passenger accommodation when they were employed on the Liverpool to London service. Later, in October 1868, the second purpose-built ship was delivered. This was the *Sheldrake*, a product of Gourlay Brothers & Company at Dundee, with a gross tonnage of 482. In 1871 the *Sheldrake*'s machinery was compounded. The *Mersey* received new compound engines in 1873.

In 1868, Mr Ferdinand Honey was recruited to the company and Colonel Alfred Read joined in 1869. Read was initially employed as cashier but by 1881 had become a partner in F H Powell & Company. His son, Alfred Henry Read, also joined the company and was made a partner in 1893. All three men were to have a significant impact on the progress of F H Powell & Company. The important post of accounts manager was occupied in the 1860s by Mr John Ellis.

The biggest ship in the fleet to date was built by Dobie & Company at Govan and launched into the Clyde on 2 August 1871 after being christened *Faithful*. She is of note for three reasons: firstly she inaugurated the nomenclature ending in *–ful*, secondly she exceeded the size of any ship previously owned by F H Powell & Company and thirdly she was specifically built to carry passengers in greater numbers and greater comfort than before, with berths for up to 60 first class passengers. She was 230 feet long by 28 feet 8 inches breadth and was of 816 tons gross. She was equipped with a compound engine built by Rankin & Blackmore of Greenock and by all accounts was a very fine ship. She was an attractive looking vessel with a whaleback poop and a well deck forward. She took her maiden voyage in October 1871 from Liverpool to London via Plymouth with departures thereafter at two to three week intervals, with some sailings to Dunkirk. The *Athlete* alone remained on the weekly Liverpool to Bristol route while the other ships ran to London and Dunkirk with occasional voyages elsewhere.

The *Faithful* had a long and profitable career. Although she only served in the Powell fleet for her first 19 years, she then started a new life in the Mediterranean working out of Alicante, firstly as *Africa*, then as *Sitges Hermanos* and she later became *Torreblanca* of Barcelona. She ended her days under the Turkish flag and was finally sold for demolition in 1933 – at the venerable age of 62. The iron hull undoubtedly enabled her longevity. The newly introduced mild steel hulls did not last as long due to impurities which encouraged corrosion, that is until the Bessemer Process was introduced, so improving the quality of the metal and its corrosion resistance.

The attractive looking *Faithful* (1871), seen as *Torreblanca* when she was owned by Linea de Vapores Tintoré, Barcelona.

The *Marley Hill* was lost on 1 January 1874. She was attempting to enter Whitehaven Harbour in a storm when she ran onto the beach, and was later declared a constructive total loss. She had left Liverpool at 10.00 in fine weather, but by 17.00 a gale had blown up from the west-south-west. At 20.15, Whitehaven Pier lights were seen close ahead while the sea was running high. When 50 yards from the North Pier, the master ordered the helm to port to enter the harbour, the distance between the two piers being something less than 200 yards. At that point, a heavy sea struck the steamer on her starboard bow, a strong gust of wind caught her at the same time; both prevented the helm from having any effect, and she was driven onto the beach. The press reported in the shipping columns on 2 January:

> Whitehaven, January 2: The *Marley Hill* in entering the harbour last night during a squall, missed the entrance and went ashore north of the harbour; crew saved.

The *Northumberland* was sold in 1874. After more than 20 years' further service as a steamship her machinery was removed in 1895 and she was used as a dumb barge. She lasted until 1917 when she grounded and later sank, at the age of 64.

The next ship to join the fleet was the former collier *Swan*, dating from 1867. She was bought in 1874, re-engined in 1875 and served the company until the turn of the century. The magnificent cargo steamer *Truthful* came next. She was built by the Barrow Shipbuilding Company and launched on 6 November 1877.

Her first master was Captain S Maddix and she was placed on the London service alongside the *Faithful*, despite having less passenger accommodation. She was a single deck iron-hulled steamer with four water-tight and fireproof bulkheads. She was of 956 tons gross and the poop was 53 feet long, the forecastle 42 feet long and the bridge deck was 60 feet long. Her compound engine had two inverted cylinders of 33 & 63 inches diameter and the stroke was 36 inches. The *West Briton and Cornwall Advertiser*, 12 November 1877, noted her launch:

> There was launched from the works of the Barrow Shipbuilding Company, on the 6th inst., a screw steamer named the *Truthful*. She is 240 feet long with a breadth of 30 feet, while the hold is 16 feet deep. The vessel, which will be propelled by engines of 150 horsepower, is intended to run between Liverpool and London, via Southampton. She has been built to the order of F H Powell & Company of Liverpool.

Frederick Powell died on 8 October 1874 at his home in Blundellsands, Great Crosby. F H Powell & Company carried on as before from its headquarters at 4 Water Street in Liverpool. Frederick Powell's shares in the ships he had part-owned were transferred to his executors to John Ellis and Thomas Wills Allen (roughly two thirds and one third respectively).

In 1876, the steamer *Athlete* was sold for further service and one year later the *Augusta* was also sold. These two stalwarts had served the company extremely well and had enabled the regular services to Bristol and to London, via south coast ports, to become established. However, with both the *Faithful* and the *Truthful* in service the original pair was thoroughly outclassed, both in capacity and in speed.

The iron-hulled cargo steamer *Hispania*, built for Mories, Munro & Company of Glasgow in 1870, was acquired in 1878. She was a valuable addition to the fleet with a gross tonnage of 420 tons. Two years later the larger steamer *Asia*, also originally built for Mories, Munro, but in 1872, was purchased. She was a substantial ship of 640 tons gross, and was 211 feet long by 25 feet breadth with a depth of 16 feet. The passenger cargo steamer *Elaine* joined the fleet the following year. She was of 544 tons gross, having been lengthened in 1871. She was unique in the fleet in that her machinery and boilers were placed aft.

The Liverpool and Dunkirk service was discontinued at the end of 1877. From 1878 it was taken up by the Cork Steamship Company Limited, which had been formed in 1872, following the split in 1871 of the Cork Steamship Company between its Irish Sea and its Continental services. The Cork Steamship Company Limited was taken over in 1920 by Amalgamated Industrials Limited, which became bankrupt in 1922. The ships and services of the Cork Steamship Company Limited were then bought by a consortium formed by the port agents to the company and rebranded as the British & Continental Steamship Company Limited, based in Liverpool.

The *Edith Owen* had quite a few mishaps. When coming up the Avon on the morning of 24 February 1876, late on the tide, she ran ashore above Horse Shoe Point, but came off on the evening's tide and proceeded to Bristol. She was undamaged. On 6 January 1878, she left Bristol in the morning for Liverpool but in passing down the Avon ran into the rocks at Chapel Pill, damaging some of her plates, and returned to the Cumberland Basin. Then, on 28 May 1878, she ran into *Hopper Barge No. 4* in the Mersey – the hopper was holed in her bow and had to be beached. On 27 June 1878, the *Edith Owen* stranded between tides at Avonmouth. She left dock at Liverpool bound for Bristol in the late morning of 21 November 1878, when she was in collision with the steamers *Mullingar* and *Colleen Bawn*. Three of the crew of the *Edith Owen* jumped for safety onto the deck of the *Colleen Bawn* and were taken to Drogheda. The *Edith Owen* was cut down to the water level and, as her fore compartment was flooding, she returned to dock.

The *Edith Owen* finally came to grief on 27 January 1879, when she ran onto the Coal Rock, the Skerries, off Anglesey. She was on passage from Bristol to Liverpool when she stranded in wind conditions north east, in calm conditions. She was carrying general cargo and passengers, all five of whom were landed safely at Cemaes, while the crew was taken to Liverpool. The following day the ship was on her beam ends and mastless with the fore part under water and the stern clear of the water.

Only one ship was bought in the 1880s, reflecting a serious downturn in business that occurred in the late Victorian period. This was the large passenger cargo steamer *Ethel Caine*, which was acquired in 1881 and renamed *Cheerful* two years later. Progress was set back that year when the *Asia*, Captain Stone, was posted missing after leaving Middlesbrough on 5 March with a cargo of pig iron destined for Liverpool. The builder's plate, which was 1 feet six inches long by 8 inches wide, was found later the same day, 4 miles north of Whitby.

At 22.30 hours on 1 February 1885, the *Cheerful*, Captain Stevens, lost her propeller off Anvil Point on passage from London to Plymouth. The *City of Hamburg*, belonging to Palgrave, Murphy & Company of Dublin, managed to get a hawser across to the *Cheerful* at 24.00 hours, but it parted at 06.00 the next morning. The *City of Dublin*, which had been on passage from Rotterdam to Dublin, lay by the stricken ship until dawn in the hope of getting another line across to resume the tow. In the attempt to get the line across, the *City of Dublin* was driven by a squall athwart the bow of the *Cheerful* and had her side cut from the deck to the water level abaft the main rigging. Water started to pour into the after hold so she was obliged to leave the *Cheerful* and make for Portland Roads, where she anchored at 21.00. The *Cheerful* was finally taken in tow at a point between the Shambles and Portland Bill by the tug *Queen* which, after several partings of the leading line in the terrific seas, succeeded in placing a tow rope aboard, and thus pulling her bows around and away from the shore. The tug *Commodore* afterwards assisted in towing the vessel to safety in Portland Harbour The Liverpool tug *Knight of St. John* was later dispatched to collect the *Cheerful* and bring her back to the Mersey for repairs.

Worse was to follow later in the year when the *Cheerful* was sunk on 21 July 1885 just after 4 am about 15 miles south west of the Longships, Cornwall, following a collision with the ironclad torpedo ship HMS *Hecla* in thick fog. The *Cheerful* left Falmouth the previous evening destined for Liverpool and had taken on board two tons of tin at Falmouth and already had a large manifest of general cargo from London. The *Cheerful* sank in just four minutes giving passengers and crew little time to evacuate the ship. Of the contemporary press reports, that in the *Glasgow Herald* for 23 July 1885 is succinct:

> The *Cheerful* at 4 o'clock was steering north-north-east while the torpedo ship was heading west-south-west. They were consequently approaching each other in a direct line, when at five minutes past four the lookout aboard the *Hecla* sighted the *Cheerful* in the fog some 400 to 500 yards distant. The *Hecla* at the time was going at nine knots, and whilst her engines were immediately reversed and put hard astern, her helm was starboarded to give the *Cheerful* a wider berth. Those on board the latter vessel appeared to sight the *Hecla* at about the same time, and ported the helm. The result of these movements was to change the relative positions of the two vessels to one of right angles, the *Cheerful* coming across the bows of the *Hecla*, which ran into her midships, striking her on the port side. Had both vessels ported or starboarded the probability is that the disaster would have been averted.

The *Evening Post* of 30 October 1885 included the following narrative by passenger Herbert White of Widnes:

> On the night of the collision there were four of us in a state room – myself, poor Mr Bernard and two others. We were all asleep but were wakened by a terrific shock. My berth was next a port-hole, and I could see the big ship outside. I ran on deck in my night-dress straight away, and I saw the *Hecla*'s bows right over us. I could have got on the *Hecla*'s deck if I had liked. I ran back into the state-room and got my two companions, and while they were turning out I slipped into my trousers. It was all the work of a moment as it were. I got Mr Bernard on deck but before we had time to make up our minds what to do the *Cheerful* went down. A large wave washed me off the deck and as I was going into the sea, one of my braces caught in the sails of the *Cheerful* and broke, else I would have gone down. I was whirled away and my brace was left behind. I was sucked into the vortex caused by the sinking ship. Luckily there were a lot of empty barrels underneath the hatches, but some of them got loose, and as I was coming up to the top of the water one of them came against me, and brought me up with it…
>
> The three gentlemen in the state-room were all drowned. There were three ladies besides the stewardess on board, and the shrieking of the passengers was something dreadful… The first mate of the *Cheerful*, assisted by one of the passengers, did all in his power to launch one of the boats before the *Cheerful* went down, but they were unsuccessful through there not being enough time. The captain was one of the last to leave the steamer and he was picked up more dead than alive. It was fully an hour before he came round. The lady passenger who was saved owes her life to having wrapped her fur cloak around her, as, when she got into the water it spread out and kept her afloat…

Thirty-six of the passengers and crew aboard the *Cheerful* were rescued by boats from HMS *Hecla* and were taken to Plymouth. Nine passengers and crew went down with the ship, and two more died shortly after being picked up. Two acts of great bravery were that of Lieutenant Rich who jumped from the bows of HMS *Hecla* to save one man, and Seaman Walsh who did the same and saved two more. During the two hour long rescue the gash in the port bow of the *Hecla*, some 10 feet long above and below the water line, was choked with timber as best as possible, but despite these efforts the fore compartment became flooded. At the subsequent inquiry into the collision neither ship's master was held to blame for the accident.

Chapter 4

F H POWELL & COMPANY – DEPRESSION & EXPANSION

The late Victorian era was a quiet period for F H Powell & Company, as it was for all traders during the Great Victorian Depression. Following the loss of the *Cheerful* in 1885, the fleet comprised just four ships: the *Elaine*, *Hispania*, *Swan*, and the passenger cargo steamer *Faithful*. The *Cheerful* was not replaced.

Fares on the London service were 25/- single, 40/- return, and meals were charged at 2/- for breakfast, 2/6d for lunch and 2/- for high tea.

Liverpool Customs Bills of Entry for 1890 illustrate the pattern of sailings, although the dates given may be the date the entry was made rather than the date of arrival. They show that *Elaine* was the mainstay on the Bristol service and the *Faithful* and *Swan* generally worked the South Coast and London service:

Elaine Bristol Jan 3, 7, 16, 23, 30; Feb 6, 12, 20, 27; Mar 6, 13, 29; Apr 10, 17, 24; May 1, 8, 13, 22, 29; Jun 5, 12, 19, 25; Jul 3, 8, 17, 22, 31; Aug 12, 21, 28; Sep 1, 11, 16, 25; Oct 2, 15, 22, 30; Nov 6, 13, 20, 26; Dec 4, 9, 16, 24, 31.
Elaine (Agent J T Fletcher & Co.) Havre Oct 7.
Faithful Falmouth etc. Jan 7, 16, 31; Feb 12, 27; Mar 13; Apr 3, 17; May 1, 22; June 5, 19; Jul 3, 17, 31; Aug 14, 28; Sep 11, 25; Oct 9, 23; Nov 6, 20; Dec 4, 22.
Hispania London Feb 6; Apr 12; May 18 (Falmouth etc.); Sep 25; Oct 9.
Hispania Bristol Apr 1; Aug 6.
Hispania Glasgow Apr 18.
Swan Arrived from London Jan 7; Sept 25.
Swan Calais Jan 20.
Swan Arrived from Bristol Apr 3.
Swan Plymouth Apr 3.
Swan London Apr 24; May 8, 22; June 5, 19; Jul 3, 17, 31; Aug 14, 28; Sep 11, Oct 23; Nov 6, 20; Dec 4, 18.
Edith Hough (Agent F H Powell & Co.) London etc. Jan 3, 21.

The use of Samuel Hough's steamer *Edith Hough* on the London service in January 1890 is evidence of a developing liaison between F H Powell & Company and Samuel Hough (Chapter 12). From December 1892, for example, Powell and Hough combined their weekly calls at Southampton into a joint consolidated service. Colonel Alfred Read also developed close links with the Cork Steamship Company and its various services to the Low Countries from Liverpool and other west coast and Irish ports. For a time F H Powell & Company acted as Liverpool agent for some of this company's services.

Transshipment was an important component of the coasting trades and regular coastal liner services were preferred for this work over the coastal tramp steamers. F H Powell & Company fostered close links with the liner companies working out of Liverpool, to service their needs for transshipment of part cargoes to Bristol, the south of England and in particular to London. The same trade was developed with London-based companies and the ships often carried fruit and vegetables brought from the Mediterranean to London as well as a wide variety of other imports destined ultimately for the north west of England.

Probably the most important transshipment customer was Elder Dempster & Company of Liverpool. An important agreement was made with Elder Dempster regarding transshipment of imports from West Africa; key imports included various vegetable oils in barrels, notably palm oil, and timber, particularly the tropical hardwood mahogany. Mahogany was shipped in long stands, much as it was felled, ready to be cut and planed at sawmills in Britain. Most of the timber was distributed to sawmills in Lancashire but a great deal of it needed to be transshipped south to the London port catchment area. F H Powell & Company became the preferred contractor for this work and as a consequence ships acquired by and built for the company tended to have one extra-long hatch to accommodate the logs below deck while logs were also stowed as deck cargo in steamers with shorter length hatches.

Powell continued to acquire second-hand tonnage rather than build anew, but the next ship to join the fleet was rather special. This was the Union Steamship Company's steamer *African*. Not only was she equipped with a modern and efficient triple expansion steam engine which drove her at 12 knots, but she also had a steel hull and berths for 112 passengers. F H Powell & Company took possession of the ship in 1893 and renamed her *Graceful*.

The *Graceful* (1886) joined the Powell fleet in 1893, when she was acquired from the Union Steamship Company. She is seen here on the Thames.

[National Maritime Museum]

Another image of the *Graceful* (1886), seen at Bristol and looking exceedingly graceful.

[World Ship Society Photo Archive]

She was a large steamer some 244 feet long by 33 feet breadth and measured 1,372 tons gross. The passenger accommodation was divided into two classes and both offered attractive and comfortable dining saloons and public day rooms. The *African* had been built in 1886 by Raylton Dixon & Company at Middlesbrough for the Union Steamship Company's South African coastal trade. She had a shallow draft in order to negotiate the sand bars at Port Elizabeth and East London, which remained dangerous before dredging operations were undertaken and protective moles constructed. She was an ideal purchase with which to develop the London passenger and cargo service. The *Graceful* replaced the *Hispania*, which was then sold for further service to owners in Newcastle. The *Western Daily Press*, 25 November 1893, reported on the new steamer:

> The vessel originally cost £40,000, was until lately employed by the Union Company in the Cape coasting trade, but, the company having built a larger steamer, the *African* was sold to F H Powell & Co. through Messrs H E Moss & Co., shipbrokers of Liverpool and London. The vessel is in all respects a first class cargo and passenger boat, her appliances for loading and discharging being of the most modern descriptions, while the first and second class cabin accommodation will be superior to most of the existing coasting lines. The deadweight cargo capacity amounts to 1,300 tons, and after some slight alterations she will travel at the rate of 12 knots. As a comfortable passenger steamer, the *African* has already earned a high reputation, and there is excellent accommodation for over 100 first class passengers. The vessel will be completely overhauled and fitted with the electric light prior to sailing on December 3, and she will then be commanded by Captain Smith, RNR, formerly of the steamer *Faithful* belonging to the same owners. The *African* will run between Liverpool, London and intermediate ports in connection with the line conducted by Messrs F H Powell & Co. and Mr Samuel Hough. The Bristol agent of this company is Mr Martin P Rowe.

Also in 1893, Alfred Read's son Alfred Henry Read was appointed a partner in F H Powell & Company. He had joined the company after serving a business apprenticeship in the offices of the Anchor Line. A notice in the *Cheshire Observer*, 2 March 1895, noted:

> A marriage has been arranged between Mr Alfred Henry Read, a partner in the firm of F H Powell & Co., Liverpool, and the eldest son of Lieutenant Colonel Read, of Derwent House, Stoneycroft, and of Kenwyn, Chester, and Miss Agnes Mary, the eldest daughter of Mr Gilbert Parry, of Farndon Hall, Farndon.

When the Manchester Ship Canal opened on 1 January 1894, Powell started to run the steamer *Swan* up to Manchester from London. Trade soon developed such that on one voyage she brought over 1,000 tons of goods up the Canal to Pomona No.1 Dock.

In May 1895, the passenger services between London and Liverpool were advertised in the press as follows:

> Delightful sea voyage by the well-known steamers *Graceful*, *Mary Hough*, *Melrose* and *Faithful*, calling at ports in the South of England, every Wednesday and Saturday, returning from London every Wednesday and Saturday. Fares including stewards fee, Saloon 23/-, return 40/-. For times of sailings and further information apply in Liverpool to F H Powell & Co., 23 Water Street, and Samuel Hough, 25 Water Street.

It was a further four years before any more ships were acquired. In January 1897, the eighteen year old cargo steamer *Mary Monica* was bought from James Carroll of Dublin. She was originally ordered from Murdoch & Murray at Port Glasgow by John G Smith of Ayr and was launched on 1 October 1879. Smith sold her in 1882 to James J Carroll with no change of name. On entering the Powell fleet, she was renamed *South Coast*, introducing for the first time the Coast nomenclature that would later be adopted by Powell, Bacon & Hough Lines Limited and later still by Coast Lines itself. The *South Coast* was specifically acquired to help develop trade out of Manchester to both London and intermediate ports, as well as to Bristol.

The next addition to the fleet reverted to the attractive –*ful* nomenclature when the *Hopeful* was bought from James Knott's Prince Line of Steamships in August 1897. She had traded for Knott as the *Belgian Prince*, and was the ship that had represented Knott at the opening of the Manchester Ship Canal in January 1894. The *Hopeful* was put on the Liverpool to London service where her luxurious passenger accommodation was much in demand.

Business was obviously on the upturn as suggested by a report in the *Bristol Mercury*, 30 December 1898:

> The [Bristol] Docks Committee has received from Messrs. F H Powell & Company, of Liverpool and this port, an application that the preferential use of a fixed shed berth be allotted to their vessels at the city quays. For very many years, and at present, Messrs Powell's weekly trader has been berthed at Mr M P Rowe's private wharf, near to the Radcliff Back ferry. The firm has recently replaced the ss *Elaine* by the ss *Faithful*, for which the wharf has not sufficient length…

A typical advertisement for the service, for example in the *Western Daily Press*, 8 November 1898, read:

> Powell line, Direct service between Bristol and Liverpool. The first class passenger steamer *Faithful*, Captain F Kolesar, (or other steamer), sails unless prevented by unforeseen circumstances, Bristol to Liverpool every Saturday, Liverpool to Bristol every Tuesday, single Saloon fare 10/-, Deck 6/-. From Bristol, Cumberland Basin, and Liverpool, Victoria Dock…

Meanwhile, the *Truthful* and *Annie Hough* served the Manchester to London route.

Also in 1898, another second-hand purchase was made when the cargo steamer *Morgan Richards* was bought. She was launched from Palmers Shipbuilding & Iron Company Limited's yard at Jarrow, on 12 May 1877, for Henry Morgan of Prestbury, Cheshire. In 1890 she was bought by R Nicholson & Sons and two years later equipped with new machinery by John Dickinson of Sunderland. The new engine was of the modern and efficient triple expansion steam type and sustained a service speed of 9½ knots. Powell & Company gave her the name *Truthful* and she was used on all routes as best needed. Another iron-hulled cargo steamer, the *Val de Travers*, was bought and given the name *West Coast*. She had been completed by D & W Henderson & Company Limited at Meadowside, Glasgow and was equipped with the then ubiquitous compound engine. She was launched on 25 December 1882 for David Slorach (A Slorach & Son) of Cork and christened *Kampokus*. She was sold two years later under mortgage by High Court Order to Charles H Sugrue, also of Cork, and resold in 1895 to John T Harrison of London and renamed *Val de Travers*. These two purchases allowed the old steamer *Swan* to be sold.

The final purchase of the decade was the iron-hulled cargo steamer *Azalea* which joined the Powell fleet in December 1899 without change of name. She was bought through Messrs Kellocks, shipbrokers. The *Azalea* got into trouble on 7 December 1899 on her first voyage for Powell which was from Rochester to Liverpool. At about 9 am she was in collision with the steamer *Federation*, of London, in dense fog about 4 miles south east of Owers Lightship. The *Azalea* came into Southampton at 16.30 hours with a bent stem but she was found not to be leaking. The *Federation* was also able to proceed on her voyage apparently undamaged.

During the year the *Faithful* (Chapter 3) was disposed of as being too small and uneconomical for passenger and cargo duties.

Competition on the Manchester-based services was fierce as both Samuel Hough and Fisher Renwick also served the same route from Manchester to London and profit margins were kept low. Sense prevailed and, by 1899, the Manchester to London service was being advertised as a joint service operated by F H Powell & Company and Samuel Hough Limited in competition with Fisher Renwick as, for example, in the *Manchester Courier* and *Lancashire Advertiser* on 2 December 1899:

> Manchester to London, Falmouth, Plymouth, Southampton and Portsmouth. Closing every Tuesday in Manchester, Friday in London. Steamships **Truthful** and **Anne Hough**, of F H Powell & Co. and Samuel Hough's Line. Loading Berths No. 4 Dock, Pomona and Wapping Basin, London.

Further consolidation of the links with Samuel Hough in 1899 was that the ownership of the *Azalea* was placed, on a 50: 50 basis, into the joint ownership of F H Powell & Company and Samuel Hough. The *Elaine* was sold in 1899 to Cuthbert Wilkinson of Sunderland, the same company that had bought the *Swan* a year earlier. Thus at the start of the new century the fleet stood at six ships: the passenger and cargo steamers **Graceful** and **Hopeful** and the cargo steamers **South Coast**, **Truthful**, **West Coast** and **Azalea**.

The twentieth century had a bad start when the cargo steamer *Azalea* went ground on 24 February 1900 on Crosby beach, Liverpool. She was starting out from Liverpool bound for Poole. Fortunately she was refloated later the same day, apparently undamaged. The *London Evening Standard*, 24 February 1900, reported tersely in the Shipping News column:

> Blundellsands, Feb. 24: *Azalea*, steamship of London, from Liverpool, for Poole, went ashore on Crosby Beach, but got off at 5.30 pm, and proceeded outward.

The *Faithful* (1900), seen as the *Thoughtful* after she had been renamed in 1906, waiting to lock in at Bristol.

The year 1900 was a year of a number of new acquisitions. The first purpose-built steamer to join the Powell fleet for some time was the *Faithful*. She was launched on 1 May by the Dundee Shipbuilders' Company Limited at Dundee. She had a triple expansion steam engine, built by Cooper & Greig of Dundee, which gave her a service speed of 9 knots. The *Dundee Evening Post*, 1 May 1900, reported:

> There was launched this afternoon from Panmure Shipyard (Dundee Shipbuilders' Company Limited), a cargo steamer built to the order of F H Powell & Co., Liverpool. Those present at the launch included Bailie Winton; Captain Lindberg and Miss Lindberg, Newport; Mr A Cooper; Mr G M Kidd, Secretary to the Shipbuilders' company; and Mr R Patterson, the manager; and also Mr J M Drake, superintendent engineer for the owners. As the vessel left the ways she was christened *Faithful* by Miss Drake, daughter of the superintendent engineer, Liverpool. The *Faithful* is 198 feet long, 30 feet broad, and 15 feet 3 inches deep, having a gross tonnage of 800. She is to be employed between Liverpool, Bristol and London. The machinery on board is of the most modern description, including five steam winches, steam windlass and steam steering gear. Electric light is fitted throughout. There is accommodation for several passengers, whilst the crew and officers are to be located in the forward and aft of the vessel respectively. After the launch 'Success to the *Faithful*!' was pledged.

Three second-hand purchases were also made in 1900, business having greatly improved since the depressed years of the 1890s. The first second-hand purchase was the *Creaden*, acquired in March 1900, but she was not renamed presumably as she was viewed as a short-term acquisition before-purpose built tonnage became available. The *Creaden* had been completed for the Waterford Steamship Company Limited by J P Rennoldson of South Shields in 1883.

The second acquisition joined the Powell fleet in April 1900. This ship was an interesting choice; it was an elderly steamer that had been built by McNab & Company at Greenock in 1867. Launched on 8 October 1867, the ship was completed for the Belfast Steam Ship Company as the *Voltaic*, a twin screw passenger and cargo steamer designed by R M Beath for the Belfast to Liverpool mail service. Her original inverted steam engines were replaced in 1882 with compound machinery. In 1896 she was sold out of the Belfast fleet to Samuel W Higginbottom of Belfast, who sold her on to Charles McIver & Company's Liverpool & Clyde Steam Navigation Company for charter to Fishguard & Rosslare Railways & Harbours Company Limited to open a new service between Wexford and Bristol via Rosslare. The Rosslare company bought her outright the following year. Still named *Voltaic*, she collided with T & J Harrison's steamship *Cognac*, off the Welsh coast on 18 November 1898. Although the *Cognac* sank, the *Voltaic* was relatively undamaged and was able to proceed to port under her own steam. The *Western Gazette*, Friday 18 November 1898, reported:

> A brandy strewn sea: The steamers *Voltaic* and *Cognac* were in collision during a dense fog in the Irish Sea on Friday, when the latter sank. All on board were saved and landed at Liverpool on Saturday morning by the *Voltaic*. The *Cognac* was coming from Charente, most of her cargo being brandy. A steamer which passed after the *Cognac* went down saw numerous casks of brandy and other spirits floating about for some considerable distance. Although the *Cognac* had a great hole torn in her side, the cases and barrels in her cargo kept her afloat for about two hours, and enabled the crew to save some of their effects.

The Wexford service was abandoned in 1900 and the *Voltaic* put up for sale. This then, was the venerable passenger and cargo ship that entered the Powell fleet in 1900 as *Voltaic*, retaining her name as she was presumably yet more stopgap tonnage until more suitable vessels could be obtained. Interestingly, her near sister the *Galvanic* joined the coasting services of M Langlands & Sons in 1899, again a short-term acquisition that was sold to overseas owners three years later.

Finally a smaller cargo steamer with the name *Watchful* was acquired in November 1900. She had been launched by the Campbeltown Shipbuilding Company at Campbeltown on 23 June 1882 with the name *Orpheus* and had been built for Francis Johnston of Liverpool. She was bought by the South Wales & Liverpool Steamship Company in 1886. She sank in the Mersey on 28 June 1900 off Rock Ferry, following a collision with the Norwegian steamship *Vigsnaes*, having just arrived from Llanelli. The hulk was abandoned to the underwriters and the register was closed. On 12 July 1900, she was successfully raised and was taken to Garston Graving Dock for repairs and refurbishment. She was bought by Henry M Grayson, ship repairer, who renamed her *Watchful* and then sold her on to the Watchful Steam Ship Company Limited, a one-ship company wholly owned by F H Powell & Company.

The *Watchful* (1882) was renamed in 1900 by Henry Grayson whilst she was being repaired and after she had been bought by F H Powell & Company.

These acquisitions brought the fleet up to an unprecedented ten ships. This allowed extra sailings on both the Bristol and London routes with time for the cargo steamers to call additionally at Manchester on a regular basis. Cargoes were plentiful inbound to Manchester but were sparse on the southward run, so the ships loaded what was available at their berth in Pomona Docks before returning to Liverpool to complete loading.

On 1 December 1900, the *Voltaic* collided off the Skerries, with T Heiton & Company's steamer *Saint Olaf*, which sank. As before, the *Voltaic* came away almost unscathed. The *Manchester Courier and Lancashire General Advertiser* carried the story on 8 December:

> A disastrous collision occurred about midnight on Saturday off the Mersey between the steamer *Voltaic*, Liverpool to Plymouth, with general cargo, and the steamer *Saint Olaf* of Dublin, owned by Robert Harper, Glasgow, and bound from France to Liverpool. The night was clear, and many of the crew of the *Saint Olaf*, thirteen in number, were in bed when the *Voltaic* struck her amidships. She sank almost immediately, most of her crew managing to jump on board the *Voltaic* but two firemen, named John Quick and John Doherty, belonging to Garston, are missing. The *Voltaic* has two holes in her bows above the waterline.

Towards the end of Queen Victoria's reign increasing emphasis was placed on attracting summer cruise passengers to the London service. A typical 1901 summertime advertisement read:

> Liverpool to London by sea four days – ss *Graceful*, sailing 3rd August, at noon, calling at Plymouth, Southampton and Portsmouth. Fare 25 shillings single, 40 shillings return. Particulars from all Tourist Agents and F H Powell & Co., 9 Albert Square, Manchester and 21 Water Street, Liverpool.

In June 1902, the company carried the advertisement:

> Coronation Procession and Naval Review. Ten days cruise, per ss. *Hopeful*, Leaving Liverpool 21st June; or four days' cruise leaving Newhaven 27th June; £5 5s for Naval Review. For particulars…

The Victorian era had ended.

Chapter 5

F H POWELL & COMPANY – 1902 to 1905

The *West Coast* sank on 23 August 1901 in the Crosby Channel. She was run down by the crack Isle of Man paddle steamer *Ben-my-Chree*. The *West Coast* had just left Liverpool bound for London and lay at anchor in the fog in the Crosby Channel. The *Manchester Courier and Lancashire General Advertiser* reported the incident on 24 August:

> Yesterday morning a disastrous collision occurred in the Mersey which resulted in the sinking of a steamer, though happily unattended by loss of life. A steamer named the *West Coast*, bound for London with a general cargo, had come to anchor in the Crosby Channel owing to a thick fog, and while in that position she was run into by the Isle of Man passenger steamer *Ben-my-Chree*, which was on the inward passage from Douglas. The *West Coast*, an iron screw steamer of 480 tons register, received such terrible damage amidships that she sank in the course of five minutes. Fortunately, all the crew, thirteen in number, were on deck at the time of the collision and all of them were hauled aboard the *Ben-my-Chree* before their vessel sank. The Manx steamer had her bows slightly damaged. There were a considerable number of passengers aboard amongst whom the collision created a good deal of excitement, but it soon subsided on it being discovered that the *Ben-my-Chree* had escaped with comparatively slight damage. The *West Coast* was owned by F H Powell & Company, Liverpool.
>
> The *Ben-my-Chree* arrived at Liverpool shortly after nine o'clock yesterday morning, three hours late. The captain declined to make any statement to the press representatives.

The wreck was later raised on behalf of the underwriter and beached at Tranmere. It was sold for repair and further trading (see Fleet Lists for details).

The *West Coast* (1883) was no match for a collision with the Isle of Man steamer *Ben-my-Chree* (1875), the latter seen here harmlessly lying at Douglas.

The steamer *Hanbury* was purchased from Edward H Stock of Bristol in 1901. She had been built for Stock and his partners by the Blyth Shipbuilding Company Limited in 1895 and was equipped with a compound engine which gave her a speed of 9 knots. Like other recent purchases she was not initially renamed but was eventually given the more corporate name *East Coast* in 1904. Another second-hand purchase was made the following year when the *Point Clear* was bought and registered under the ownership of the Point Clear Steamship Company Limited, with F H Powell & Company as managers. She was almost a new ship, equipped with a triple expansion steam engine that provided a service speed of 9½ knots. She was a typical machinery aft bridge forward of amidships cargo steamer and had been completed by Ritson & Company at Maryport for Kilgour & Baker of Glasgow in 1901. She was later renamed *Hopeful* during 1904. These acquisitions made the *Voltaic* surplus and she was put on the For Sale list. She was bought by V. Tolstopjat and registered as *Prince Oldenbourgsky* at Kertch, Russia, in 1902. The *Prince Oldenbourgsky* was wrecked in the Black Sea during the following year.

The *Hopeful* (1901), formerly the *Point Clear*, seen off Pill in the River Avon.

The impressive broadside launch of the *Point Clear* (1901) from the yard of Ritson & Company of Maryport in January 1901. She was ordered by Kilgour & Baker, Glasgow.

On 10 February 1903, the *Watchful* (formerly *Orpheus*) was in collision with and sank the coasting steamer *Arthur* of Dublin. The collision happened near Sully Island in the Bristol Channel. The Board of Trade Enquiry, which found the mate of the *Watchful* mostly to blame for the incident, states:

The *Arthur* was a British screw steamship, built of steel, by Messrs Murdoch & Murray, at Port Glasgow, in the year 1894... Her gross tonnage was 511.31 tons... She was owned and managed by Mr Michael Murphy, of 94, North Wall, in the City of Dublin, and was registered at that port, her official number being 99756.

The *Watchful*…carried a crew of twelve hands all told, Mr John Brew, who holds a home trade certificate of competency as master, No. 103962, dated 7th June, 1899, being in command.

The *Arthur* left Newport, Mon., at 4.20 a.m. on 10th February last with a cargo of coal for Dublin, her draught of water being 12 ft. 6 ins. forward and 16 ft. 1 in. aft. The weather was fine and clear with a light breeze from WSW, and lights could be seen nearly, if not quite, at their full range. The master, the second mate, and the steersman were on the upper bridge, the master being on the starboard side and the second mate on the port side while one AB was on the look-out on the lower bridge. Shortly before six o'clock the *Arthur* was to the southward of Sully Island, about 1½ miles distant, proceeding on her course W ½ N (magnetic), full speed, about ten knots, while the tide, which was about an hour and a-half ebb, was also in her favour, to the extent of from one to two knots.

In these circumstances, the masthead and green lights of a steamer, which afterwards proved to be the *Watchful*, were observed about a point on the port bow, and as they drew ahead, or even a little on the starboard bow, the master of the *Arthur* stopped his engines and blew two short blasts on the whistle to indicate that he was directing his course to port, at the same moment ordering the engines to go full speed ahead, the helm being hard-a-starboard. Just as the *Arthur* starboarded and had signalled the same by the whistle, the red light of the *Watchful* appeared about one and a-half points on the *Arthur's* starboard bow, and at the same time the *Watchful* gave one short blast on his whistle to indicate that he was directing his course to starboard. In the positions in which the vessels now were a collision was inevitable, and the *Watchful* came stem on into the starboard bow of the *Arthur*, making such a breach that in two or three minutes afterwards the *Arthur* foundered, carrying with her five hands, who had attempted to launch a boat over the vessel's port quarter, but were unable to do so, owing to the *Arthur* listing over so much to starboard. They accordingly got into the boat, expecting it to float clear as the vessel went down, but unfortunately the boat got entangled in some way and went down with the ship. The five hands found themselves in the water, and after about half an hour, during which some of the men supported themselves on pieces of wreckage, four of them were picked up by a pilot boat and landed in Barry. One of the four, Hamilton McCoy, second engineer of the *Arthur*, was so exhausted that he died two hours after being landed. The man who was not picked up was William Henry Seymour, first mate of the *Arthur*, who was never seen after the men were thrown into the water, nor has his body been recovered.

Under the circumstances of wind, weather, and tide already related as existing about 6 a.m. on 10th February last, the *Watchful* was proceeding up channel on a E ½ N course on a voyage from Manchester to Bristol. She had a part cargo of about 130 tons on board, and her draught of water was 6 ft. 9 ins. forward and 11 ft. aft. Breaksea Lightship had been passed about half a mile off on the *Watchful's* starboard hand, the mate, Mr Thomas Henry Green, who holds a home trade certificate of competency as mate, No. 104546, dated 28th February, 1901, being in charge of the deck. The passage, until well into the Bristol Channel, had been impeded by fog, and the master, Mr John Brew, had been about 18 hours continuously on deck, when at 1.45 a.m., on the aforementioned day, he turned in. He came on deck, however, several times in course of the early morning and satisfied himself that the weather was clear, and that the vessel was proceeding on a safe and proper course. When between Breaksea and Flatholm, the mate of the *Watchful* saw the masthead and red lights of a steamer (which proved to be the *Arthur*) on his starboard bow, and estimated to be about 1½ miles away. The mate knew that it was his duty to give way to the other vessel, and he states that 'almost immediate', he ordered his helm to be ported, and that the order was executed, and that the *Arthur* was brought on his port bow. He was just about to steady his helm when he heard two short blasts from the *Arthur* indicating that that vessel was starboarding, and then, for the first time, the mate of the *Watchful* indicated by the prescribed signal that he was porting. In the circumstances then existing, though both vessels stopped and reversed their engines, the disaster, as already related, could not be avoided. The master of the *Watchful*, hearing and realising the import of the conflicting signals, hurried on deck, but reached the bridge only in time to see his vessel crash into the *Arthur*. He immediately ordered his engines, which had been reversed, slow ahead, in order to keep the vessels in contact long enough to allow the crew of the *Arthur* to escape to the *Watchful*; but owing to the serious injury inflicted on the *Arthur*, that vessel rolled clear of the *Watchful* before the complete rescue of the crew could be effected, and, falling alongside the *Watchful* was quickly carried astern, and appears to have immediately foundered, for the boat which was as quickly as possible lowered from the *Watchful* in charge of the master of the *Arthur*, and with a combined crew of the two vessels, failed to find any trace of her or of the remainder of her crew, though they rowed about for upwards of two hours. The shock of the collision broke the main steam-pipe of the *Watchful*, and that vessel had to anchor until repairs could be effected.

Three days later, on 13 February 1903, the steamer *Hopeful* was lost in a collision in circumstances that should never have happened. Initial statements from Penzance issued that day and the next read:

> Penzance 13 February. Steamers *Hopeful*, Liverpool for London, and *Raloo*, St Malo for Troon, collided this morning. Former struck starboard side abreast funnel. *Greencastle* [Captain Anderson]… left Benwick for scene. *Hopeful* sank shortly after [*Greencastle*] arrival. Position Longships N, Runnelstone buoy E by N ½ N. Some barrels, sundries and logs mahogany floated; Anderson recovered some. *Raloo* in ballast, stem broken, plates adrift and twisted. Captain engaged Anderson to wedge up and paulin over. Work done satisfactorily, and vessel proceeded destination 12.15. *Greencastle* landed *Hopeful*'s crew and two passengers at Penzance.

> Penzance 14 February. The steamer *Hopeful* sank in deep water, probably 35 fathoms, and it is feared that the salvage will be very small.

The *West Briton and Cornwall Advertiser*, Thursday 19 February 1903, embellished the story:

> In bright sunshine, on Friday morning, a collision took place off Porthgwarrs, near Land's End, between two steamers, under circumstances which at present have not been fully explained, which resulted in the sinking of one vessel and only comparatively slight damage to the other. About ten o'clock in the morning, the *Hopeful*, a steamer of about 1,200 tons gross, bound from Liverpool to London, with a general cargo, was it appears, run into by the *Raloo* of Belfast, on her way to Troon, Scotland, in ballast. Apparently the *Hopeful* was attempting to cross the bows of the other vessel, which struck her amidships, making a hole which one of the crew described as big enough for a man to walk through. The forepart quickly filled, and in about half an hour the crew had to abandon her, and she went down head first, the whole of the stern part of the vessel being visible until the boilers exploded, when she disappeared. Captain Edwards, a native of Liverpool, the crew of 21, and two passengers, were taken on board the *Greencastle* salvage boat and brought to Penzance. Captain Anderson of the *Greencastle* was engaged to patch up the injuries to the bows of the *Raloo*, and she proceeded on her voyage. It is stated that the Chief Engineer was on watch at the time, and his life was probably saved by the fact that he had left the deck just before the collision to go to his room. The *Hopeful* was owned by F H Powell & Co. of Liverpool.

On 5 March the *Cornishman* reported:

> Quantities of oranges, apples, onions and bags of flour, have been washed ashore at St Buryan during the past week supposed to have come from the steamship *Hopeful*.

The loss of the *Hopeful* was a setback for the company which meant it could not so easily sustain its regular cargo service to London. However, Powell had a new ship building at Newcastle that was intended for the London passenger and cargo service that would be ready in time for the summer tourist season. This was the purpose-built passenger cargo steamer *Powerful*. She was a large ship which measured 1,612 tons gross.

The *Powerful* (1903) waiting to lock in on arrival at Bristol.

The *Powerful* was launched from the yard of Swan Hunter & Wigham Richardson Limited, Newcastle-on-Tyne, on 28 May 1903. The *Shields Daily Gazette*, 29 May 1903, reported:

> An addition to the fleet of Messrs F H Powell & Co, of Liverpool, Manchester and Bristol, was launched on the Tyne yesterday by Wigham-Richardson & Co Ltd. The vessel is intended for the coasting service carried on by Messrs. Powell from Liverpool to London and the South Coast of England. The *Powerful*, as the vessel was gracefully named by Miss Drake, daughter of Mr Drake, is a very finely modelled steamer 280 feet in length by 36 feet beam, and will be propelled at a speed of over 12 knots by a set of triple expansion engines, which are also being constructed by Wigham-Richardson & Co. Ltd. The vessel will carry over 2,000 tons of cargo, and the passengers, 60 in number, will be accommodated in state rooms, and will have a spacious dining saloon in which all can dine together. In addition there will be a cosy smoke room and a ladies' room, besides a good sheltered promenade deck. Amongst the company present at the launch were Mr Alfred H Read, of the firm of F H Powell & Co., and Mr Drake of Liverpool, their Superintendent.

In anticipation of the *Powerful* being commissioned, the elderly *Graceful* stood down from the London service and was sold in November 1902. In 1903, the steamer *River Tay* was bought from the Steamship River Tay Company Limited. The ship had been launched from the Ardrossan Drydock & Shipbuilding Company at Ardrossan on 26 April 1902. Powell did not immediately rename their new steamer but in 1904 she finally adopted the name *West Coast*. She had a compound engine situated aft and was good for 10 knots. She was of typical size for the Powell fleet of cargo ships with a length of 166 feet and a beam of 26 feet; her gross tonnage was 467 tons.

A new service was commenced in September 1903 by the *Watchful*. This was a fortnightly departure on Tuesdays from Bristol, Cardiff and Swansea for Falmouth, Plymouth, Weymouth, Poole, Southampton, Portsmouth and London. Towards the end of the year the company suffered another serious accident with the loss of the steamer *Azalea*. On 24 December 1903, the *Azalea* sank in the Crosby Channel, Liverpool, after collision with Mersey Docks & Harbour Board's steam hopper *No. 21*. She had been on passage from Liverpool to Exmouth, Newhaven and London. The *Edinburgh Evening News*, Thursday 24 December 1903, reported the incident:

> The coasting steamer *Azalea*, outward bound for Newhaven and Gravesend with a general cargo, sank after a collision today in the Mersey Channel with a Dock Board hopper. The steamer was struck on the port side, and commenced to sink almost at once, but the crew was saved by the hopper, which was only slightly damaged at the bow. The *Azalea* was about 500 tons register built seventeen years ago at Sunderland, and owned in Liverpool.

The wreck was dispersed between 6 February and 1 March the following year.

The cargo steamer *Mindful* was added to the fleet in 1904. She was a small steamer 142 feet in length with a beam of 24 feet and a depth of 10 feet, built by Murdoch & Murray at Port Glasgow in 1893. Her compound engine sustained a good speed of nearly 12 knots. As the *Maggie Barr* she had worked for Glasgow owners until sold in 1898 to William Postlethwaite of Millom, who sold her on to the Watchful Steamship Company Limited (F H Powell & Company, managers) in 1904 when she was renamed *Mindful*.

The *Mindful* (1893), seen in her former guise as *Maggie Barr*, in the River Avon below Bristol.

[World Ship Society Photo Archive]

An interesting new ship was completed for F H Powell & Company in 1904. This was the engines aft cargo ship *Cornish Coast*. She was 180 feet long by 29 feet beam with a depth of 13 feet. Her gross tonnage was 676 tons. She was launched from the yard of W Harkess & Son Limited at Middlesbrough, on 29 September 1904. Equipped with the now common triple expansion steam engine, she was a state-of-the-art ship in the coasting trade. Shortly after she was accepted from the shipyard her ownership was registered as F H Powell & Company and Samuel Hough Limited (Chapter 11). A sister ship, the *Devon Coast*, was launched into the Tees by W Harkess & Son Limited six months later on 4 April 1905.

During the summer 1904, the *Powerful*, under Captain John Edwards, was advertised to sail from Liverpool for London via Plymouth on alternate Thursdays, returning the following Thursday also via Plymouth. The *Powerful* was regarded as the flagship with the best passenger accommodation for the cruise traffic.

The *Manchester Courier and Lancashire Advertiser*, 30 March 1905, announced the death of Colonel Read:

> The death is reported at his residence Kenwyn, Deebanks, Chester, of Mr Alfred Read, who was senior partner in the firm F H Powell & Company, steamship owners, of Liverpool, Manchester, and Bristol, and was well known as a colonel in the 1st Lancashire Artillery Volunteers. Colonel Read was 59 years of age.

The association with the Harkess yard on the Tees was set to continue with a succession of orders over the next eight years. Indeed all but one of the orders placed by Powell up to the formation of Powell, Bacon & Hough Lines Limited in 1913 were placed with W Harkess & Son Limited.

The Middlesbrough yard launched the passenger and cargo ship *Masterful* on 28 September 1905, designed as a running mate for the *Powerful*, on the London passenger and cargo service. She was 280 feet long by 36 beam, had a depth of 20 feet and was of 1,794 tons gross. The triple expansion steam engine provided a service speed of 12 knots. She was some ten feet longer than the *Powerful* and had accommodation for 80 passengers. On delivery the ships settled into a routine with *Masterful* sailing from Liverpool on Wednesdays and *Powerful* on Saturdays, returning from Regent's Canal Wharf in London on Saturdays and Wednesdays respectively. The service proved extremely popular and full passenger complements were common on the summer Saturday sailings both north and south.

The passenger steamer *Masterful* (1905) was sold shortly before the formation of Powell, Bacon & Hough Lines Limited, and was lost in the Great War.

An advertising postcard for the 'Powell Line Liverpool and London Steamers: Best route to Cornish Riviera and Sunny South'.

The new ship *Masterful* was described in an article in the *Portsmouth Evening News*, 7 December 1905:

Lying well up Portsmouth Harbour yesterday and in the berth usually occupied by the Royal Yacht was the ss *Masterful*, the largest steamer engaged in the British coasting trade. She has a peculiar interest to Portsmouth, for it is the intention of her owners, F H Powell & Co., of Liverpool, to employ her regularly, summer and winter, in the trade between Liverpool, Plymouth, Southampton, Portsmouth and London. The vessel represents the company's latest effort in manning this line, both in respect to her passenger accommodation and cargo capacity; and whereas the *Augusta*, one of the first steamers in the service, was a vessel of 188 tons gross, and 50 horsepower, the *Masterful* has a gross tonnage of 1,794, whilst her horsepower is 1,300.

A representative of this paper had the pleasure of a visit to her, in company with Mr J Taylor, manager for the local agents, Messrs Powell & Hough, of 116 High Street, Portsmouth, and aboard they enjoyed the guidance of Captain Edwards, the captain and Commodore of the fleet, and Mr Hynes the purser. The *Masterful* has exceedingly graceful lines, and what she loses in appearance from the shortness of the thick business-like masts, with derricks sprouting out all around, she fully makes up for when one gets a view of her unobstructed promenade decks, and broad look-out space for passengers right forward. The vessel, which has a speed of 14 knots, is of the shelter deck type, and is 291 feet long, with 36 feet beam, and 19 feet draught. With extra-large cubical capacity she has a net tonnage of 1,020, and a gross tonnage of 1,794.

The passenger accommodation is for 80 persons, and is of an exceptionally handsome character, all the woodwork being of unstained brightly polished oak. On the shelter deck is a really charming smoking room, with a piano, and below, on the main deck, is the roomy dining saloon, to seat 40 passengers at swinging dining chairs. All the ceilings are of panelled lincrusta, and the floors of a patent linoleum-like material, cemented down hard and known as lino-silo. The flooring is of a pleasant green and blue studded colour, and is covered here and there with bright Axminster carpet. Each state room has two berths, and like the other accommodation, is comparable in quality to that of a liner. The old-fashioned bunk gives place to a neat iron bed with a spring wire mattress. In the shelter deck are deck state rooms, and above, on the upper deck, the captain's state room. The officer's accommodation is 'tween decks; and the crew, according to the new style, are berthed in a deck house right aft. Already Captain Edwards has been in two gales with the *Masterful*, and she has acted fully up to her name. She is a capital sea boat, free from vibration...

The Promenade Deck aboard the *Masterful* (1905).

Chapter 6

F H POWELL & COMPANY – FINAL YEARS

The upgrading of the fleet allowed the *Creaden*, which had been renamed *North Coast* in 1904, and *Truthful* to be sold in 1905 and 1906 respectively. In 1906, the *Hanbury*, renamed *East Coast* two years earlier, and the *Watchful* were both sold. In the meantime new ships were delivered by W Harkess & Son Limited on a regular basis. The big steamer *Faithful* was delivered in 1906, to work mainly on the Bristol Channel services from Liverpool. She was followed in late summer 1907 by the *Sussex Coast*, a slightly smaller ship but to the same bridge forward of amidships and machinery aft design.

The *Faithful* (1906) about to lock in to enter the Cumberland Basin at Bristol.

The *Truthful* (1907) was built for F H Powell & Company as *Sussex Coast*.

The *Sussex Coast* was sold almost immediately to Samuel Hough Limited but came back into Powell ownership in 1908 without change of name. Later that year she was renamed *Truthful*, and shortly afterwards her ownership was changed to the Watchful Steamship Company Limited managed by F H Powell & Company. A sister to the *Sussex Coast/Truthful* was launched on 30 May 1908 and christened *Dorset Coast*. She was almost immediately 50% sold to Samuel Hough Limited.

A similar ship to the new cargo ships was ordered from Harkess at Middlesbrough for a new company, the British & Continental Steamship Company Limited. This appears to have been a holding company under the management of Alfred H Read, and was dissolved in 1910. The ship was delivered in 1909 with the name *Graceful*. She did not remain long on the Continental services and was sold first to F H Powell & Company later in 1909 and then to F H Powell & Company and Samuel Hough Limited in the same year. In 1910 she was renamed *Devon Coast*.

Seen in the Avon on her approach to Bristol Docks is the *Devon Coast* (1909), formerly *Graceful*. She was sold in 1934 and renamed *Devonbrook*.

One ship had been lost, again highlighting the dangers of the coasting trades in the days before radar and other aids to navigation. The *Devon Coast* was sunk on 4 November 1908, following a collision in fog with the steamer *Jeannie*, 5 miles south south east of Newhaven. The *Devon Coast* had left Swanscombe Jetty, Kent, loaded with a cargo of cement bound for Liverpool. The *Yorkshire Post and Leeds Intelligencer*, 5 November 1908, offered the following:

London 4 November: The steamer *Devon Coast*, bound from Swanscombe for Liverpool with a cargo of cement, was in collision off Beachy Head early this morning with the Cardiff steamer *Jeannie*. The *Devon Coast* was cut down to below the water line, but her pumps were kept going, and she was towed towards Newhaven for three hours when the *Jeannie* had to abandon her. The crew were taken off before the *Devon Coast* foundered in deep water several miles from the shore, and were landed at Newhaven by the tug *Alert*. The *Devon Coast* was a steel screw steamer of 668 tons register, owned by Messrs F H Powell & Co, and valued, including cargo, at about £27,000. The *Jeannie* which is of 1,793 tons, owned by Messrs E R Care & Co. of Cardiff, is reported badly damaged.

In July 1910, a new, but short-lived, service between Bristol and Havre was started, calling at Cardiff and Swansea, with other ports added by inducement. The French agent was E Grosos et fils, 26 Place de la Hotel de Ville, Havre.

Two identical steamers, both with the name *Hopeful*, were delivered by Harkess in 1910. This pair has long been a source of confusion to shipping historians, although the difference between the two is apparent. The first *Hopeful* was launched on 24 March and the second was also christened *Hopeful* at her launch into the Tees on 3 September. By then the first *Hopeful*, which had been delivered to the British & Continental Steamship Company, had been renamed *Devon Coast* and then transferred to F H Powell & Company. Before the end of the year she was sold to the Union Steamship Company of New Zealand Limited releasing her name to the former *Graceful*. The second *Hopeful* never actually sailed under her original name and was completed as the *Norfolk Coast*. Harkess also delivered the big cargo steamer *Hampshire Coast* the following year and yet another *Hopeful* in 1913. All were engines aft and bridge amidships type ships.

The *Norfolk Coast* (1910) was launched with the name *Hopeful* but completed as *Norfolk Coast*. She is wearing the grey hull applied to some ships during the Great War.

The *Hampshire Coast* (1911) passed to Powell, Bacon & Hough Lines Limited in 1913 and later to Coast Lines. She was eventually sold in 1936.

On 7 February 1911, the **Norfolk Coast** was the scene of a fatal accident. She was alongside at Liverpool loading for London and various ports along the south coast. A mooring chain, weighing between 3 and 4 tons, destined for the Naval Harbour at Dover was to be loaded from a barge from the Manchester Ship Canal using one of the ship's derricks. Just as the chain had been hoisted above the barge the slings snapped and it fell onto three men working on the barge. Sadly two of the men were killed instantly while the third died later in hospital. The chain was eventually unloaded at Dover on 11 February.

Only one steamer was delivered by a builder other than Harkess, the **Graceful** which was built by Sir Raylton Dixon & Company, also at Middlesbrough, under sub-contract from Harkess. The **Graceful** was launched on 21 September 1911, exactly two weeks after the **Hampshire Coast** slid down the ways – busy times for the Teesside shipyards. The **Graceful** was an identical sister to the **Hopeful** which was completed by Harkess two years later. Both ships had accommodation three quarters aft and had a small number of passenger berths. Several ships were sold as the new vessels were commissioned, the **West Coast** in 1908, and the elderly **Mindful** and the **Hopeful**, formerly the **Point Clear,** in 1909.

The *Hopeful* (1913) seen approaching Bristol in 1913 before she was renamed *Western Coast* later in that year.

In August 1911, the steamer **Suffolk Coast**, built at Dundee in 1900 as the **Faithful**, was sold to J & P Hutchison for £6,500. She later went to Norwegian owners and in February 1916, during the Great War, was bought by another Norwegian company for £44,500, a greatly increased price that reflected the massive increase in cost per ton of merchant shipping caused by increased demand and war losses.

The **Masterful** of 1905, was sold to Chilean owners in 1912. The sale of the flagship of the fleet, was in anticipation of the merger with Samuel Hough Limited and rationalisation of the prestigious Liverpool to London passenger service. She was sold prior to the slack winter passenger season. The twice weekly passenger service was reduced to weekly with Hough's steamer **Samuel Hough** retained at that stage only to serve as relief during the annual survey and refit of the **Powerful** working alongside Hough's newer steamer **Dorothy Hough** (Chapter 12).

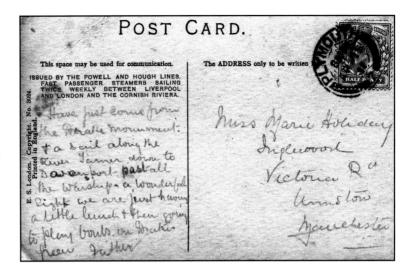

A picture postcard issued by the Powell and Hough Lines. Fast passenger steamers sailing twice weekly between Liverpool and London and the 'Cornish Riviera'.

In March 1912 the *Western Daily Press* advertised 'The Powell Line' Bristol services as:

> Liverpool and Manchester Service: The fine modern steamers *Faithful*, *Graceful*, *Truthful* and *Powerful*, or other vessels of this line, will sail as follows: Bristol to Liverpool (direct) every Saturday; Bristol to Manchester every Monday and Thursday; Liverpool to Bristol (direct) every Tuesday; Manchester to Bristol (direct) every Tuesday and Saturday. For rates and all particulars apply F H Powell & Co, The Grove, Bristol.

A number of corporate changes were made before 30 September 1913, when a newly merged company called Powell, Bacon & Hough Lines Limited was registered. This company included all the assets and goodwill of F H Powell & Company, Samuel Hough Limited and John Bacon Limited. The main changes prior to the creation of the new company had involved liaison first with Samuel Hough Limited and then also with John Bacon Limited, both companies operating in similar trades to Powell. Competition on the Manchester to London trade was consolidated shortly after the Manchester Ship Canal opened to trade in 1894 by offering a joint service by both Powell and Hough. This was seen as the best way to take on head-to-head the direct competition from Fisher Renwick & Company Manchester-London Steamers Limited. Fisher Renwick operated the same route and had used Saltport near Runcorn from December 1892 until January 1894 when the canal was finally opened to Manchester.

Further collaboration with Samuel Hough Limited led to the joint ownership of the five cargo ships by F H Powell & Company and Samuel Hough Limited between 1904 and 1911. The ships were jointly owned on a 50:50 basis. This allowed the pooling of resources in order to tackle competition for trade in the interests of both organisations. In 1912 F H Powell & Company acquired John Bacon Limited, allowing for further consolidation and pooling of resources. The *Shipping Gazette*, 19 October 1912, reported on the deal:

> A local shipping deal of some magnitude, the negotiations in connection with which have been going on for some time, is now reported as having been brought to completion, subject to the approval of three-fourths of the shareholders of the selling concern. The deal in question is the acquisition of the well-known coasting fleet and business of Messrs John Bacon Ltd., known as the Bacon Line, whose steamers trade regularly between Liverpool and Swansea, Liverpool and Wexford, Liverpool and Bristol, and Wexford and Swansea and Bristol. The purchasers are Messrs F H Powell & Co. Ltd., who own one of the premier transport coasting lines, and they are particularly well known in the trade with London, Bristol and South Coast ports, and have already a fleet of ten large modern coasters, many of them passenger vessels. The addition of the Bacon Line fleet to that of the Powell Line will just double the number of vessels and bring F H Powell & Co. to the forefront of local coasting concerns. For many years back they have displayed a policy of extension and modernisation, so that this last and most important acquisition will not cause great surprise in local shipping circles.

Henry Tyrer & Company at Preston agreed to sell its Preston to Hamburg and Preston to London rights to F H Powell & Company in 1912. Tyrer's *Prestonian* was displaced by Powell and Bacon vessels and resorted to tramping duties mainly to North European ports. This purchase gave Powell further access to the Continent although the Hamburg service was not continued after the Great War. More importantly it gave access to Preston Dock, an important port with a major industrial hinterland, albeit also within the Liverpool port catchment, but providing shorter journeys to many customers. The issue of road transport and the provision of a door-to-door parcels service was finally resolved in 1913 with the purchase of the Liverpool Cartage Company, the first of several such acquisitions.

The *Manchester Courier and Lancashire General Advertiser*, 2 February 1912, recorded:

> At the annual meeting of the Liverpool Steamship Owners Association, yesterday, Mr E Lionel Fletcher, one of the managers of the White Star Line, was appointed Chairman, and Mr Alfred H Read, of Messrs F H Powell & Co, vice-chairman for the ensuing year. To the retiring chairman, Sir Percy E Bates, Bart., a vote of thanks was accorded.

Five days later the same paper noted:

> The Annual meeting of the Manchester Steamship Owners Association was held yesterday at the Chartered Accountants' Rooms, Spring Gardens. The Report and Statement of Accounts were presented and adopted. The following were elected officers for the year: President, Mr Alfred H Read (Messrs. F H Powell & Co.), Vice-President Mr W V Bacon (Messrs, Sivewright, Bacon & Co.), Hon Treasurer Mr G M Milroy (Messrs. Donald Currie & Co.), Hon Secretary, Mr A A Ashton (F H Powell & Co.)…

Alfred H Read was honoured in 1913 by his name being given to the new Liverpool Pilot Cutter, No. 1. Launched by Murdoch & Murray at Glasgow on 17 May 1913, the new pilot cutter was duly christened **Alfred H Read**. Sadly the cutter was sunk by a mine south of the Bar lightship in December 1917 with the loss of 38 men.

Powell and Bacon took over Samuel Hough Limited in 1913 to create Powell, Bacon & Hough Lines Limited, itself the forerunner to the iconic Coast Lines Limited that was to be formed in 1917 (Chapter 14). However, before that took place, the King and Queen reviewed a line-up of over 100 merchant ships in the Mersey after opening the new Gladstone Dock on 11 July 1913. The steamer **Powerful** represented F H Powell & Company.

ENGINES OF THE STEAMSHIP *GRACEFUL* from *The Engineer* 1 October 1909

The set of engines illustrated in a supplement (and left), has recently been fitted into the ss. *Graceful*, a quarter-deck type steel vessel 195ft. by 30ft. by 13ft. 10in. moulded depth, built by W Harkess and Son, Limited, Middlesbrough, to the order of Messrs. F H Powell and Co, Liverpool, under the superintendence of Mr. W L Roxburgh. The vessel is specially designed for the coasting trade, having large capacity and being able to carry 1,000 tons of cargo in addition to bunkers and stores on a very light draught. The engines, which have been built by Richardsons, Westgarth and Co, Limited, Middlesbrough, represent the latest design for cargo boats, and have cylinders 16in., 27in. and 44in. diameter respectively, with a stroke of 30in., and are supplied with steam from two boilers working at 180 lb. pressure.

The feature of particular interest about the engine is the condenser, which, though of the Contraflo type, is novel in many respects. It is designed with the object of making the air passing to the air pump as dense as conditions will permit, and this it effects, of course, by reducing the temperature and removing as far as possible all water vapour. Broadly speaking, the condenser, whilst being of the ordinary Contraflo type, is provided with two extra chambers, one above the other, at the bottom. These chambers are fitted with tubes passing between plates just as in the ordinary part of the condenser. Through these tubes the circulating water flows first, and they are therefore always at the lowest temperature. Connecting the bottom of the condenser proper and the lowermost chamber is a pipe fitted with a cylindrical valve.... The water of condensation passes from the condenser through this valve into the lowermost chamber, where it is further cooled by its passage amongst the tubes. From this lower chamber this cooled water finds egress into the chamber immediately above through a comparatively small aperture. Now to this second chamber none of the water of condensation finds admission in the ordinary way, it contains only air and water vapour, and the cold water rising from below condenses the vapour and leaves little or nothing but air. Hence the air pump which draws from this chamber receives its charge in as dense a condition as possible. That is, very broadly, the construction of the condenser; we hope to be able to deal with it more fully on another occasion.

The point of great interest is the control valve to which we have already referred. It can be adjusted to permit just so much of the water of condensation to pass into the lower chambers as may be desired, so that the air pump discharge may be maintained at a practically constant temperature, notwithstanding considerable variations in load and temperature of the circulating water. Speaking of this device recently at the Liverpool Engineering Society, Mr. Morrison said:

> If the air leakage is within the capacity of the air pump, or if the required vacuum of, say, 26in. to 27in. can be maintained in a boat fitted with reciprocating engines when the condensed water at maximum temperature passes through the pump, the regulating valve is lowered and the regulating tank becomes inoperative, but if the air leakage is sufficient to lower the vacuum below the desired amount, the pump may be increased in effective capacity by by-passing a portion of the condensed water through the regulating tank.

> Again, if the air leakage is normal, but the vacuum falls by reason of high temperature of sea water increasing the volume of the aerated vapour in the condenser base, the by-passing of a portion of the condensed water through the regulating tank will suffice to raise the vacuum to the desired standard. The arrangement, in fact, provides an air pump of great flexibility in capacity, whereby the highest temperature of feed can be obtained for a given vacuum with a given air leakage in varying temperatures of sea water.

So satisfied are the makers with this system that they have, they inform us, practically adopted it as their standard practice. Broadly, the results claimed are that the most economical vacuum can be maintained in all temperatures of sea water – in other words, the power efficiency of the engines as affected by the vacuum is constant in all sea waters, thus favourably influencing the average speed of a ship on her voyage. In cargo boats especially the prevailing practice is to maintain a comparatively low vacuum in order to obtain high temperature feed-water, but if this high temperature of feed-water can be obtained by utilising the waste heat in the engine-room auxiliaries, such as the steam from the evaporator and the various high temperature drains, the relation between low vacuum and hot feed can be severed, and that degree of vacuum can be carried which is best adapted to the power efficiency of the engines. In tropical waters there is invariably a considerable fall in vacuum, and in practically all cases this fall is attributable to insufficiency of air pump. Mere increase in size of pump has, it is said, but little influence, but its air withdrawing capacity is quickly responsive to decreased temperature; therefore, if the temperature of the pump can be regulated to meet the requirements of the air leakage prevailing, the highly detrimental effect of surplus air to the condenser is obviated and a steady vacuum is maintained.

On the loaded trial which took place on Saturday, 25th ult., a speed of 10.6 knots was maintained with 709 indicated horsepower, and at a vacuum of fully 28in., the temperature of the hotwell was within 3 deg. of the corresponding temperature.

We understand Richardsons, Westgarth and Co, Limited, have now on order at their Hartlepool Middlesbrough Works seventeen sets of marine engines ranging up to 2,500 indicated horsepower which are to be fitted with this system.

Chapter 7

THE EARLY WEXFORD AND LIVERPOOL TRADE –

JOHN REDMOND AND FITZSIMONS, APPLEBEE & COMPANY

John Edward Redmond 1837 - 1856
Fitzsimons, Applebee & Company 1852 - 1860
Wexford Steam Ship Company Limited 1860 - 1864
John Bacon & Company 1860 - 1887
Joseph Wright (executor of John Bacon) 1887 - 1890
John Bacon Limited 1889 - 1913

The purchase of John Bacon Limited by F H Powell & Company in the last quarter of 1912 identifies the second thread of predecessors of what eventually would become Coast Lines Limited. John Bacon Limited, like Powell, was a long established company and could trace its roots back to the 1830s.

The origins of the so-called Bacon Line go back to John Edward Redmond, of Wexford, who entered the Wexford-Liverpool trade in 1837. John Redmond was a Wexford banker, who later became Member of Parliament for Wexford from 1859 until his death in 1865. He had already been instrumental in the development of port facilities at Wexford, as reported by Samuel Lewis (1837):

> A quay extends for nearly half a mile from the bridge, having a general breadth of 60 feet, except near its middle, called the Crescent, where it widens to 80 feet. On the opposite shore has been raised the ballast quay, so called from being formed by the ballast deposited there by the shipping: it serves as a breakwater for the protection of the vessels moored on the side towards the town. The former of these quays has received a considerable extension to the south-west by an embankment raised by J. E. Redmond, Esq., which carries it on in a direct line to the end of Fishers' Row, whence a communication with that part of the country will be opened by a road in the same direction to the rock of Maudlintown … The shipping interests have been materially promoted by the construction of a patent slip and ship-building yard, by Mr Redmond, at the southern extremity of his new embankment, from which a vessel of 70 tons has been already launched...

At Liverpool, John Redmond's first agent was Thomas Richards. In 1838 or 1839, Thomas Richards was replaced by Thomas McTear, who had been the agent for the 'opposition' ship *Antelope*, and was also the agent for the Cork Steam Ship Company. It seems probable that the change of agency occurred as a result of the withdrawal of *Antelope*. Thomas McTear went out of business in June 1846, and was replaced as agent by William Fitzsimons and William Daunt Applebee, who traded as Fitzsimons & Applebee. William Fitzsimons had been trading as an agent for sailing ships operating between Wexford and Liverpool since before 1830. William Applebee had been John Redmond's agent at Bristol. In late 1850, the name of the partnership was changed to Fitzsimons, Applebee & Company, implying the admission of at least one more partner - possibly the occasion when John Bacon was admitted to the partnership. The partnership was renamed John Bacon & Company in 1860, implying that Messrs. Fitzsimons and Applebee had withdrawn from the business.

In his early years in charge, John Bacon himself held only a minority of the shares in his ships. Later, however, he was often their sole owner. After the death of John Bacon in 1886, his ships were registered in the name of his executor, Joseph Wright. During this period, Joseph Wright took delivery of new vessels which were also registered in his name as executor. In 1889/90, the entire fleet was transferred to a limited company, John Bacon Limited.

A service between Liverpool and Wexford had been started by the Saint George Steam Packet Company, which operated its small paddle steamer *Kingstown* on the route. In 1828, the newly built vessel, *Marchioness Wellesley*, spent some time on the service. The early services do not appear to have lasted long, but there were two further attempts at a service in 1831. The Saint George Steam Packet Company made a second attempt with its ill-fated *Rothesay Castle*, which was wrecked later in the year in the Menai Straits with heavy loss of life. Another new vessel, *Magdalena*, also attempted the service later in 1831, with Thomas Richards as Liverpool agent. In 1832, the service was operated by *Harriet*, with William Fitzsimons as Liverpool agent. In 1833, *Harriet* continued on the route, but with a different agent. Thomas Richards became agent for an interloper, the Liverpool vessel *Abbey*. In 1834, yet another vessel, *Ormrod*, attempted the route, with another agent, Peter Haskayne (a shareholder in *Ormrod*), who had never previously been involved with the route. Fares by the *Ormrod* were advertised at fat cows and cabin class 10s, store cattle 6s, deck passengers 2s 6d, and pigs 1s 6d.

After a lapse in 1835, there were some sailings in 1836 by *Abbey*, in which Peter Haskayne also owned some shares, and yet another ship, *Eclipse*. Later in the year, Thomas McTear became the Liverpool agent for *Antelope*, this time owned in Belfast. During occasional absences of the *Antelope*, reliefs were given by an assortment of Belfast and Glasgow vessels - *Rapid*, *Ailsa Craig* and *Belfast*. John Redmond entered the Wexford-Liverpool trade in 1837, with his new wooden-hulled paddle steamer *Town of Wexford*, launched at Wexford on 19 January 1836. As originally built by Archer and Leared, she was 126 feet long by 20 feet breadth, but Redmond had her lengthened by 26 feet in 1838 bringing her up to 337 tons gross; she was re-measured at 362 tons gross in 1842. The service operated by the *Antelope* lasted for only a short period after the introduction of *Town of Wexford*, which became the first ship to have anything more than a short-term association with the route. Dr David McNeill wrote of the *Town of Wexford* in the second volume of *Irish Passenger Steamship services*:

> The arrival of this steamer in August 1837 caused great excitement. On 6 September the *Wexford Conservative* reported 'On Friday last as the steamers were about to sail from the Quay, a fine little boy happened to 'Harrah for the *Antelope*' when a ruffian seized the poor little fellow and threw him into the river. A boatman hastening to his relief was severely pelted with stones for his laudable exertions by some of the unfeeling rabble in the interests of the *Town of Wexford*...'

John Redmond's second ship, *Brigand*, an early iron-hulled paddle steamer, was completed in 1840; iron was chosen in preference to wood to reduce her draught, which could be a problem when crossing Wexford Bar. He placed her on a service between Bristol and Liverpool via Wexford. An advertisement in the *Liverpool Mail*, during the summer of 1840 read:

> Liverpool and Bristol, Liverpool and Wexford. The new and powerful iron steamer *Brigand*, E Goff, Master, and *Town of Wexford*, Andrew Jones, Master, are intended to sail from the Trafalgar Dock, with goods and passengers, for Bristol every Saturday evening and from Bristol for Liverpool, every Thursday, calling at Wexford each way, and for Wexford, every Thursday... Apply to Robert Bruce & Company, Bristol, John Leared, Wexford, or to Thos. M'Tear, 25 Water Street Liverpool.

The Wexford-Bristol leg appears not to have been very successful, and within a few years, the emphasis was on the Liverpool-Bristol service, which normally called also at Swansea and Milford. A third ship, another iron-hulled paddle steamer, the *Troubadour*, was added in 1841. There was more competition on the Wexford route from another company, the Wexford & Liverpool New Steam Navigation Company, which had acquired the steamship *City of Carlisle*. However, the new company did not last into 1842. Despite the removal of the competition, there appeared to be over-capacity with three ships, as *Town of Wexford* was chartered to the Saint George Steam Packet Company during the summer of 1842 for its North Wales service. After *Town of Wexford* had completed her charter, *Brigand* was sent on a voyage from Liverpool to St. Petersburg, only to be wrecked off the Isles of Scilly on 12 October 1842 during her outward voyage.

The Victoria Tower at the entrance to Collingwood Dock, the Liverpool berth for the Wexford Steamship Company's *Troubadour* (1841) in 1860.

The sinking of the *Brigand* (1840) after she had drifted off the Crim Rock near the Scilly Isles on 12 October 1842. No lives were lost.

[*Illustrated London News* (**Vol. 1**)]

The *Bristol Mercury*, Saturday 22 October 1842, reported:

Intelligence reached Bristol on Saturday morning last, of the loss of the new iron-steamer *Brigand*, on the Wednesday preceding, near the Scilly Isles. This news created considerable excitement in the mercantile world, and more particularly so for the fact of the *Brigand* having been built to trade between Bristol and Liverpool, calling at Wexford, in which trade she had been employed for the last two years, having left the station only a fortnight since for the purpose of proceeding from London for St Petersburg, for which port she was intended to sail from St Katherine's Dock, London, on Thursday last. The *Brigand* was one of the largest and most beautiful steamers ever yet built, being 600 tons burthen, and of 190 horsepower, and was remarkable for the beauty of her workmanship, the splendid fittings of her saloon, and her extraordinary speed. She cost in building £32,000…

It appears that the *Brigand*, having taken in upwards of 200 tons of coals, and a large quantity of patent fuel, for her consumption on her voyage to St Petersburg, sailed from Liverpool for London at two o'clock on Monday afternoon, and proceeded safely on her voyage until five o'clock on Wednesday morning, when they saw the St Agnes' light, which, from the refraction of light, the weather being very hazy, they conceived to be at a considerable distance – they were then steaming at 12 knots. The wind was light, but there was a strong current setting in for the Bishop's Rock. Suddenly the man on the look-out on the bow shouted 'Breakers ahead!' which they distinctly saw, but too late, unfortunately, for the rate at which they were going was such that they could not stop her, and although they put the helm hard aport, to endeavour to shave the rock, the vessel immediately afterwards struck most violently, and two plates of the bluff of the bow were driven in. She rebounded from the rock, but in an instance afterwards, such was the force of the current, she struck again, broadside on, the force of which blow may be in some measure conceived from the fact that it actually drove a great portion of the paddle wheel through her side into the engine room.

It was realised that the construction of the ship kept her afloat longer than a simply constructed wooden-hulled vessel would have lasted. The article continued:

The vessel was built in four compartments, the plan adopted in iron ships, or she would have gone down instantly, two of her compartments being now burst, and the water rushing into them at a fearful rate. By the two shocks, four and a half plates were destroyed, and four angle irons were gone in the engine room. The two compartments aft, still water-tight, she continued to float, and every exertion was used by her commander, Captain Hunt, for upwards of two hours, to save her, when the crew took to the boats, and shortly afterwards she went down, about seven miles from the rock, in forty five fathoms of water…

In 1844, the services were advertised in the *Wexford Independent*, for example, 8 May 1844, as:

Superior Steam Communication between Wexford and Liverpool, Wexford and Bristol and Wexford and Dublin. First class powerful steam packets, *Town of Wexford*, Captain Williams, and the *Eclipse* sail regularly from the Packet Wharf, Wexford, for the following ports: for Liverpool [every Friday] returning every Tuesday, cabin fare 10 shillings, deck fare 5 shillings, stewards fees 2s 6d. The *Eclipse* for Dublin [every Sunday] cabin fare 7s 6d, deck 3 shillings… The proprietor of these steamers has also a steamer plying regularly between Liverpool and Bristol by which all goods left at this office will be forwarded with dispatch and on the most reasonable terms…

The *Brigand* was not replaced until 1845. The *Eclipse* did not sail to Liverpool in 1844, being half owned by Thomas McTear. John Redmond then bought the wooden-hulled paddle steamer *Erin*, formerly owned by the Saint George Steam Packet Company. She had been built in 1826, so was elderly and only gave a few years' service, being broken up by 1851.

The replacement for the *Erin* in 1850 was the newly-built *Glendower*, which most unusually was built at Swansea. The normal pattern at this time was for the Wexford service to be operated by *Town of Wexford*, with the other two ships sailing to the Bristol Channel. The trade on that route appears to have been building up at that time, and on occasion *Troubadour* served only Bristol, with the Swansea sailing being taken by *Glendower*. This pattern was interrupted on 4 January 1852, when *Town of Wexford* was wrecked. The *Cork Examiner*, Wednesday 7 January 1852, reported:

> The *Town of Wexford*, steamer of Liverpool, was wrecked on Sunday morning on the rocks in Holyhead Bay: It appears that she was seen in the distance near Carvel Point, as early as half past eight am (Sunday), blowing a gale at north-north-west, but no information reached Holyhead 'til about 10.30 am, when she had anchored among the rocks at a point called Clipperia, east side Holyhead Bay. The lifeboat went out, but not near enough to render any service, and returned again to harbour. Steam was got up in the *Anglia*, railway steamer, which took the lifeboat in tow, and slipped her as near as was prudent to go, and the crew and passengers (about 43 in all) were safely landed on the Anglesey side. At 2.30 pm, she seemed waterlogged, filled and turned round, stern to the sea, and was then level with the water edge (being nearly low water). This morning (5th January) she has parted, and will be a total wreck, the gale having shifted to about west-south-west. It appears she had become leaky on the passage from Waterford to Liverpool, so much so, that cows and pigs, it is said, had to be thrown overboard, as the fires were nearly extinguished in the engine room. Several pigs, poultry, etc., have floated to the shore since. She has since gone to pieces.

The *Glendower* made some relief Wexford sailings after the loss of the *Town of Wexford*. Nevertheless, the service was suspended from the end of April until mid-August, when the wooden-hulled Thames paddle steamer *Emerald* was chartered to re-open the route. *Troubadour* was off the service between February and May 1855, and was replaced by the Cork Steam Ship Company's former vessel *Blarney*, partly owned by William Daunt Applebee since 1854. *Glendower* became John Redmond's third casualty on 29 July 1855, when she was wrecked off Anglesey on passage from Bristol to Liverpool. Happily all passengers and crew were safely landed. The Swansea newspaper *Cambrian*, Friday 3 August 1855, reported:

> The *Glendower* was a paddle wheel iron passenger boat, having been built in the Iron Shipbuilding Yard, Swansea, under the superintendence of Mr Spencer. She was a faithfully built ship, both in model and strength, and did much credit to her builder. She is about four years old, and was built expressly for trading between Bristol and Swansea, and Liverpool. Her engines were of about 140 horsepower; she was of 315 tons register, being capable of carrying from 250 to 300 tons in addition to her complement of coals, etc. She afforded excellent accommodation for a large number of passengers, whilst her internal arrangements and fittings generally were seen as to give every satisfaction.

> The *Glendower*, Captain John Wallace, left this port on Saturday morning last, about five o'clock, for Liverpool, having on board no less than 140 passengers. Her cargo consisted of general merchandise, in addition to which she carried a considerable quantity of manufactured copper, iron and tin. All went on well until the vessel arrived at about two miles south of Holyhead, when, unfortunately, a very thick fog came on suddenly, and was of such density that the crew were unable to see half the ship-length, and, in an unprecedented short space of time, she ran upon a rock. Immediately when she struck, the captain, with his usual coolness and precision, gave directions to get some spars to form a stage to land the passengers over, as there was some risk of landing in his boats, having a little ground sea. The landing was done with the greatest care and attention by Captain Wallace and his crew.

Evacuation of the ship was essential as it was feared she might slip off the rocks into deep water. No blame was attached to the captain and his officers, the accident being ascribed to 'the unfortunate setting in of a dense fog shortly before arriving off Holyhead'. The loss of the *Glendower* was covered by a series of charters, first the City of Dublin vessel *Diamond*, and then the Glasgow vessel *Auguste Louise*.

William Applebee first took an interest in a steam ship in 1852, when he acquired 16 shares in the paddle steamer *Emerald*, which had immediately been chartered to John Redmond as a replacement for the lost *Town of Wexford*. Applebee acquired a shareholding in two further ships, *Iron Prince* in 1853 and *Blarney* in 1854. *Iron Prince* never served on John Redmond's routes, but was sent straight out to Australia to find a buyer.

Blarney was chartered briefly to John Redmond for his Bristol Channel service before being sent out to the Crimea, where she was later sold. In July 1855 the brand name Liverpool and Wexford Steamship Company appeared in John Redmond's name and it advertised the *Emerald*, Captain Clarke, and *Blarney*, Captain Cademy, as sailing from Liverpool every Tuesday and from Wexford every Friday.

The first ship, in which John Bacon had a shareholding, to be employed regularly on the Liverpool-Wexford/Bristol Channel service, was the iron screw steamer *Sovereign*. She began her first voyage to Bristol on 9 August 1856. John Redmond's last remaining ship, the paddle steamer *Troubadour*, had been withdrawn from the Liverpool to Bristol Channel service in May 1856, being replaced by the iron-hulled screw steamer *Montagu*, which was operated by Fitzsimons, Applebee & Company. Initially, John Redmond had no shareholding in *Sovereign* or *Montagu*, so this appears to be around the date when he handed over the Wexford-Bristol-Liverpool services to Fitzsimons & Applebee. The chartered ship *Emerald* was withdrawn from the Liverpool and Wexford trade in August 1856, and was replaced by *Montagu*. The *Emerald* re-appeared in 1857, this time on the Bristol Channel service, mainly to Swansea, having in the meantime been acquired by various individuals associated with Fitzsimons, Applebee & Company. The *Wexford Independent*, Wednesday 20 August 1856 carried a description of the *Montagu*:

> We have today been favoured by the following particulars of this fine vessel, which is to leave Liverpool on the 26th inst., for Wexford, for which station the Liverpool and Wexford Steam Packet Company lately bought her, and are now fitting her out with every modern improvement for cattle, which will be able to walk in and out of each hold, and thus avoid all necessity for slinging. She will carry 300 head of fat cattle and 1,500 pigs and sheep; has good cabins for 30 passengers, and a house on deck for 100 steerage ones. Her speed is expected to enable her to make the passage at all times under sixteen hours. We also understand that our old and well-tried friend *Emerald*, is at once to be laid up for an entire new outfit, and then to be kept as stand-by, to help the *Montagu* if the trade requires it…

In 1857, John Redmond acquired a small shareholding in *Sovereign*, and also in the newly-built *Gipsy*, but he had no shareholding in the other vessels acquired by William Applebee and others in that year.

John Bacon first acquired a shareholding in a steamship, *Isabella Croll*, in 1854. She was not involved initially in either the Wexford or the Bristol Channel service. He followed this with shareholdings in *Annie Vernon* and *Sovereign* in 1856, and in *Montagu*, *James Kennedy* and *Emerald* in 1857.

Since the withdrawal of John Redmond's *Troubadour* from the Bristol Channel service in May 1855, the *Troubadour* had been chartered out and served on other routes including Liverpool to Dundalk and Liverpool to Sligo. In June 1858, she was sent to Belfast to be lengthened and was then chartered to John Redmond's nephew, William Archer Redmond, and entered the Liverpool and Wexford service in competition with the sailings of *Montagu*, every other Tuesday evening from Trafalgar Dock, Liverpool, and alternate Fridays from Wexford. Unfortunately the *Troubadour*, Captain Edmond Roach, working under the banner, the Wexford Steamship Company, sailed on precisely the same schedule as the *Montagu*, rather than taking the alternate week when no sailing was offered.

Advertisements for the Liverpool to Wexford service, now with the ships trading under the slightly different banner Liverpool and Wexford Steam Navigation Company, reflected severe competition against the two ships as, for example, in the *Wexford Independent*:

> Great reduction in freights and fares by the new and powerful steamer *Montagu*. The Liverpool and Wexford Steam Navigation Company beg to inform their friends in Wexford, Enniscorthy and neighbourhood, that until further notice, Freights on Flour, Indian Corn and Grain will be reduced to 4 shillings per ton, to and from Liverpool. Livestock as per agreement before shipment. Other goods one half the former rates. Cabin passage 7s 6d, Deck 2s 6d.

> This company now have two well tried and efficient vessels ready to take the station when required, so that shippers of Stock will be secured from disappointment. Powerful steamships *Montagu*, Captain Wm. Clarke, and *Emerald*, Captain G H Tallan, or some other suitable vessel, is intended to sail from Wexford [Fridays] and from Liverpool [Tuesdays]. Goods and stock intended for the above Steamer must be at the Steam Packet Wharf, two hours before the advertised hours of sailing. Apply to Fitzsimons and Applebee, 20 Water Street Liverpool…

The *Montagu* had enjoyed only a limited period without competition on the Wexford route. *Fire Fly*, operated by Richard & Robert Allen, of Wexford, was introduced onto the service in October 1856, and remained on it until the end of 1857. Fares with both companies were reduced from 12s 6d to 7s 6d saloon and from 6s steerage to 5s, and both steamers sailed on the same days, Fridays from Wexford. Eventually, early in 1858, the *Fire Fly* was sold to the Bristol General Steam Navigation Company for its Bristol - Wexford service, with calls at Tenby and Carmarthen on the run to Wexford and just Tenby on inducement on the return leg.

In January 1860, William Applebee sold most of his remaining shares in *Gipsy* to John Bacon. At the end of February 1860, John Bacon took over the agency for the two services from Fitzsimons & Applebee. On Saturday 21 February 1860 a report in the *Wexford Independent*, signed by John Bacon, pledged to keep the *Montagu* on the Wexford to Liverpool service:

> At a meeting of the owners of the *Montagu* steamer, lately at Liverpool, it was determined to continue her on the Wexford Line and not to be deterred by the opposition of any company however formidable it may appear.

> The principal owners are proprietors of several other steamers, and they consider they would better serve their interests to bear on opposition for even ten years, than be beaten off any line; and these parties have now purchased the shares of such as do not wish to encounter further opposition.

> The loss of the small shares held by the other parties is nearly compensated by the advantages they derive from their connection with the steamers.

> As the *Montagu* is a modern boat, fitted up in the best manner to ensure cheapness and efficiency, her expenses are much less than vessels of more antiquated construction; and as she has since the opposition received great support from her friends, and as the strictest economy has been used in her management, the loss by continuing the contest will be comparatively small, particularly, as during the opposition she has been able to combine occasional trips to other ports, with her weekly trips to Wexford.

> The owners of the *Montagu* return their friends their sincere thanks, for the support they have received, and can assure them that they will not be deprived of that vessel, for although the owners are well aware that the station will not be worth the expense of a protracted contest, still other considerations make it in their interest to run for the time named, rather than suffer a defeat.

> They also pledge themselves to have good and efficient vessels on the Line; and being shipowners and merchants they know the value of giving parties engaged in the trade every facility.

> Signed JOHN BACON, Liverpool

'Vessels of more antiquated construction' was, of course, a reference to the paddle steamer *Troubadour*, and its operator, William A Redmond and his Wexford Steamship Company. The *Montagu* was an iron-hulled screw steamer. The sailings of the two lines were both out from Liverpool on Tuesday (*Montagu* from Trafalgar Dock, *Troubadour* from Collingwood Dock) and back from Wexford on Friday and they were both still sailing on the same weeks from the same ports.

Chapter 8

JOHN BACON IN CHARGE

The year 1860 sees, for the first time, John Bacon in charge of the *Montagu* sailing between Wexford and Liverpool every other week. The title Fitzsimons, Applebee & Company was restyled John Bacon & Company although the trading name Liverpool and Wexford Steam Navigation Company was retained. The fortnightly round trip was increased to weekly in March with the addition of the screw steamers *Annie Vernon* and *James Kennedy*. They were iron-hulled screw steamers built by Thomas Vernon at Liverpool for John Bacon & Company in 1856 and 1857 respectively. They had been used primarily on John Bacon's new Bristol to Liverpool service until they both came onto the Wexford service. The *James Kennedy* was slightly larger but they were well matched for the Wexford trade although neither was advertised to carry passengers.

Competition for trade on the route was from the Wexford Steamships Company managed by William A Redmond, also agent at Liverpool, and ironically the cousin of one of the former proprietors of the Liverpool and Wexford Steam Navigation Company. A new limited liability company, the Wexford Steamships Company Limited, was formed in January 1860, and 300 shares of £100 each were issued. By the end of June, the Wexford Steamships Company had chartered the Clyde Shipping Company's screw steamer *Vivandière* for a two ship weekly service with the paddle steamer *Troubadour*, Captain Edmond Roach.

A contemporary illustration of the Wexford Steam Ship Company's *Vivandière* (1856)

The *Vivandière* was replaced by the *Colonist* in August, Captain Beckett, with some sailings proceeding to Ayr with a connection to Glasgow by the steamer *Ayrshire Lass*. Nevertheless the *Vivandière* returned to Wexford in 1861 having been bought by William Redmond. She commenced from Wexford on Thursday 26 September with her first departure for Liverpool for her new owners.

Despite earlier promises to the contrary, John Bacon withdrew from Wexford quite quickly, leaving the *Troubadour* in charge. In the meantime he put his energies towards developing his service between Liverpool and Bristol. Advertisements in the *Western Daily Press*, for example, 9 December 1861, showed a weekly service:

Average passage to Bristol, 28 hours. Steam communication between Bristol and Liverpool, Swansea and Milford for the month of December 1861. Reduced fares to Swansea, Cabin 4s, deck 2s. The Liverpool and Bristol Steam Navigation Company's steamships *Sovereign*, *Montagu*, *Annie Vernon*, *James Kennedy* and *Briton Ferry*, or some other suitable vessels, are intended to sail from Cumberland Basin with goods and passengers (unless prevented by any unforeseen occurrence) as follows… [weekly on Tuesday from Bristol and weekly from Liverpool on Saturdays] landing passengers at the Mumbles for Swansea weather permitting… From Liverpool to Swansea direct, the *Briton Ferry*, with cargo only, on Wednesday, returning from Swansea on Sunday.

Fares: Bristol to Liverpool cabin 12s 6d, deck 5s; Liverpool to Milford or Swansea (including boat hire) cabin 15s, deck 7s; Bristol to Swansea, cabin 4s, deck 2s; Bristol to Milford, cabin 8s 6d, deck 5s; Swansea to Milford cabin 5s, deck 3s; Swansea to Liverpool, cabin 13s, deck 7s…

The service had originally been operated by Fitzsimons & Applebee using steamers such as the *Emerald*, *Sovereign* and, of course, the *Montagu*. John Bacon acquired shares in these three steamers in 1856 and 1857. On 1 March 1860, John Bacon & Company took over the Liverpool agency from Fitzsimons, Applebee & Company with the *Montagu* running to Wexford and the *Annie Vernon*, *Artizan*, *Sovereign* and *James Kennedy* running to Bristol and Bristol Channel ports. In addition J Bacon rather than John Bacon & Company acted as agents for the *Briton Ferry* owned by H K Vivian of Swansea. She was a small cargo steamer of just 200 tons gross that dated from 1852 and did a weekly return trip with cargo only to Swansea. In August 1861 the *Annie Vernon* was chartered to bring 546 tons of Welsh coal into the Mersey from Briton Ferry, destined for the bunkers of the *Great Eastern*. She arrived two days after the big ship had set sail to cross the Atlantic. That same year the main Bristol service was maintained by the *Sovereign* with a weekly departure from either port.

In June 1862, John Bacon & Company invested in the share sale for the flotation of the United Kingdom Screw Collier Company Limited, John Bacon later becoming a director of that company. A major import into Liverpool was coal from Cardiff and other Welsh ports brought in by the collier *Isabella Croll* and also by the *James Kennedy*. John Bacon had been involved with the *Isabella Croll* since 1854 when he bought 8/64th shares in her. Lancashire coal did not have the best calorific properties for the furnaces of the big passenger steamships that had started to cross the Atlantic, and supplies of high grade Welsh coal were always in demand at Liverpool. The *Isabella Croll* pursued the trade throughout much of the following year, 1863, and in October 1864 she was sold for further service with Scottish owners. She was returned to John Bacon in default of the mortgage and sold in 1866 to none other than the United Kingdom Screw Collier Company Limited.

John Bacon could call upon a core fleet of ships by January 1864: *Sovereign, Montagu, Artizan, Briton Ferry, Gladiator, Annie Vernon, James Kennedy, Thomas Powell* and *Helena*. Some of them were available through partners or associates but most were majority owned by John Bacon. The *Briton Ferry* was still owned by H K Vivian of Swansea, while the *Windermere* was a more substantial steamer of 339 tons gross that was on charter from H W Schneider of London although not used on the Liverpool to Bristol service.

In January 1864 the *Montagu* went back to the Wexford to Liverpool route, running alongside the *Troubadour* for some time in the summer. John Bacon was the Liverpool agent for the *Montagu* while W A Redmond retained the agency for the *Troubadour*. By this stage the paddle steamer *Troubadour* had become thoroughly outdated and inadequate for the cattle trade and the ever increasing one-way exodus of Irish emigrants destined for transhipment at Liverpool. From late summer 1864, the *Troubadour* was employed on a variety of work including Dublin to Liverpool cattle runs and was eventually sold to Malcomson Brothers of Waterford. Thus, in the summer of 1866, the sole steamer on the route was the *Montagu* under John Bacon's management and the name 'Wexford Steamships Company Limited', that had been adopted by W A Redmond, disappeared from the companys' register. John Bacon was now operator of services between Liverpool and Bristol and Liverpool and Wexford.

An important event took place on 28 February 1865, when the steamer *Jane Bacon* was launched from the yard of Bowdler, Chaffer & Company at Seacombe. She was especially designed and constructed for John Bacon although he initially owned just 20/64th shares, later increased to 44/64th. She was a substantial steamer of 505 tons gross and was a valuable addition to the fleet with accommodation for a small number of cabin passengers and a larger complement of deck passengers. She was followed at the end of April by the smaller single deck steamer *Swansea*, of just 309 tons gross, built by the same yard.

In 1865, the *Sovereign* performed the weekly run to Bristol and the *Montagu* to Wexford. The new steamer *Jane Bacon* took up the Cardiff coal roster alongside *Isabella Croll* and *James Kennedy*, while the *Swansea* worked between Liverpool and Swansea, taking copper ore north to Liverpool and the smelters in Lancashire, returning with refined metals and general goods. The *Artizan* and the *Helena* did some coal runs during the spring. The *Helena* had earlier been bought by John Bacon in 1863 (all 64 shares) and was an interesting little ship having been built by George Cram at Chester in 1854, with her 30 horsepower steam engine built and installed at Liverpool. The *Helena* was initially used to serve the smaller ports of the Bristol Channel such as Barnstaple and Llanelli, but in 1865 she was on the Liverpool to Swansea service instead of the *Swansea*. However, in April 1865 she was sold to James Graham of Londonderry, although John Bacon retained a mortgage against the sale. The *Helena* still worked some of the Bacon rosters after her sale.

Another new steamer the *Agnes Jack* was delivered by Bowdler, Chaffer at the end of the year. She was another large ship, 181 feet long by 27 feet beam with a depth 16 feet contributing to a gross tonnage of 574 tons; she completed her maiden voyage to Swansea early in January 1866. The year 1866 saw pretty much the same pattern of sailings as 1865, again with *Sovereign* the mainstay of the Bristol service and *Montagu* the Liverpool to Wexford route.

Business continued through 1867 much as before. One new steamer was accepted from Bowdler, Chaffer in March, the *Bristol*, which then took up a charter in the Mediterranean. She returned home in the late summer and on a voyage from Middlesbrough to Briton Ferry foundered off Start Point on 30 November with a crew of nineteen aboard. The *Morning Advertiser*, 6 December 1867 noted:

The most disastrous accounts keep coming in from all points of the coast of the effect of the heavy gales. Yesterday telegrams were received announcing the loss of two iron screw steamships. One was the *Smyrna*, from Odessa bound for Hull… The other ill-fated steamer is reported to be the *Bristol*, from Middlesbrough bound for Briton Ferry. She is stated to have foundered in the Channel, and the telegram speaks of the master and two men having perished. The remainder of the crew were saved by a Danish vessel, and landed at Cherbourg.

Shortly afterwards, the relatively new steamer *Swansea* was lost in collision in the Mersey, but this accident could not be blamed on the weather. The *Manchester Courier and Lancashire General Advertiser,* Tuesday 24 December 1867, reported as follows:

A collision, resulting, it is feared, in the total loss of a steamer, with a cargo of copper ore, occurred in the Mersey on Saturday. The steamers which came into collision were the *Magnetic*, belonging to the Belfast Steamship Company, and the *Swansea*, belonging to Messrs. Bacon & Co., of Water Street, engaged in the copper ore trade.... The collision occurred about half past eight o'clock in the morning, in the Victoria Channel, midway between the Crosby and the Rock lightships. The *Magnetic* was returning to this port from Belfast, with a general cargo and a number of passengers, and the *Swansea* had left Liverpool for Swansea, when at the point above indicated she came into collision with the *Magnetic*, which ran into her amidships, the *Swansea* being, it is stated, on her wrong side of the channel. There was no fog at the time of the collision, and the vessels could be seen from each other for a long distance.

The *Swansea*, a somewhat smaller boat than the *Magnetic*, which is 311 tons register, was completely stoved in, and her crew, about twelve in number, had only just time to save themselves by getting on board the *Magnetic*, when it sunk, five or six feet of her masthead alone remaining out of the water. The *Magnetic*, which sustained some damage to her port bow, proceeded to the Clarence Dock, where she landed the crew of the *Swansea* and was discharged. The *Swansea* lies in a dangerous position, having sunk in mid-channel.

During the following year, the wreck of the *Swansea* was dispersed with explosives so that the channel was completely clear by November 1868.

The steamer *Llewellyn* was delivered in March 1868. This ship was a departure for John Bacon & Company as she had been built speculatively by Thomas Charlton at Grimsby and was bought by, and fitted out for, Bacon. She was a direct replacement for the *Swansea* on the copper ore and coal run to and from Swansea. She was only small, a single deck ship, and was just 125 feet long and 20 feet broad with a depth of 9 feet.

Fares by the *Montagu* to Wexford in 1868 were still advertised at 12s 6d cabin, return 18s, deck 7s 6d. Early in the year the *Annie Vernon* was sold to an owner in Briton Ferry. Thereafter business continued much as before with the *Sovereign* on the Bristol route and the *Llewellyn* serving other Bristol Channel ports.

Three times in quick succession, the *Montagu* went aground on Hanton Bar off Wexford during 1868. The first was on 22 February when she waited to be floated off on the next tide. Then on 23 March, inbound to Wexford, she needed to have some of her cargo removed before she was freed, and the same happened on 16 June, outbound.

In 1869, Samuda Brothers of London speculatively built the steamer *Plantagenet* which they were able to charter to John Bacon on completion. John Bacon acquired the *Louisa* in October 1870 and the *Heptarchy* in 1871 from the same source, initially both jointly owned with Joseph D'Aguilar Samuda. In 1872, each partner took 100% ownerships of one of the vessels, with John Bacon taking over the *Heptarchy* and Joseph Samuda taking the *Louisa*. The three Samuda ships were big single deck cargo ships, ideal for use in the coal trade and wherever bulk cargoes or heavy cargoes needed to be shipped.

Disaster struck in 1870. On 2 April the iron-hulled *Sovereign* sailed as normal on her Saturday departure from Liverpool for Bristol and quickly encountered increasingly thick fog as she attempted to round Anglesey. Misjudging the position of the ship, the *Sovereign* went aground at Dulas Bay that evening. The weather was quiet and all personnel were safely evacuated in the lifeboats. Salvage of the vessel later proved impossible and she was declared a constructive total loss. Saleable items recovered from the wreck comprised a variety of provisions and other goods which were auctioned at Liverpool on 25 April.

A number of charters were made from the Belfast Steamship Company to cover the Bristol passenger and cargo service. In May the *Arbutus* came onto the service followed by the *Electric*, *Voltaic* and *Semaphore* in quick succession, the latter a schooner rigged three-masted screw steamer dating from 1855 while the *Voltaic* was state-of-the-art being commissioned only in 1868. Nevertheless there were gaps in the service and a replacement vessel for the hapless *Sovereign* was hastily sought. The two year old iron steamer *Sunlight* was the answer and was bought from her owners Laurence Hill & Company of Port Glasgow and re-registered at Liverpool. She made her first Bristol sailing from Liverpool at the end of July. The *Sunlight* was a little smaller than the *Sovereign*, being 340 tons gross, but she was fit for the weekly general cargo trade then on offer between Liverpool and Bristol and offered comfortable berths for a small number of passengers.

The new Belfast steamer *Voltaic* (1867) was chartered to maintain the Wexford service after the loss of the *Sovereign* in 1870.

[*DP World*]

The *Sunlight* (1868) was bought in 1870 for the Liverpool to Bristol service. Typical of her day she had a whaleback fo'c'stle and boat deck in order to shed water. She is seen at Bristol.

[*World Ship Society Photo Archive*]

A rather telling court case took place in 1870, as reported in the *Morning Advertiser*, 22 April 1870:

> John v. Bacon: The defendant was the owner of the steamers *Gipsy* and *Sovereign*, and by agreement with Captain Williams, the owner, he had the use of the hulk *Empress*, which lay in the Channel at Milford Haven. The *Gipsy* carried people to the hulk, when they remained until the *Sovereign* came and took them to Liverpool. On the night of 6th May 1868, the plaintiff, with his nephew, went on board the hulk, and there took tickets for Liverpool. Whilst there the plaintiff fell down a hatchway into the hold and severely hurt himself. The action was to recover damages for his injuries and at the trial before Mr Barren Channell, of Haverfordwest, the verdict was for the plaintiff for £100. Afterwards a rule for a new trial was obtained upon the grounds that the defendant was not the owner of the hulk nor responsible for the way in which it was kept, and that the plaintiff had contributed to the accident by his own negligence, because he went between decks, although cautioned not to do so until an attendant accompanied him and the other passengers. For the plaintiff this latter statement was denied, and it was further said that by a written agreement with Captain Williams the defendant was to light the hulk and that he had omitted to do this properly…

The *Gipsy* was a 33 tons gross iron-hulled tender that had been built in Glasgow for William Applebee in 1857. She was deployed at Milford until the wooden steam barge *Pembroke* was commissioned for John Bacon in 1872, at which time use of the hulk *Empress*, with all its apparent hazards, still continued.

The Wexford service continued as before, with sailings by the *Montagu*. Ambitions of completing the triangle with regular sailings between Wexford and Bristol had always been thwarted by the existing and reliable service offered by, for example, the paddle steamer *Briton* operated by the Bristol General Steam Navigation Company.

The Bristol General Steam Company's paddle steamer *Briton* (1862) operated between Bristol and Wexford and prevented Bacon ships from completing the Liverpool-Wexford-Bristol triangle. She grounded on the Wexford Bar in 1892 and her hull was badly strained; she was scrapped shortly afterwards.

Nevertheless a few sailings were operated as inducement offered. The *Sunlight* settled into the Bristol routine and the company's other ships served as required on Bristol Channel coal runs and occasional tramp-type sailings to the near continent. The small single deck steamer *Llewellyn* was sold to the Antrim County Iron Ore Company Limited in 1871.

In 1872, the Wexford service was still Tuesday from Liverpool and Friday from Wexford. The current advertisements in the *Wexford Constitution* noted:

> Free passage to Liverpool is allowed to the owners or their men solely with the intention of their taking of the animals. Servants in cabin, full fare. Fares cabin 12s 6d, return ticket 18s, deck 6s.

The small iron-hulled passenger and cargo paddle steamer *Pharos* was acquired in February 1872 from the Aberdeen, Newcastle & Hull Steam Navigation Company. Despite her having been built in 1846, originally for the Commissioners of the Northern Light Houses, she was ideal as a relief steamer for the Wexford service and for general duties elsewhere. She stood in for the *Montagu* in July, for example, while the *Montagu* did a number of cattle runs from Scotland and Cumbria into Liverpool. The tenure of the *Pharos* in the fleet was brief, however, and she was sold in 1873.

Business carried on as before, with *Sunlight* and *Montagu* providing the key services to Bristol and Wexford respectively. *Agnes Jack* was the main ship used on the coal runs up to Liverpool and both *Plantagenet* and *Heptarchy* supported this work.

The *James Kennedy* was lost on 30 November 1873. The *Shields Daily Gazette*, Wednesday 3 December 1873, reported:

> Loss of a Tyne-bound steamer: The screw-steamer *James Kennedy*, of Liverpool, from Rotterdam for the Tyne, ballast, was abandoned on Sunday morning off the Dutch Coast, having sprung a leak in the engine room. In a very short time the water rushed in and extinguished the fires. The crew were saved by the smack *William & Louise*, of Lowestoft, and landed at the latter port yesterday.

The *James Kennedy* later drifted ashore across a stone dam at Petten, on the Dutch coast about 18 miles south of Nieuwe Diep. By 6 December she had broken her back and attempts at salvage were given up.

The steamer *Furness Abbey* was bought from Mories, Munro & Company of Glasgow in 1873. She was a small ship of just 178 tons gross but a useful unit for the copper ore trade into Liverpool. She did not serve the company long as the *Glasgow Herald*, Monday 27 April 1874, reported:

> St Davids, April 25: The *Furness Abbey*… from Swansea for Garston, with copper ore, struck last night during a thick fog on Bishops, and sank in ten hours. All hands saved.

The Whitehaven Shipbuilding Company delivered the new cargo steamer *Muncaster* to John Bacon in 1874. She was another big steamer measuring 233 feet long with a beam of 30 feet and a depth of 16 feet. She was mainly deployed on tramp duties and charters. Although the small paddle steamer *Pharos* had been sold in 1873 she was chartered back during December 1875 so that the *Montagu* could attend for refit. Coal runs were still mainly operated by the *Agnes Jack* supported by *Jane Bacon*, with the *Sunlight* running the coastal liner service to Bristol.

John Key & Sons of Kinghorn completed the big steamer *Tudor* for John Bacon in 1876, the builders initially retaining part ownership in the vessel. She was 223 feet long with a beam of 29 feet and a depth of nearly 18 feet. Like the *Muncaster* before her she was mainly deployed on tramp duties.

Services remained much as before with the *Sunlight* serving Bristol and *Montagu* on the Wexford station. The coal work became less important, presumably as dedicated colliers were able to work the cargo more efficiently. However, a regular weekly general cargo and passenger service to Swansea was introduced in 1878 by the *Jane Bacon*, with calls at other ports in the Bristol Channel by inducement.

On 24 July 1875, the *Montagu* went aground on the North Bar at Wexford. She soon flooded up to the 'tween decks while the passengers were safely landed along with a consignment of sheep. All lighters that could be procured were sent to help and steam pumps were requested. The crew was taken off in the evening by the local lifeboat *Ethel Aveline*. In October 1875 the *Montagu* was successfully raised and moved two lengths astern with the deck just two feet above the water at high tide. By mid-month she was pumped out and brought into Wexford where she was beached. Temporary repairs were made so that she could be towed to Liverpool for survey and repairs. She left Wexford under tow on 25 October and was back in service early the next year.

The *Montagu* was again in the news when she stranded on the East Bar coming into Wexford on the morning of 24 April 1878. It was expected that she would float off on the next tide and tugs were sent to assist her. However, the wind had risen from the east, the sea became rough and the attempt had to be abandoned. The *Montagu* finally got off the Bar the next day and anchored in the south bay to lighten ship.

The steamer *Plantagenet* was lost on 14 October 1880 on passage from Newport to Barcelona with a cargo of coal. She foundered near Cape Palos at about midnight, but Captain Campbell and his crew were all landed safely at Porman. The ship apparently struck a sunken hazard off Cape Palos and sank within an hour in deep water.

On Thursday 26 January 1882, the *Aberdeen Evening Express* reported:

> During the dense fog that prevailed yesterday two steamers, *Lara*, from Waterford, and *Jane Bacon*, outward bound, collided at the entrance to Bristol port. Both were much damaged, but no one was injured.

On Friday 30 November 1883, the *Aberdeen Evening Express* reported:

> Early this morning a collision occurred in the Bristol Channel, resulting in the foundering of the barque *Lord Marmion*, and out of the crew of forty, six were lost namely, Captain Evan Evans, the first mate, three able seamen and a boy. The *Lord Marmion* was on her way from Swansea to Valparaiso, and about midnight, when off the Helwick lightship, was struck by the steamer *Jane Bacon*, of Liverpool, and sunk in two minutes. The steamer also was much injured.

On 27 January 1883 the big steamer *Agnes Jack* was lost at Port Eynon Point, Oxwich, on the Gower. She was on passage from Cagliari to Llanelli with iron and lead ores. An initial report from Swansea issued on 27 January at noon read:

> A three-mast ship, name unknown, is ashore on Port Eynon Point; hull under water; crew in rigging; rocket apparatus cannot reach her from mainland; tide ebbing; may save some crew if mast holds.

This was followed in the evening by:

> Our representative has returned from Port Eynon with proofs of loss of *Agnes Jack*. Ship gone to pieces, crew all lost. He picked up ship's articles, some clothes and one sail. No further news of a second steamer reported.

Later newspaper reports stated:

> The Steamer *Agnes Jack*, of Liverpool, was wrecked in Port Eynon bay, on the Gower Coast, today and all hands were lost. Residents of Port Eynon heard cries of distress at sea about 05.00 and when day dawned saw a vessel with only one mast above water and eight men clinging to it. One fell off into the sea. The others remained there until 11.00, when the mast fell over and carried them with it. Four rockets were fired, but not one reached the ship. The sea was so high that it was impossible to send off boats. The vessel was not identified until after she sank, when a boat with the name on was washed ashore… It is reported that a Llanelli pilot was on board when the steamer sank.

Many years later the following brief report was published in *The Times*, 17 May 2012:

> A 10ft tall anchor dedicated as a memorial to eight sailors who drowned off Swansea in 1883 has been stolen by scrap metal thieves. The anchor, from the SS *Agnes Jack*, was recovered last year and had been placed at the entrance to the Port Eynon boat club. Police believe that the thieves used a crane to lift it onto a lorry.

Four new steamers were commissioned in 1883 and 1884: the *Plantagenet* in 1883, the *Stuart* in April 1884, *Vigilant* in June and *Slaney* in August 1884, the latter designed for the Wexford service. They were iron-hulled ships, all but the *Vigilant* built by William Allsup & Sons at Preston. The *Vigilant* was built at Low Benwell, Newcastle-upon-Tyne, by T & W Toward & Company. The steamer *Sunlight* received a new set of compound engines in 1883 increasing her service speed slightly, to just over 9 knots.

The new Wexford steamer, the *Slaney*, finally allowed the faithful *Montagu* to stand down in the early summer of 1884. The *Slaney* was built at Preston by William Allsup & Sons and was an iron-hulled steamer, some 180 feet long by 27 broad with a depth of 12½ feet. She was equipped with a modern compound engine that gave her sufficient speed to maintain the service to Wexford in time to be able to land her passengers in the morning after an evening sailing from either Liverpool or Wexford. She had permanent stalls fixed in the 'tween decks with adjacent accommodation for the drovers and was a fine vessel for the route. Meantime, the *Montagu* took up service between Liverpool and Swansea allowing the *Jane Bacon* to take up the Bristol service, displacing the *Sunlight*.

The new steamer *Slaney* was lost early in 1885 as reported in the *Freeman's Journal*, Friday 16 January 1885:

> This morning [Thursday] the steam tug *Ruby* left Wexford for the purpose of discovering what vessel it was that showed signals of distress on the previous evening. She proved to be the new steamer *Slaney*, from Liverpool to this port, with passengers and a general cargo. The vessel stuck on the bar in attempting to cross it on the previous evening and became unmanageable. After striking, she drifted onto the Dogger Bank, where she remains in a very critical position. During the night Mr Briggs, HMC, and Cox of the two Royal National Lifeboats stationed at Rosslare Fort, made an attempt to reach her in the large lifeboat, but the sea being too bad they had to return. About 9 o'clock this morning, the *Ruby* (Captain Ennis) called at the fort and took out the small lifeboat, and after great difficulty succeeded in taking off the passengers, nineteen in number, some of them being children in arms, and placed them in safety aboard the *Ruby*. Again the lifeboat took off for the steamer. The ebb tide was running stronger and the sea had got up. After two attempts, Mr Briggs with his gallant crew took off Captain Devereux and his crew, 15 hands all told, and placed them on board the *Ruby*. The lifeboat was then taken in tow and brought to her station. The passengers and crew of the steamer were brought to Wexford this evening and landed at the Liverpool Steam Packet Wharf. The *Slaney* left Trafalgar Dock, Liverpool, on Tuesday night, with nineteen passengers… with a general cargo consisting principally of bacon, sugar, flour, iron, etc. On Wednesday evening she arrived in Wexford Bay, and was boarded by Moses Murphy, Bar Pilot. The steamer when she left Liverpool was drawing 11 feet 5 inches, at the time she came for Wexford Bar the signal at Rosslare pilot station indicated that there was only 10 feet of water on the bar, and the danger signal was hoisted to show that the sea was very bad on the bar. In attempting to cross it the steamer struck the ground heavily… Should the weather become bad she will in all probability become a total wreck. Even at present very little hopes are entertained of getting her off. Some of the cargo is only partially insured. None of the passengers' effects have been landed, and the vessel has been abandoned. The *Slaney* was only built last year, principally for this trade, and had not made more than 25 voyages. She belonged to Messrs. John Bacon, and Co., Liverpool.

In 1886, the *Jane Bacon* offered passengers on the Bristol service a fare of 12s 6d between Liverpool and Bristol and Liverpool and Milford, cabin, deck 6s.

John Bacon died at his residence, Clwyd Hall near Ruthin in North Wales, on 28 November 1886. He was 67 years old.

Chapter 9

JOHN BACON & COMPANY - 1886 TO 1913

Following the death of John Bacon in November 1886, the ownership of the ships in which he had been a majority shareholder was vested in his executors. Joseph Wright, as executor and manager of John Bacon & Company, thus became nominal owner of the ships during 1887 until the formation of John Bacon Limited in 1889. The ships involved were the *Montagu*, *Jane Bacon*, *Sunlight*, *Heptarchy*, *Muncaster*, *Plantagenet*, *Vigilant*, *Eden Vale*, and the Milford steam tenders *Pembroke* and *Cleddau*. The fleet was, for the most part, modern, with three ships having been built since 1880, and a fourth, the *Slaney* built specifically for the Wexford service but already lost (Chapter 8). The funnels of the ships were quite distinctive being black with two equally spaced white bands, the upper two black bands the same width as the white ones, and said to resemble streaky bacon.

Joseph Wright was not content with his fleet, particularly with the stopgap steamer *Vigilant* running the weekly cattle run from Wexford. He ordered a new ship for delivery in 1889. This was the small steamer *Eden Vale*, the first ship in the fleet to be equipped with the modern triple expansion steam engine. She was 180 feet long and 27 feet broad with a depth of 13 feet. She was launched from the yard of Samuel McKnight & Company Limited at Ayr on 29 January 1889 and, when accepted shortly afterwards, was placed on the Wexford service. This allowed the new steamer *Vigilant*, which had been especially adapted by her builders for the route following the loss of the *Slaney* in 1884, to stand down. The *Eden Vale* had a shallow draught suitable for negotiating the Hanton Bar at all but the lowest of tides, she was equipped with livestock stalls and carried portable sheep pens that could quickly be erected in the 'tween deck. Accommodation was provided for the drovers but passengers were no longer carried. However, the same weekly roster was maintained.

The *Sunlight* was on the Swansea route with a weekly departure from Liverpool. The *Montagu* was still running to Bristol and the *Jane Bacon* maintained her Liverpool to Milford and Swansea service. The *Vigilant* supported the *Eden Vale* at Wexford during the height of the livestock season during the summer months. The big single deck ships were mainly employed on tramp duties with cargoes of coal and iron ore. The *Heptarchy* and *Plantagenet* operated in the Bristol Channel area at times but were mainly employed elsewhere.

The *Stuart* was sold in 1888 to German owners and renamed *Borgefelde*, but in July that year she went aground on Hillswick Ness in St Magnus Bay on the Orkney Islands and became a total loss. The *Brunswick* was sold later in the same year.

The *Manchester Courier and Lancashire General Advertiser*, Wednesday 3 July 1889, reported:

> Wreck in the Mersey: On Monday morning the steamer *Tudor*, when going up the Mersey to Garston, got ashore at a place known as Devil's Bank, not far from Garston. It was thought that she would be got off all right in a tide or two, but during the night she broke in two pieces. This was owing to the very heavy nature of her cargo, which was iron ore. This she was bringing from Sestrilevanti. The crew reached the shore in safety, and were received at the Sailors' Home. Salvage operations were afterwards commenced for the recovery of the cargo. The *Tudor* was an iron screw steamer of 924 tons gross register… She was built at Kinghorn in 1876.

In 1890, the *Montagu* was shortened by 11 feet to reduce her loaded draught and deadweight capacity so that she could again serve on the Wexford cattle and sheep runs. The need for the extra ship was not deemed necessary the following year and in 1891 she was sold for further service as a dumb lighter.

In June 1892, a new *Tudor* was commissioned; modern in every way she had a triple expansion steam engine that provided a service speed of 10 knots. The big steamer *Salerno*, built in 1882, was bought in August 1892 to support the collier trades and sold five years later as demand for her services dropped. In 1893 the wooden steam 'flat' *Edith* was purchased from Salt Union Limited. She was a typical Mersey flat, built at Northwich in 1879 for the salt trade and she sailed south to take up duties alongside the steam barges *Cleddau* and *Pembroke* at Milford.

In 1894, John Bacon Limited accepted another large steamer which was given the name *Stuart*, the second ship to be given that name. She was 230 feet long by 33 feet beam with a depth of just under 15 feet. She was equipped with the now standard triple expansion steam engine which drove a single propeller to maintain an impressive service speed of 11 knots. Also in 1894 the small, two year old steamer *Kelvinside* was acquired. She was 120 feet long with a beam of 20 feet and a depth of just 9 feet, and the machinery and accommodation was aft. Her intended role was feeder ship on the Bristol Channel, but she was sold in 1898, later coming under the ownership of the General Steam Navigation Company of London.

The *Stuart* (1894) spent her first sixteen years in the service of John Bacon & Company, and under Italian ownership was lost in the Great War.
[World Ship Society Photo Archive]

The *Kelvinside* (1893) was bought in 1894. She is seen at Preston in the colours of the General Steam Navigation Company after 1906.
[David Whiteside collection]

Another small engines-aft steamer, the *Talbot*, had been built for John Bacon Limited in 1890. In addition another Mersey flat joined the fleet, the wooden sailing flat *Invincible*, and like the steam-powered *Edith*, built originally for the salt trade. The *Invincible* was employed on the Mersey for feeder services to the main line services.

In 1895, the small iron-hulled vessel *Tivyside* was bought to support the Bristol Channel smaller ports and feeder services. She had been built as long ago as 1869 and had spent her entire career working in the Bristol Channel and Cardigan Bay area. The big collier *Muncaster* was sold in 1896.

The wooden steam barge and tender *Pembroke* was wrecked on 9 December 1896 at Popton Point, Angle Bay, Milford Haven. She was lost in wind conditions north west force 10, on passage from Neyland to Angle. She was literally blown ashore; the cargo hold was flooded from a gash on the port side, while the keel was also broken. The crew was saved by soldiers from nearby Popton Fort using a line. The wreck was raised in 1901 and repaired; the ship started a new career based in Fowey.

In the last few years of the nineteenth century the company was beset by a series of ship losses that reflected the difficulties of the coasting trades in those days. The first occurred on 20 March 1897 when the *Plantagenet*, Captain Jones, was wrecked on Black Head near Coverack, Cornwall, on passage from St Valery to Runcorn, with a cargo of flints. The *Liverpool Mercury*, Wednesday 24 March 1897, reported:

> The *Plantagenet* is another steamer belonging to Liverpool which has been wrecked on our own coast within the past couple of days, making the list within that time four steamers actually sunk, apart from several which have been damaged by stranding, mishaps to machinery, or injured by fire. The *Plantagenet* was an iron screw steamer of 619 tons, belonging to J Bacon Limited of this city. She was coming to the Mersey from France, and got ashore at Blackhead, not far from Falmouth, where the crew landed. The *Plantagenet* remained on the rocks for some time, and then went down in deep water. She was built at Preston in 1883, and was classed 100A1 at Lloyd's.

By the 22 March the ship was reported to be filling with the tide and likely to become a total wreck. Later in the day she turned on her starboard side with masts and funnel below water and the hull completely submerged at high tide. The ship was abandoned as a total wreck.

Later that same year, on 23 December 1897, the *Jane Bacon* sank in the Crosby Channel. The *Liverpool Mercury*, Friday 24 December 1897, reported:

Yesterday morning in thick weather a collision occurred off Crosby between the steamer *Jane Bacon*, belonging to Messrs John Bacon Limited, steamship owners in Water Street, inward bound from Bristol, and the steamer *Lombardy*, inward bound from Montevideo with cattle. Both vessels were steaming slowly up the Channel, the weather at the time being very foggy and thick, and it is suggested that the *Lombardy* struck the *Jane Bacon* somewhere about the starboard beam. It was soon seen that the *Jane Bacon* had been seriously injured. Water poured into her through her side, and she at once began to settle down stern first. The *Lombardy*, which was very little injured, gave what assistance was necessary, and, after taking off the crew of 13, later on transferred the men to the tug *Weathercock*, which was quickly on the scene. The *Jane Bacon*, as mentioned above, lies midway in the Crosby Channel, and until removed will be a danger. Mr Ashton, the Assistant Surveyor for the Dock Board, and Lieutenant Simpson, RN, the water bailiff, were early on the scene to make some arrangements with regard to the wreck.

The small steamer that succeeded the *Jane Bacon* on the Liverpool to Bristol weekly sailing was completed in 1898 for John Bacon Limited and given the name *Brunswick*. Her triple expansion engine maintained a speed of 11 knots. She was a two deck ship and like the *Jane Bacon* had accommodation for a small number of passengers.

On 13 February 1899 the *Stuart* was blown ashore between Osmington and Preston, Dorset, in a gale, after her anchor cables parted. Press reports stated:

During the heavy squall last night a steamer, name unknown, parted from her cables in Portland Roadsteads, and at high water was carried over the rocks forming part of the new breakwater. Fearing the vessel was damaged the crew got on board a tug. The steamer continued to drive, and this morning went ashore near Osmington. Tugs are endeavouring to render assistance.

The *Stuart* had been in ballast. An unsuccessful attempt was made at high water, at midnight on 14 February, to pull her off the shore. She was finally refloated on 10 April and taken for survey and repair before taking up service with her owners again.

The little *Tivyside* was not as fortunate as the *Stuart* when she stranded on 15 June 1900, at Overton Cliffs, Port Eynon, Gower, on passage from Carmarthen to Bristol. The *Western Mail*, Saturday 16 June 1900, reported:

The *Tivyside*, a steamer of 66 tons register, in ballast, from Carmarthen to Bristol (master Harvey), went ashore at Porteynon Point on Friday morning. The crew, numbering six, and seven passengers, were all saved. The Rhossilly and Oxwich rocket companies were both in attendance, but their services were not required, as the crew and passengers came ashore in the ship's boats. The steamer is a total wreck, her masts and funnel only being visible.

The tragic loss of the regular weekly Liverpool and Bristol steamer *Brunswick*, when only two years old, was one of the worst accidents in the history of John Bacon & Company. It occurred on 24 December 1900. The ship was wrecked on the Hook Sands about 8 miles off Clevedon in the Bristol Channel, on passage from Liverpool to Bristol, as encapsulated in this report in the *Western Daily Press*, Thursday 27 December 1900:

There seems very little prospect of salving the steamer *Brunswick*, which capsized on the Welsh Hook, on Monday morning, or of recovering the bodies of the four missing men. The vessel is gradually disappearing beneath the sand, and the boisterous weather of Tuesday night added to the difficulty of making a satisfactory survey. Yesterday Captain Wade went d to the scene of the wreck, but nothing practical could be done. Of the three bodies lying at Bodminster Mortuary, only one has been identified…

The bodies of four men in the engine room are buried beneath enormous quantities of sand, which have been swept into the hull by the tide. The only passenger was Thomas Cooper, a boilermaker, of Liverpool, who, instead of being below at the time of the accident, was on deck. He leapt into the only boat that could be got off, and, as he jumped, heard the cries of the poor fellows in the engine room as the sea swept upon them.

The *Western Daily Press*, Wednesday 26 December 1900, sombrely described what had happened:

> In the West of England the festivities marking the final Christmastide of the century have been rendered distinctive by a sombre note of tragedy. Whilst those secure on land were preparing, or looking forward to the preparations, for the great festival of the year, a vessel went to her doom within sight of land, and almost within touch with the agencies that connect the city of Bristol with its maritime outposts near the mouth of the river. Unfortunately the wreck of the steamer *Brunswick* was not unattended with loss of life. Seven men out of a crew of fifteen have perished under circumstances of an unusually pathetic character. The *Brunswick*, a Liverpool and Bristol vessel, was steaming up the Channel early on Monday morning, those on board no doubt rejoicing in anticipation of spending a happy Christmas Day in Bristol. By a terrible stroke of fate the cheerful prospect was suddenly obliterated by death and disaster.
>
> The *Brunswick* grounded on a sandbank between the English and the Welsh Grounds, not far either from Clevedon or Portishead. Many vessels have just touched these perilous shoals, and managed to get clear before much damage had been done. With the *Brunswick* it was different. As soon as she touched the sandbank she was caught by a very swiftly flowing flood-tide, and capsized. The captain, a passenger and seven seamen, who were on deck at the time of the accident, succeeded in launching and getting into a boat, in which they reached a haven of safety. But the other seven were drowned – caught, it is conjectured, in the interior of the vessel when she turned over. The whole tragedy was enacted with an appalling suddenness, and the pathos of it is that the victims were denied the smallest chance of escape. The gale which swept across the country during the latter days of last week was followed by a fog of unusual density. It was in this early morning fog that the *Brunswick* essayed to reach a safe anchorage at the mouth of the river, and it may not be amiss to assume that the thick atmosphere was responsible for the disaster...

The *Prestonian* was bought from Henry Tyrer & Company of Preston in 1900. In 1913 she was renamed *Sir George Bacon* and shortly afterwards Powell, Bacon & Hough Lines Limited gave her the name *Gower Coast*. Henry Tyrer & Company replaced her with a new, and slightly large *Prestonian* which was commissioned in 1901; two ships now with the same name. The small steam lighter *Taurus* was purchased in 1901 for use at Swansea and elsewhere. She was an iron-hulled vessel completed in 1890 and was good for a speed of 7 knots. She was sold locally for further service in 1909.

The *Prestonian* (1899) was bought in 1900 and was renamed *Sir George Bacon* in 1913, and then *Gower Coast* within the merged fleets of Powell, Bacon & Hough Lines Limited.

[World Ship Society Photo Archive]

An important new steamer, the ***Wexford*** was delivered at the end of 1901 by Samuel McKnight & Company Limited of Ayr. She was specifically designed for the Irish Sea cattle trade and had a loaded draught such that she could cross the bar at Wexford at most states of the tide. She was a shelter deck ship with two cattle decks, both accessed by large doors set in the hull through which the cattle could walk on board at Wexford and disembark at the lairage at Birkenhead the same way. Her arrival in service allowed the ***Eden Vale*** to take up general duties except when an extra ship was required for cattle work. Apart from Wexford, cattle were also carried from Waterford either to Birkenhead or occasionally to Bristol or Swansea.

On 1 December 1903, the *Heptarchy*, Captain Brody, grounded off Troon Harbour on the rocks abreast Troon Harbour Light on arrival in ballast from Belfast. The weather was hazy. She was refloated without damage on the next tide. Just ten days later, on 11 December, she was in collision off Caldey Island, with the German sailing ship *Roland*, on passage from Cardiff to Cape Town with a cargo of coal, the wind conditions being west force 8. At the time the *Heptarchy* was on passage from Newport, Monmouthshire, to Waterford also with a cargo of coal, and was attempting to tow the sailing ship *Roland*, of Bremen, to Milford Haven. The *Roland* had lost her rudder. The collision occurred when the tow rope fouled the propeller, the impact stove in the stern and damaged the port bulwarks of the *Heptarchy* causing considerable damage and carrying away the mizzenmast and a lifeboat. As a consequence the *Heptarchy* was rendered unmanageable. The *Roland* was towed into Milford by three tugs, while the *Heptarchy* was herself towed to Swansea by the Glasgow steamship *Miner*. The *Heptarchy* was further damaged while changing berths at Swansea on 16 December when she hit the quay hard, damaging the stem of the bow and adjacent plates. Repairs were beyond the value of the ship and she was sold for demolition at Liverpool in March 1904.

In 1904, the *Eden Vale* was sold as surplus since the dedicated cattle carrier *Wexford* had been commissioned three years earlier. A neat little steamer, *The Lady Belle*, was acquired from W T Ferris of Newry, also in 1904. Her machinery was aft and the bridge and deck crew accommodation forward of amidships. The bridge had an upper flying bridge the full width of the ship to facilitate docking. There was a deep well deck with No. 1 hatch forward, and No 2 hatch-aft of the bridge. She had two 5 ton derricks supported on the forward mast and the same arrangement at the mizzen. There was a small signal mast aft and like many ships of this era she carried a foresail to assist in steering. She was sold in 1912.

The Lady Belle (1900) was bought in 1904 and remained in John Bacon & Company service until 1912 when she was sold to owners based at Cardiff.

[David Whiteside Collection]

The *Vigilant*, Captain Curwen, was wrecked on 25 July 1906 about 8 miles south of Roches Douvres (a group of islands between Guernsey and northern Brittany). She struck the Gautier Rock, while on passage from Cardiff to Saint Brieuc with a cargo of coal. She sank within 5 minutes, but all the crew evacuated the ship in one of the lifeboats and were later safely landed at Loguivy by the pilot vessel *Leroy*. Although the Gautier Rock was well charted it was not marked by a warning buoy and any error in navigation in the vicinity could, as in this case, be fatal. *The Board of Trade Wreck Report* for the sinking of the *Vigilant* records:

> The *Vigilant* left Cardiff on the 24th of July last, bound for St. Brieuc, France, with a cargo of 405 tons of coal, drawing 11 ft. 6 ins. forward, and 12 ft. 10 ins. aft, and was under the command of Mr Robert Curwen, who holds a master's certificate of competency, No. 09122, and had a crew of 11 all told. All went well up to 8.15 p.m. of the 25th July last, when Roches Douvres light was sighted, bearing about three points on the starboard bow, her course being then SE ½ E magnetic. The master stated that at 9.40 pm he took a four-point bearing; at 10.20 pm the light was abeam and the distance run by log 4½ miles, and that he made various alterations in the course to round the light about the same distance off.

> At 10.55 pm the course was set S by W, magnetic, to sight Grand Lejon light. The weather at this time was dark and clear with a moderate breeze from ESE with smooth sea. At 11.30 pm the vessel, being still on the same course, struck some unknown object, which the Court is of opinion was probably the two fathoms patch to the southward of the Barnouic Beacon, and which was marked on the chart by which the vessel was navigated. The blow did not appear to be a heavy one, nor was the way of the vessel apparently stopped, but immediately afterwards the engines were stopped and orders given to sound the wells. Before this could be done the chief engineer came on deck and reported that the vessel was sinking and the fires were out. The starboard lifeboat was at once launched and all hands got into her and left the vessel. By this time the water was up to the engineers' rooms in the engine-room

and nothing further could be done, the vessel sinking fast and disappearing stern first at about 11.45 pm, the tide being about 2½ hours ebb. At 5 am of the 26th July, when making for the shore, a French fishing vessel took them in tow and landed them at Loguivy in France…

If the vessel struck the patch above mentioned, this was due to the fact that she had passed much nearer to the Roches Douvres light than the master calculated, and was carried to the westward by the ebb tide, whose force the master under estimated, having no information either on the chart or in the sailing directions which he used, as to the strength of such tide. As the exact cause and precise locality of the foundering of the vessel are only matters of conjecture, the Court does not feel justified in attributing the loss of the vessel to the wrongful act or default of the master.

The small steam barge *Pennar* was commissioned in 1907 for use at Milford. She was built by W & J Yarwood at Northwich, Cheshire and equipped with a compound engine, built by Yarwood, placed aft. There were two hatches forward of the bridge structure, separated by a single steam crane. Similar vessels, the *Enniscorthy* and the *Harfat*, were delivered by the same builder in 1908 and the summer of 1911 respectively, joining the *Edith* and *Pennar* at Milford.

The steam barge *Pennar* (1907) was built for service in the Milford area and is seen here in Powell, Bacon & Hough Lines Limited / Coast Lines Limited colours.

Between 1910 and 1913, a major rebuilding programme was undertaken. This started with the acceptance of the aptly-named livestock carrier *John Bacon* from the yard of Murdoch & Murray at Port Glasgow early in 1910. Like the *Wexford* before her, she had two clear upper decks with cattle stalls and room for portable sheep pens, all accessed by two large doors in the hull for the animals to walk on and off the ship. Unlike her predecessor she was built as a shade deck vessel, the hull being open beneath the sheerstrake to allow ventilation to the upper livestock deck, with a partial deck above to protect the livestock. She served mainly between Birkenhead and Wexford but was subject to tidal restrictions entering and leaving Wexford due to her draught. The triple expansion steam engine was placed aft and maintained a service speed of 11 knots. The bridge was between the forward hatch and the aft hatch, each plumbed by a single 5 ton derrick to access general cargo stowed in the two deep holds. Crew accommodation was situated in the poop. The *John Bacon* had accommodation for men accompanying livestock and also had a few berths for fare-paying passengers. Two years after the *John Bacon* was commissioned, the older cattle carrier *Wexford* was sold as surplus.

The livestock carrier *John Bacon* (1910) at Wexford. Note the long ports, beneath the sheerstrake, that open to the shade deck.

The *John Bacon* was joined by a series of engines aft, bridge amidships two deck steamers: the sisters *Lady Bacon* and *Lord Bacon*, completed by George Brown & Company at Greenock, and in December 1912 the new steamer *Sir Roger Bacon* was registered, having been laid down as the *Clydeholme*, and a few days later the larger *Sir Edward Bacon,* built in 1899 as the *Birker Force*, joined the fleet and finally *Sir Walter Bacon* was completed in 1913. George Brown delivered the first two in 1911, each 142 feet long by 24 feet broad with a depth of 10 feet.

The *Lord Bacon* (1911) was sold in 1913 to James Henry Monks (Preston) Limited and renamed *Elizabetta*, as seen here.

[World Ship Society Photo Archive]

The *Sir Roger Bacon* (1912) in F H Powell & Company colours following that company's takeover of John Bacon Limited.

The *Sir Walter Bacon* (1913) was renamed *Gloucester Coast*, as seen here, when she joined the merged fleet of Powell, Bacon & Hough Lines Limited just eight months after she was commissioned.

The **Sir Edward Bacon** was slightly larger in capacity than the first pair and was built by Irvine Shipbuilding & Engineering Company in Ayrshire. She had an outdated compound surface condensing engine with cylinders of 18 inch and 42 inch diameter and a stroke of 30 inches working at a pressure of 140 pounds per square inch. The **Sir Walter Bacon** was another product from George Brown & Company but was much bigger, with a length of 210 feet, a breadth of 33 feet and a depth of 13 feet.

The commissioning of the new ships allowed a number of older vessels to be sold. The big collier **Stuart** was finally sold in 1910 to Joseph Constant of London, and the same year the **Tudor** was sold to owners in Russia.

In the late evening of Saturday 7 September 1912, the steamer **Talbot** was lost in the Queen's Channel, Liverpool. She sank following a collision with the big passenger and cargo steamer **Kent**, belonging to the Federal Steam Navigation Company. The **Talbot** was on passage from Cardiff to Birkenhead with a cargo of coal. A boat from the **Kent** took off the crew while the **Talbot** drifted outside the main channel and sank. The Dock Board Marine Surveyor considered the wreck an obstruction and requested permission from the underwriters to remove the wreck which was later dispersed with explosives. The work started on 12 September and was completed by 30 September.

In October 1912, John Bacon & Company Limited was bought by F H Powell & Company but allowed to trade as a separate entity under the continued management of Robert Mountfield, but under the close scrutiny of Alfred H Read the manager of F H Powell & Company. The steamship services of the two companies were consolidated and further disposals were proposed and carried out in 1913 while discussions also took place with Samuel Hough regarding a merger of interests between all three companies. In the event, it was agreed that the Bacon interests in collier work to and from the Continent should be dropped in order to focus on the core coastal cargo and passenger liner service based on Liverpool and working down as far as London but including existing services to Waterford and Wexford and between those ports and the Bristol Channel. Ships sold in 1913 were the **John Bacon**, **Lady Bacon**, **Lord Bacon** and **Sir Edward Bacon**.

From the Board of Trade wreck report on *Brunswick* held in January 1901

The Court, having carefully inquired into the circumstances attending the above-mentioned shipping casualty, finds, for the reasons stated in the Annex hereto, that the loss of the said vessel was due to the negligent navigation of her by her master, Mr. John Richard Wade, whose certificate, numbered 102,148, the Court suspends, but having regard to his previous career, only for a period of three months from the date hereof. The loss of the said lives was due to the capsizing of the vessel…

The ***Brunswick*** was employed in a regular service running between Liverpool and Bristol, and, on the 22nd day of December last, she left Liverpool for Bristol with a general cargo of about 676 tons, and a crew of fifteen hands, all told, and one passenger, and under the command of Mr. John Richard Wade. Her draught of water on leaving Liverpool was 15 feet 8 inches aft, and 12 feet 10 inches forward. The 676 tons of general cargo was distributed as follows: 351 tons (of which 125 tons was pig lead) was carried in the lower holds, 258 tons in the 'tween decks, and 67 tons of bacon and porter on the main deck. The master was appointed to the command of this vessel in January, 1900, and with the exception of about five weeks had been in command, running constantly between Liverpool and the Bristol Channel, and, in addition to this, had been in command of other boats belonging to the same Company, running on the same route for the last six years. All appears to have gone well on the voyage in question, and at about 4 am of the 24th December last, the Breaksea Light Vessel was passed on the starboard side at an estimated distance of one and a half miles, the weather at this time being fine with a slight haze, and the sea perfectly smooth. The vessel was at full speed, making about 10 knots through the water. In due course the vessel passed through the Barry Roads, and Flatholme Light was also passed on the starboard side. From this position a SE by E course was steered until the English and Welsh Ground Light Vessel was sighted, when it was kept slightly on the port bow. At 5.25 am the light vessel was abeam on the port side, at an estimated distance of half a mile, whereupon the master stated that he set a course E by N which, allowing one point for easterly deviation, would make the magnetic course due East. The tide at this time was about half flood and the top of the spring tides. The master was on the upper bridge, and the man at the wheel was also on the same bridge steering by steam. There was no look-out man stationed forward, the master conducting the whole of the navigation, and keeping the look-out himself, and the mate (whose watch it was) was by the master's orders superintending the rigging of the derrick, and getting the hatches cleared for the unloading of the cargo.

The master stated that in his opinion, based upon previous experience, the E magnetic course would, with the flood tide setting him slightly to the northward, take the vessel up in mid-channel and at a safe distance off Blacknore Point. At the time of taking his departure from the English and Welsh Grounds Light Vessel, the master stated that the Clevedon Red Light was in sight but that he did not see the Blacknore Point Light until after the stranding. The weather at the time of arriving at the light vessel is described by the master as being still fine with a slight haze, but that, in about eight minutes after passing the light vessel, a fog set in which obscured both lights and he thereupon went to the compass and saw that the vessel was to the northward of her course. He spoke to the helmsman about this, and upon going a second time he noticed the same thing, whereupon he remonstrated with him telling him if he did not mind he would have the ship ashore. Thirteen to fourteen minutes having elapsed since passing the light vessel, and no lights coming in sight, the master gave orders to keep the vessel ESE, intending if nothing was seen in a few minutes to bring the vessel head on to the tide. The order had scarcely been executed before the vessel was felt to take the ground, whereupon the engines, which had up to this been going full speed ahead, were stopped, the helm put hard aport and the engines again put at full speed ahead. Finding she did not move, the engines were put astern and the vessel then canted broadside on to the tide and immediately went over on to her port side, the water almost coming up to the starboard bulwarks. Upon the vessel taking the ground the mate went into the chart house for the lead and line, but so suddenly did the vessel capsize that before he got the lead and line he was immersed in the water and was with great difficulty rescued. The second mate was sleeping aft on the starboard side, and he with the steward got out of the cabin, walking on the starboard bulwarks to the bridge. The men in the forecastle could not be reached, neither could those who were on duty in the engine room, and although the Court are clearly of opinion that everything was done that could be done to save the lives of those in peril, the result was that seven lives were lost, the names and ratings of which will appear hereafter. The master and eight others reached the starboard lifeboat and hung on to the ship for a time in the hopes of still doing something to save those on board, but finding it useless they cast adrift and pulled towards Blacknore Light, which by this time had come in sight. When getting near the land they saw a tug which took them in tow and they (the nine survivors) were all landed in safety. During the afternoon of the same day, viz., the 24th December, the master visited the wreck at low water in a tug, when he found the vessel submerged in the sand, and was enabled to recover the bodies of the three men in the forecastle but none of those in the engine room. Finding the vessel so submerged she was abandoned, and the ship and cargo have become a total loss…

The stranding of the vessel was due to her not making good the course set from the English and Welsh Lightship. The capsizing of the vessel was due to the effect of the strong tide on the vessel as she lay aground on the edge of the bank. One man who was on watch at the time appears to have been washed overboard and carried away when the vessel capsized. Three sailors were drowned in the forecastle and three hands in the engine room, none of these being able to make their way out.

Chapter 10

SAMUEL HOUGH BECOMES A SHIPOWNER

Thomas McClune and Frederick Augustus Tamplin (McClune & Tamplin) 1856.
Frederick Augustus Tamplin & Company 1856 - 1865.
Pennington & Company 1864 - 1865.
Pennington & Hough 1865 - 1867.
Samuel Hough 1867 - 1902.
Richard George Hough (executor of Samuel Hough) 1902 - 1904.
Samuel Hough Limited 1904 - 1913.

The third strand leading to the formation of Powell, Bacon & Hough Lines Limited in 1913 was Samuel Hough Limited. The founders of the group of owners leading to Samuel Hough's ownership were Thomas McClune and Frederick Augustus Tamplin, who traded under the name McClune & Tamplin. They were originally shipping agents, but later moved into shipowning. Between 1847 and 1850, they were agents for the short-lived Dublin and Liverpool Steam Ship Company and its ships *Dublin*, *Liverpool* and *Water Witch*, which had been set up in opposition to the City of Dublin Steam Packet Company. They became the Liverpool agents for the British & Irish Steam Packet Company (B&I) when it started a Liverpool-Waterford service, B&I extended its Dublin to London service to Liverpool, and McClune & Tamplin were appointed Liverpool agents for that service. They were also agents for the Cambrian Steam Packet Company Limited, of Aberystwyth, which operated a service from Liverpool to north and mid Wales with the steamship *Plynlimon.* The firm acquired its first ship in 1854. Thomas McClune died on 9 November 1856, and thereafter the business was carried on by Frederick Tamplin in his sole name.

In September 1864, Tamplin sold half his shares in the steamship *East Anglian* to William Pennington, and the other half to Samuel Hough, who was an employee of Frederick Tamplin's firm. He also sold the business, which traded initially as Pennington & Company; the identity of the other partner(s) is not clear, but Samuel Hough was probably one of them. The firm was re-styled as Pennington & Hough in 1865. When William Pennington died on 25 March 1867, the firm thereafter traded under Samuel Hough's name. Initially, Samuel Hough was a minority shareholder in the ships which he managed, but gradually he acquired sole ownership. On his death in 1902, Richard George Hough was appointed as executor. He managed the ships for Samuel Hough's estate until 1904, when they were transferred to a limited company, Samuel Hough Limited.

McClune & Tamplin began its service on the Liverpool to London route in March 1856. B&I had withdrawn from the Liverpool to Dublin section of its service in 1855, due to a shortage of ships following the loss of one vessel and the charter of two others for use as transports in the Crimean War. Once it was clear that B&I did not intend to resume its sailings from Liverpool, the way was clear for McClune & Tamplin, as B&I's former Liverpool agents, to operate the service to London in their own right. However, to avoid any conflict with B&I, their ships did not call at Dublin. Their service included calls at some south coast ports, including Penzance, Falmouth, Plymouth, Dartmouth, Torquay and Portsmouth. Initially, the chartered Bristol ship *Rose* was employed; she operated the service intermittently until November 1855. In June, she was joined by the firm's own vessel, the iron-hulled screw steamer *Loire*. She was 177 feet long by 25 feet broad with a depth of 13 feet and had two hatches, one forward and one aft of the central island. The second ship to be owned by McLune & Tamplin, *Empress Eugenie*, was completed in 1855, and joined the Liverpool to London service in July. Of similar design to the *Loire*, the *Empress Eugenie* was a slightly bigger ship 187 feet long by 26 feet in the beam with a depth of 14 feet. The steamer *Antelope*, in which both John Bacon and McClune & Tamplin held some shares, made a single round voyage to London in August 1856.

In 1857, the service continued with *Loire* and *Empress Eugenie*. There were two further appearances by the chartered *Rose*, in March and April. In August and September, there were three round trips from London by *Kangaroo*, chartered from Malcomson Brothers, of Waterford, replacing *Empress Eugenie*, which was off service.

The *Loire* was wrecked on the Wirral peninsula at the start of a sailing to London on 27 January 1858. The *Liverpool Mail*, Saturday 30 January 1858, reported the incident:

> We have to record the loss of the screw steamer *Loire*, at the Hoyle Bank at the mouth of the Mersey, at 10 pm on Wednesday night last. The *Loire* struck on the bank during thick weather, while bound for Penzance, Plymouth, Falmouth and London, with a dozen passengers, and a general cargo of fine

goods, salt, soda ash, etc. Though a gale had been blowing for several days previously, the sea was not rough when the steamer struck, but she immediately broke in two amidships, all the butts starting on the port side. The passengers remained quietly on board, till they were taken off next morning by the Hoylake lifeboat. Since then a portion of the cargo has been safely removed, but the greater part of it will be much damaged. The steamer was injured, and so was the greater part of the cargo. She was built in 1854 by Thomas Vernon & Son of this town.

Two flats went to the wreck on 29 January and took off the deck cargo and whatever else they could salvage, including 136 tons of soda ash in casks. The ship was declared a total constructive loss.

Following the loss of *Loire*, the Belfast steamship *Ossian* was chartered in mid-February and she remained on the London service until early May. In March, the Glasgow vessel *Genova* was bought as a permanent replacement for the *Loire*. She had been built in 1850 for the Anglo-Italian Steam Navigation Company, and traded to the Mediterranean. Her principal claim to fame was that in 1853 she had been chartered to the Canadian Steam Navigation Company to inaugurate its service from Liverpool to Canada. In doing this, she became the first steamship ever to sail from Liverpool to Quebec and Montreal. She only made a single round trip to Canada, and then returned to her usual duties. In McClune & Tamplin's service, the *Genova* occasionally called at Cowes in addition to the usual south coast ports.

In 1859, *Genova* was off service for most of the first three months of the year. To cover her absence, three rare visitors made appearances on the Liverpool to London service. The first was Thomas Wilson's Hull-based steamship *North Sea*, which made two round voyages in January. She was followed by two Stockton steamships, *Cleveland* and *Ironmaster*, each of which made a single round voyage in February and March respectively. In May 1859, the Bristol vessel *Rose*, which had been chartered by F A Tamplin for a few voyages in 1856 and 1857, was sold to him by the ship's mortgagees. She made several more voyages to London in January, September and October 1860. The *Rose* was a wooden-hulled paddle steamer built in 1842 for the Bristol General Steam Navigation Company. She originally had an American style beam engine but this was replaced with more conventional machinery in 1856. In 1860 Frederick Tamplin commissioned the small wooden passenger and cargo screw tender *Young England* but she was sold two years later. She was used in Cardigan Bay mainly at Aberystwyth. She worked in conjunction with the passenger service run by the steamer *Plinlymon* which was owned by W S Crealock of Aberystwyth, and which was agented at Liverpool by Tamplin.

In 1860, the iron-hulled steamer *Liverpool* was delivered to Frederick Tamplin by Marshall Brothers of Willington Quay. She was a substantial ship 202 feet long, 27 feet broad with a depth of 16 feet. She had two masts and was rigged as a brigantine. She had a straight stem with no figurehead to get in the way when berthing. Fine cabin accommodation was provided for the passengers. The *Liverpool* immediately became popular both with passengers and shippers on the Liverpool to London service.

The *Empress Eugenie* was lost on 25 January 1861. The *Liverpool Mercury*, Monday 28 January 1861, reported:

Intelligence reached Liverpool on Saturday of the loss of the screw steamer *Empress Eugenie*, off Point Lynas. The *Empress Eugenie* was an iron vessel of about 425 tons burthen, belonging to the General Steam Packet Company, for which Mr F A Tamplin is the manager. She was under the command of Captain Higgins, and plied between this port and London, Plymouth, Penzance, etc. From the particulars of the occurrence, as reported by the captain, it appears that the vessel left this port on Thursday last, on her usual trip, about half past ten in the forenoon. At midnight she passed the Fairway buoy, Queen's Channel. The following day, Friday, it came on to blow violently from the south west, and at about 3 o'clock in the morning the engineer reported that the ship was making a great deal of water in the engine room – the pumps, though constantly going, being unable to keep her free. This state of things continued until about six am, every effort being made by the crew to reduce the leakage, but without success. It was then ascertained that the water had put out the fires, and the engines consequently became useless.

The mainsail was set in order to keep the vessel's head to sea, but she still laboured heavily, the water gaining rapidly in the hold, notwithstanding the exertions of all on board to check it. Under these circumstances it was deemed advisable, there being no hope of saving the ship, to lower the lifeboats. This was accomplished, and the crew and passengers, numbering 34 persons, got safely into the boats.

About half past five they finally left the vessel, which very shortly afterwards settled down and sank. She was then about 30 miles north east of Point Lynas. The crew and passengers in the boats rowed in a north east direction until 2.15 am, on the 26th, when the foremost boat fell in with the steamer *Countess of Galloway*, Captain Broadfoot. With some difficulty the occupants of the boat were got safely on board the steamer.

The fact of the other boat being still missing, having in her 15 of the passengers and crew of this ill-fated ship, being communicated with Captain Broadfoot, he immediately proposed going in search of her. The steamer was put round in the direction where the *Empress Eugenie* had foundered, and after a search of about two hours, Captain Broadfoot had the satisfaction of falling in with the other boat. The sufferers, consisting of nineteen persons, were rescued, and taken on board the *Countess of Galloway*. The whole of the party during the stay on board experienced the greatest kindness from Captain Broadfoot, his officers and crew, who supplied them with food and clothing and everything which their unfortunate position demanded.   The sufferers were entirely destitute, having in consequence of the heavy seas, been obliged to throw all their clothing and other effects overboard, in order to lighten the boat. They reached this port in the *Countess of Galloway* on Saturday morning. The *Empress Eugenie* had a large cargo, consisting of general goods, the loss of which, with the vessel, is covered by insurance.

On 6 January 1863, the fine new steamer *Liverpool* foundered after a collision at sea with the barque *La Plata*. The *North London News*, Saturday 17 January 1863, reported:

Lloyd's agent, on hearing of the collision, dispatched vessels to the spot, where the steamer and barque had foundered, with a view of ascertaining the possibility of recovering either of the ships or portions of the valuable cargo, but it is feared that both are a total loss, owing to the great depth of water in which the wrecks have sunk. It appears that the steamer lies in 17 fathoms. The latter, with the cargo, is valued at £60,000, and the *La Plata* and cargo at £36,000. In the course of Friday the Receiver of Wrecks for the district of Holyhead proceeded to examine the crews with reference to the collision, and the sub-joined depositions of the two masters and the chief officer of the *La Plata* taken on oath, have been forwarded to the marine department of the Board of Trade:

Captain William Charlesworth, late master of the *Liverpool* steamer, states: We left London on 30th December… the crew mustered 23 hands and there were three passengers. We called in at Plymouth and Penzance, and at 10 pm on the 6th we were off Port Lynas, which bore SSE, three quarters of a mile distant, the wind blowing fresh from SSE. The steamer's course was SE by E, when a light was seen right ahead about half a mile distant. We ported our helm, which put her head SE, and in about four minutes afterwards the helm was put hard a-port until her head was SSE. The other vessel (which proved to be *La Plata* from Liverpool) starboarded her helm, and seeing that a collision was certain, I stopped and reversed the engines full speed. We had stopped her way and the engines were reversing when the barque struck us on the port midships with great force. Finding we were fast sinking, we got the boats out and had the passengers and crew safely put into to them. Soon afterwards she went down. We were picked up by a schooner and landed the next morning at Holyhead.

Mr Enos Faulkner Mackintosh, chief officer of the barque *La Plata*, who was in charge of the watch at the time of the collision, states the ship was bound to Lima, with a general cargo, consigned to different merchants in Peru. She was built of iron, 275 tons register, and the owner were Messrs Imry Tomlinson, at Liverpool. We left Liverpool on the 6th. At 9.50 pm on that day, the ship was lying three miles off Point Lynas bearing SSW, the weather was hazy, with a fresh breeze from the NE. The course we were steering was N by W, when a light was seen right ahead. At first it seemed to be a fixed light, and we expected that it was that at the Skerries. About two or three minutes after ten o'clock we saw the light a little on the starboard bow, as also a green light, which proved to be the steamship which had recently crossed the barque's brow. I immediately starboarded the helm a little, and directly I had done so I saw the steamer's three lights and her red and bright light. Seeing that a collision was inevitable if not quickly prevented, the helm was put hard a-port. After this was done some person in the steamer shouted out to me to port the helm, but in another minute the vessels came in collision, the barque's bow striking the steamer in the main chains. The barque's fore compartment was stove and immediately filled. We took to the pumps and endeavoured to keep her afloat, but she sank about ten o'clock in the morning. We were picked up in our boat by a steamer.

The *Liverpool* was replaced by the purchase of the steamer *East Anglian* from John Johnson of London. She was a considerably smaller steamer than the *Liverpool* being just 148 feet long by 23 feet broad with a depth of 14 feet and was equipped with a compound engine. She was not unknown on the service, having made four round sailings in 1861. Her first sailing in 1863 from Liverpool for London was in early February 1863.

The Liverpool to London steamer *Liverpool* (1862) depicted in collision with the barque *La Plata* off Port Lynas, Anglesey, on 6 January 1863.

[Illustrated London News]

In 1865, the iron-hulled steamer *Edith* dating from 1861 was purchased by Messrs. Christopher M Webster, Charles B Harrington, John D Hewitt, Charles R Fenwick, Samuel Hough (8 shares), William Pennington & others (as Fenwick & Company). She was 181 feet long by 28 feet broad with a depth of 17 feet and a useful size for the tramp trades as well as supporting the coastal liner trades. In 1865 and 1866 she traded to Valencia as well as to London.

In 1866, the **West of England** was delivered by Bowdler, Chaffer & Company of Seacombe. Launched on 30 April 1866 for Pennington & Hough, Samuel Hough initially owned 32 shares and later 27 shares. In 1867 the ship became the property of Samuel Hough & Company, following the death of William Pennington. Samuel Hough then owned 43 shares in her. She served on the core liner service between Liverpool and London with a maiden voyage at the beginning of June 1866. The *Cheshire Observer*, Saturday 5 May 1866, reported on the ship's launch:

> The **West of England**, a new iron screw steamer, was launched on Monday from the shipbuilding yard of Messrs Bowdler and Chaffer, at Seacombe, in the presence of a large number of ladies and gentlemen. The steamer has been built for Messrs Pennington and Hough, of the Liverpool and London Steamship Company, Liverpool, and is intended as a trade between this port and London. She is 185 feet on length, with a beam of 28 feet, and a depth of 17 feet, and is fitted up with excellent accommodation for first and second class passengers. She is built so as to permit of the introduction of water ballast, and has a registered tonnage of 700 tons. Messrs Bowdler and Chaffer have had the steamer about four months on the stocks, and up to the present time they have given the utmost satisfaction to the owners. The launch was very successful, with the exception of a slight hitch that occurred as the steamer fell over the wall and took the water. This was caused by the breaking of the cradle, and after a slight oscillation, the **West of England** recovered her position, and glided into the watery element amid the cheers of the spectators. The steamer was christened by Miss Pennington, daughter of one of the owners…
>
> Although intended for the carrying trade between this port and London, she was by her construction capable of carrying water ballast; and, although this principle was seldom adopted, she had this advantage that in case of anything falling short in the particular trade for which she was intended, she could be used for heavier trades, such as carrying iron or coal. In fitting out the vessel, great attention had been paid to all the recent improvements. She has a windlass upon a patent principle, and her sails would be worked by patent gear, and was as complete a vessel for the purpose as could be well devised. The engines had been made by Messrs. Jack and Co, and were quite ready for the vessel – in fact the engineers expected to have them on board within the present week. It was expected that the **West of England** would be ready for sea within a month.

The newspaper report concluded with a description of the reception held after the launch. It is noteworthy that the response from the Chairman of the reception, Mr Bowdler, representing the shipbuilder, was invited from 'Mr John Bacon, of the Bristol and Wexford line of steamers' who applauded the introduction of the double bottom ballast tank arrangement if for no other reason that it would ensure a stronger and safer vessel. Notable then, that John Bacon was a guest at a launch for Pennington and Hough in 1866, suggesting that the Bacon and Pennington/Hough interests had more than a respect for each other's businesses, perhaps also that they were happy on occasion to help each other out – even at that early stage.

The main London service of Pennington and Hough had been operated by the **Genova** and **East Anglian** with a weekly departure from both London and Liverpool with calls at Penzance, Plymouth and Falmouth at least once during the round trip. The **Edith** supported the route as required while the other steamers were employed in tramp duties. From June 1866 the new **West of England** joined the service and the **East Anglian** stood down, although she still made occasional sailings on the service.

Two ships were lost in quick succession in January 1868. On 12 January the **East Anglian** left Porthcawl with a cargo of coal in heavy seas and strong winds, started to make water and foundered on 14 January, off Lundy, when the lighthouse bore north east. The 16 crew members were all saved in their own two lifeboats and landed at Lundy.

On 16 January 1868, just four days after the loss of the **East Anglian**, the **Genova** (Captain Maycock standing in for Captain Hoskins – see below) was wrecked at St Michael's, Penzance. She was on passage to London from Liverpool with a cargo mainly consisting of fruit. She had been on a fortnightly departure for London since July 1867 calling at a variety of intermediate ports. A report dated 28 January stated that the 'Genova hove up her moorings and was steaming out of the breakwater this morning when her rudder chains parted and she drifted on the rocks near the quay. She has holes in her bottom and is filling as the tide rises. Crew saved and labourers endeavouring to save part of cargo, in a damaged state'. By the end of the month the ship had been condemned and sold with the cargo remaining on board. Part of the cargo was removed in its damaged state and was sold.

The *Genova* had earlier been in the news on her passage to Liverpool as reported by the *Royal Cornwall Gazette* on Thursday 2 January 1868, reporting on the recent gales:

> Several vessels in Falmouth were damaged, and two were stranded, but no lives were lost. The *Genova*, London and Liverpool steamer put back to that port, after the renewal of the gale the following Monday, having lost overboard the captain's son. Her mate was so injured by the sea which washed young Hoskins over, that he also died.

For the remainder of the decade the London service thereafter fell principally to the *Edith* and the *West of England*, happily without further incident.

Samuel Hough had inherited a coastal liner trade, it would seem, that was fraught with maritime hazard. The weather was the greatest danger to shipping, due both to poor visibility and high seas whipped up in gale force winds, but human error was always present in the days before there were many foolproof aids to navigation. Coastal navigation not only required precision tracking of a ship's course by compass and measuring the distance run, it also required bearings of available fixed lights and headlands to be taken, and it needed exact compensation for tidal flow especially in the more confined waters where fast and changeable tides prevailed.

Busy shipping channels were always a danger when visibility was poor and the approaches to Liverpool were treated with great respect by all experienced masters when the weather was 'thick'. Nevertheless, the ships that were operated on the Liverpool to London service by Hough and his predecessors, once the B&I company had withdrawn in 1855, seem to have had a particularly bad run of luck. This apparently poor record of safety does not reflect on the managers or the ships' officers, but rather on the everyday conditions in which the vessels operated. Ships and their cargoes were indeed lost, but happily loss of life was restricted to only a few of the incidents.

It is interesting that the economic margins in the coastal liner trades were such that expansion could at best be slow but hopefully steady. The initial two ship service operated by McClune & Tamplin eventually became a six ship fleet falling back to five at the time of the merger of Samuel Hough Limited with the Bacon and Powell interests in 1913. Ships became larger as time went on, so that the aggregate tonnage grew disproportionately to the number of ships. The graph showing the progress of the Hough interests is broadly the same shape as that for the Powell and Bacon threads; modest in comparison to companies such as M Langlands & Sons and the Clyde Shipping Company, both of which were able to develop new trade as the Victorian era progressed.

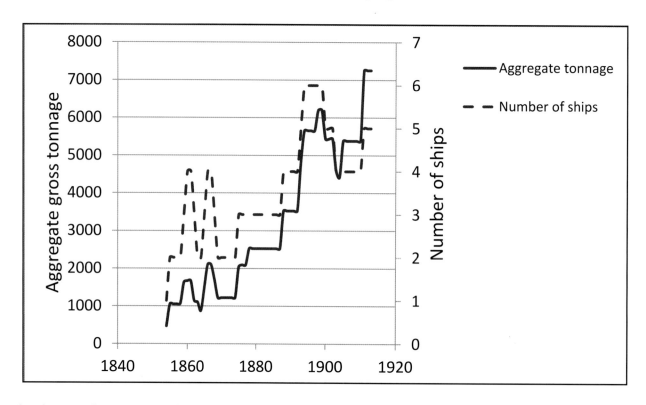

The slow but steady expansion of the Hough interests illustrates the low margins that the coastal liner trades attracted.

Chapter 11

SAMUEL HOUGH IN CHARGE

Samuel Hough had assumed sole responsibility for the Liverpool to London coastal liner service in 1867, when his partner William Pennington died. At first Hough was not a major shareholder in the ships operating under his management but in time he was able to increase his shareholdings and soon became the majority owner of the ships themselves. The core service between London and Liverpool was operated by the passenger and cargo steamers *Edith* and *West of England*, with a sailing every Saturday from both ports. The service was operated under the banner Liverpool and London Steam Packet Company. This remained the case for some years until a new steamer, the *South of England*, was ordered for delivery in 1875.

The *South of England* was a schooner-rigged iron-hulled vessel, some 219 feet long by 29 breadth and with a depth of 16 feet. She was launched from the yard of R Irvine & Company at West Hartlepool on 20 February 1875. The *South of England* was equipped with a compound steam engine of 110 horsepower driving a single screw to maintain a normal service speed of little over 11 knots. The new ship offered comfortable cabin accommodation for passengers while space was provided also for a number of deck passengers. The *Cheshire Observer*, Saturday 27 February 1875, reported:

> A new steamer called *South of England*, and intended to run between Liverpool and London, calling at various stations in the English Channel, has been launched from the dockyard of Messrs Irvine & Co., West Hartlepool. The vessel, which belongs to Mr S Hough of Liverpool, is fitted with all the newest appliances, and will have accommodation for about 50 first class passengers.

On acceptance by Samuel Hough & Company, the *South of England* took up the London to Liverpool service alongside the *West of England*, with the *Edith* reduced to relief duties. The new ship was welcomed on the service which was now considered to be modern, comfortable and reliable. The *South of England* was initially owned 42/64ths by Samuel Hough, 12/64ths by Mr R Irvine (the ship's builder), and 10/64ths by Mr J T Warrington.

On 2 February 1876 the new steamer *South of England*, bound to London up the River Thames, came into collision with, and sank, the sailing barge *Edwin* from Lambeth The collision occurred off Limehouse and the crew of the barge were rescued unhurt. Subsequently, on 26 March 1876, the *South of England* towed the barque *Mary* into Holyhead following a collision between the *Mary* and the steamship *Newton*.

The tenure of the *South of England* was to be a short one. On 3 July 1876, the *South of England* foundered off Milford Haven on passage Liverpool to London. During a dense fog, which had lasted all day, distress guns were heard about 3 miles south west of St. Ann's. A pilot lay off, but could not pick up the vessel firing the guns, the fog being so dense, when an officer at St. Ann's reported the vessel to have been the *South of England*, which struck on the Smalls at 13.30 on 2 July and sank at 04.00 the following morning while trying to reach Milford. The crew were all saved, and landed at St Ann's. The *Liverpool Mercury*, Wednesday 12 July 1876, reported on the subsequent enquiry into the loss:

> A Board of Trade Enquiry was opened at the police court, yesterday afternoon, before Mr Raffles, Stipendiary Magistrate, and Captains Harris and Whyte, nautical assessors, into the circumstances attending the loss of the steamer *South of England*, on the 3rd inst. Mr Tyndall appeared on behalf of the Board of Trade, and Mr James… for the captain… She [*South of England*] sailed between Liverpool and London, and on the 1st instant, she left this port with a general cargo of about 750 tons, with 19 of a crew all told, and about 40 passengers on board. She was commanded by Captain William Wraight. The ship was in good condition and well found in every respect.

> She sailed on the afternoon of the 1st instant and passed the Carnarvon Lightship three miles distant, the course then set being SW by S, which was continued unto 4 am of the 2nd, when it was altered to SW by ½ W. The weather became thick about 10 am, and the course was altered to SW by W. About noon a very dense fog came on, when the engines were at first eased and then stopped; and soundings were taken about 25 minutes past 12 o'clock. The lead showed between 49 and 50 fathoms. This was the only time the lead was used, although the weather continued very thick.

About 1.25 am, the look-out saw something on the starboard bow, which he immediately reported, and the helm was put hard aport. It was then seen the ship was on the Smalls, and as she was coming round she grated on one of the Smalls rocks. As the steamer made no water for the next half hour, she was again put on her course, SW by W, but in half an hour it was reported that there was half a foot of water in the fore hold. The pumps were set to work, but the water continued to increase. The steamer was then headed for Milford, and she went on until seven or eight o'clock, when the water came in to such an extent as to put out the fires. She then came to anchor. The passengers were placed in the lifeboat, and the master and the crew took to the other boat. They rowed about until half past three or four o'clock on the 3rd instant, when the ship went down, head foremost…

A passenger wrote in the *Manchester Courier and Lancashire Advertiser*, 10 July:

…Minute guns were fired from the steamer… Unfortunately there were only seven charges of powder on board for the guns. During the night blue lights were burned… and finally her stern lifted up as if some powerful machine had been placed to hoist her, until we could see the whole length of her keel. You must imagine the sound of the crockery, the machinery, the fittings, hundreds of boxes of bacon and cheese, pig iron, besides tons on tons of other merchandise, bursting up her deck and sides, and picture to yourself the noise of this rushing down deep into water 50 fathoms …

The *Edith* was employed elsewhere at the time so could not be deployed back onto the London to Liverpool service. In the event, the *South of England* was replaced on the London service by the *Farnley Hall*, chartered from the West Hartlepool shipbuilder R Irvine. This ship was a cargo ship of 954 tons gross dating from 1871, and so the passenger service only operated on alternate weeks until, in August, the *Swan* took over. The *Swan* was chartered from F H Powell & Company and provided both cabin and deck passenger facilities. In mid-November the new steamer *Mary Hough*, named after the owner's wife, was delivered and the London service again adopted some semblance of stability.

The *Mary Hough* was an attractive looking single screw passenger and cargo steamer that measured 226 feet long by 29 feet broad with a depth of 15 feet. The *Liverpool Mercury*, Saturday 7 October 1876, reported on the launch of the ship on 4 October:

At Renfrew, on Wednesday, there was launched from the yard of Messrs. Löbnitz, Coulborn & Company, an iron screw steamer of 900 ton, built to the highest class at Lloyd's, and elegantly fitted up for 50 first class passengers. She has been built to the order of Mr Samuel Hough, of Liverpool, and is intended for his line of steamers between Liverpool and London. She will be fitted with the builder's compound engine of 135 hp nominal. As she left the ways she was christened the *Mary Hough*. After the launch she was at once towed into the builder's tidal basin, where she will receive her masts and machinery. She will be commanded by Captain William Wraight, well known on the Liverpool and London station.

Indeed it was Captain Wraight that had been in charge when the *South of England* had been lost earlier in the year; Samuel Hough obviously held a high opinion of him. The *Mary Hough* carried out her maiden voyage, then operated the London service single-handedly.

The *Maggie Warrington* was delivered in 1878 by R Irvine & Company at Hartlepool. She was a big cargo steamer that was intended to bolster the tramp initiatives undertaken by Hough. She was launched on 4 April and undertook her acceptance trials on 8 April. Part-payment for the steamer was the *West of England* which came under Irvine's ownership with Samuel Hough retaining just 5/64th shares in her; she remained effectively a Hough fleet member. The *Northern Echo*, Friday 5 April 1878, reported on the *Maggie Warrington*:

Yesterday Messrs R Irvine & Co. launched from their yard at West Hartlepool, the second new iron screw steamship ordered by Mr Samuel Hough of Liverpool. She has been designed to the highest class at Lloyd's, and is 232 ft. long, 30 ft. in her beam, and 16 ft. 11 in. in her hold, her deadweight carrying capacity being 1,303 tons. She will be rigged as a schooner, with iron main deck, four hatchways, a similar number of steam winches (Irvine's), and all the latest improvements for fitting her for the general carrying trade. Engines 120 horsepower nominal, by Blair & Co, of Stockton. The christening ceremony was performed by Miss Pyman, the daughter of Mr George Pyman, JP.

The *Edith* was sold late in 1878. The cargo steamer *Zakynthos* was bought from W Glynn & Sons of Liverpool and renamed *Edith Hough*. These fleet changes meant that between 1878 and 1880 the *Mary Hough* maintained the core coastal liner service with the other ships tramping mainly to near continental ports. From 1876 onwards the service was maintained collaboratively with F H Powell & Company, the *Mary Hough* working alternate services with the *Faithful* until 1878, then the *Truthful* until 1881, after which the *Faithful* took over again. This was an excellent example of collaboration between two competing companies and was often upheld as a fine example whenever shipping companies continued to vie with each other and enter into severe loss-making rate wars.

The *Edith Hough* also made a number of coastal trips including collier work from South Wales. It was while on tramp duties in July 1880 that the *Edith Hough* stranded in the Baltic, under circumstances that remained largely unexplained. She was under the command of Captain G C Hawkins and the first officer was S J Delaney. The *Liverpool Mercury*, Wednesday 25 August 1880, reported in detail from the subsequent Board of Trade Enquiry:

On 5th July last the vessel left Riga with a cargo of about 750 tons of sleepers, part of which were on deck, bound for Liverpool. She had a crew of 13 hands, and the captain had with him his wife, three children, and a servant. At seven o'clock on the morning of the 6th, a light at the head of the Gulf of Riga was passed, and the master took his departure from it, estimating its distance as seven miles. He set his course west by south, three quarters south by standard compass, and proceeded under steam and sail. Between ten and eleven o'clock the wind increased to a moderate gale and sail was taken in. At noon the master found the vessel had a list to starboard, and he put her head to the south east for an hour, changing her back to her original course at one o'clock. That course was kept until midnight, the vessel going full speed, or about eight miles an hour. About a quarter past ten o'clock the island of Gothland was sighted about six points off the starboard bow, distance from 15 to 20 miles. The master took the mate into the chartroom and pointed out to him the vessel's position, at the same time giving him certain instructions. The master then retired, leaving word that he was to be called at midnight, and that the vessel's course should be changed once the revolving light was made.

According to the evidence of the crew, a light was made about half past ten o'clock, but the mate said that it was half past eleven when it was first reported. That light was about three quarters of a point off the starboard bow, bearing west by north, about 15 miles distant, according to the master's statement. Shortly after the light was sighted, the mate made out that it was a flash light instead of a revolving light. By the time the mate had ascertained this, the light was broad on the starboard bow and about ten miles off. The ship was then headed round to south west by west half west, and the master was called. There is some discrepancy in the evidence as to how long the master was on deck before he gave any order, but the master admitted that he at once saw the vessel was in danger, and he went to the chartroom to verify his position. He then gave orders for the helm to be put to starboard, and immediately after that was done he telegraphed the engineer to stop and reverse the engines. Before that order could be carried out the vessel struck on what proved to be Melgrue Shoal off the island of Gothland. She remained there fast, and the deck cargo had to be thrown overboard. Eventually she was taken off by the salvage steamers and taken to Stockholm, where she was repaired, and proceeded on her voyage to Liverpool.

Master and mate were both found to blame, the mate for not following a proper course and the master for not properly prescribing the course.

Shortly afterwards, on 15 September 1880, the *West of England* was lost in the North Atlantic about 100 miles west of Ushant. She was on passage from Villa Real to Liverpool with copper ore. All but one of the crew and passengers were rescued by a German ship and taken to Madeira; one man was drowned. Since 1878 the *West of England* had been wholly owned by R Irvine & Company and in 1877 had been displaced from the London service by the *Mary Hough*.

On 28 May 1881, the *Mary Hough* was sunk off Formby in the Mersey following collisions with both the *Africa* and the *Castilian*. She had just started on a voyage from Liverpool to London. One fireman died in the sinking, having been overcome as the engine room flooded. The owner, Samuel Hough, was a passenger on board. The *Liverpool Mercury*, Monday 30 May 1881, reported:

A collision of an alarming character, which resulted in the sinking of a steamer and the narrow escape of her crew and passengers, occurred off the port on Saturday. It seems that the Liverpool steamer *Mary Hough* left the river in the forenoon for London. She had a full cargo and a number of passengers, among the latter being Mr Hough, the owner. The steamer proceeded down the river, and all went well until she reached the Crosby lightship. The weather was fine at the time, but there was a thick haze prevailing. Those on board the *Mary Hough* were alarmed by seeing a large inward bound steamer, (which turned out to be the *Castilian* from Oporto, belonging to the Leyland Line) coming towards them. It was at once apparent that a collision was inevitable, and the *Castilian* struck the *Mary Hough* on the bow.

The occurrence caused the greatest alarm to those on board the *Mary Hough*. Among them were several ladies and gentlemen who had gone for a pleasure trip to London. It appeared that both steamers were much damaged, and what increased the consternation of those on the *Mary Hough* was a cry raised that the water was rushing in at the bow. Fortunately a tug – the *Hercules* of Liverpool – was observed approaching. She was skilfully brought alongside the *Mary Hough*, and the passengers from the latter were safely got on board the tug. The captain and the crew of the *Mary Hough* determined to stand by their vessel. The tug, however, had scarcely got clear when another steamer – the *Africa*, outward bound for the west coast of Africa – was seen near, and she too, collided with the *Mary Hough*, striking her violently, it is said, amidships.

It soon became apparent that the *Mary Hough* had been so damaged in the two collisions that she was in a sinking state. The captain, who acted throughout with the greatest coolness and bravery, gave the orders for the boats to be lowered. This was done and some of the crew got into the boats; but before all could get off, the *Mary Hough* sank, and the captain and several of the crew could be seen struggling in the water. They were promptly rescued by boats that had been lowered by the other steamers, and taken on board the tug, where they received every attention…

The Leyland Line's *Castilian* (1862) standing off the *Mary Hough* (1876), which had been cut down to the water level at her starboard bow when the ships collided off Formby.

[from an oil painting by Nick Robins]

Details of the incident became apparent at the subsequent Board of Trade Enquiry (for more detail see the transcript in *Coastal Passenger Liners of the British Isles*):

The collision, then, between the *Mary Hough* and the *Castilian* was, in our opinion, caused partly by the fact that the *Mary Hough* was going down on her wrong side of the river, and partly to the great speed at which both the vessels were going, and to the thick fog which prevented their being able to see one another until they were too close to avoid a collision.

Secondly, as to the collision between the *Mary Hough* and the *Africa*. The *Mary Hough* as we have seen, after her collision with the *Castilian*, proceeded up the river, keeping, however, near to the Formby Bank, in case it should be necessary to beach her. At first, when she thought she was going to sink, the engines were put on full speed, but as she proceeded up the river they were reduced to half speed. After porting to clear a small yacht, she starboarded her helm with a view of running on the Bank, it having been reported that the water was increasing rapidly; and at this moment the *Africa* was observed coming down the river and a little on her starboard bow. She accordingly hard-a-ported her helm, but owing to the vessel being down by the head she refused to answer her helm; and although the engines were thereupon stopped and reversed full speed, it was not possible to avoid a collision. The *Africa*, for her part, which was going down the river on her own proper side of the channel, and was keeping very near the line of the Black Buoys, observing the *Mary Hough* ahead and nearly end on, ported her helm; on finding, however, that the head of the *Mary Hough* was paying off to port, apparently under a starboard helm, she at once stopped her engines and reversed full speed, but too late to avoid a collision. The *Mary Hough* then, can hardly be said to have been to blame for the collision, as, owing to her disabled condition, she was not able to answer her helm. Nor can the *Africa* be deemed to be in fault, for she ported her helm, as she was bound to do; and when at length she saw that the *Mary Hough*'s head kept paying off to port, she stopped and reversed full speed, but too late to avoid a collision.

…Lastly, it is said that the Board of Trade are of opinion that the certificates of the masters of the *Mary Hough*, *Castilian*, and *Africa*, should be dealt with. As regards the master of the *Africa*, we are not aware that he is in any respect to blame for the collision which took place between his vessel and the *Mary Hough*, and we shall, therefore, certainly not deal with his certificate. As regards the master of the *Castilian*, if he is to blame at all, it is for not at once ordering the helm to be put to port and the engines full speed astern when the *Mary Hough* first came in sight, and when he was in sole charge of the vessel; but this amounts at the utmost to only an error of judgment; and for the undue speed at which she was proceeding, the pilot is alone to blame. As regards the *Mary Hough*, no doubt the master is greatly to blame for having allowed her to get over to the wrong side of the Channel, and for having navigated her at too great a speed through a dense fog. But under all the circumstances, we are not prepared to deal with his certificate.

The wreck lay level fore and aft, with a slight list off-shore, port side of her deck being awash at low water. The first collision cut the vessel down on the starboard bow about 14 feet deep by about 15 to 20 feet wide at the bow. The second collision, on the port side, just abaft of the bridge, caused a hole about 3 feet square at the gunwhale. Cargo was discharged as rapidly as possible, and preparations made to raise the hull. The wreck was raised on 10 June and beached at Egremont, while discharge of more of the cargo and temporary repairs allowed her transfer to Herculaneum Dock the next day. The *Mary Hough* was repaired and back in service by the end of the year.

Chapter 12

SAMUEL HOUGH LIMITED - DEVELOPING TRADE

Throughout the 1880s, the *Mary Hough* provided the majority of London sailings supported mostly by the *Maggie Warrington*. It was an unbalanced service but an understanding developed with F H Powell & Company that their main passenger steamer would jointly run the passenger service on the alternate week to the *Mary Hough*. The Powell steamer *Faithful*, therefore, became partner to the *Mary Hough*. It was a comfortable arrangement for both companies, lessening the competition between them and providing the optimum service for their clients, both cargo shippers and passengers. The single cabin fare between Liverpool and London was maintained at 25/-. Meanwhile the *Edith Hough*, which was re-engined by D Rollo & Sons in 1884, tended to operate to and from the Continent as well as occasional duties on the core coastal liner service.

The *Mary Hough* attended the sinking barque *Earl of Aberdeen* on 15 May 1886. The barque had a crew of 29 and a full cargo of 3,100 tons of coal loaded at Barry and was bound for Montevideo. The *Earl of Aberdeen* struck the Hat & Barrels Reef off Pembrokeshire on her maiden voyage and began rapidly to sink. Despite rescue attempts by the *Mary Hough* and HMS *Foxhound*, both ships being in the vicinity, sixteen men including five apprentices were lost. Captain W Patrick and the first officer were amongst the survivors.

The *Baidar* (1871) was purchased in 1888 and remained in Hough service until she was wrecked in 1897.

[from an oil painting by Nick Robins]

During 1888 Samuel Hough bought the steamer *Baidar*. She had been built in 1871 for W N Smith of Hull and was bought by the newly formed Hull company W H Cockerline & Company in 1885 along with the *Spark*. Walter Cockerline was just 29 at the time, a former clerk working for J W Smith. She was essentially an iron-hulled cargo steamer being 232 long by 28 feet breadth and 16 feet deep and had a compound engine driving a single screw. Cockerline replaced the *Baidar* with a new purpose built ship and so enabled Samuel Hough to purchase her. She was a useful acquisition offering two hatches forward and two aft, each served by single 5 ton derricks mounted on the fore and main masts. Accommodation was provided for a handful of passengers.

In 1893, the steamer *El Dorado* was bought from Scrutton, Sons & Company of London. She had been built in 1882 by T & W Smith at North Shields and was equipped with a compound steam engine, and patent steam steering gear by Messrs Muir & Caldwell of Glasgow. She was an iron-hulled cargo steamer some 240 feet long by 34 feet breadth and 18 feet deep and was described at her launch as 'beautifully modelled'. She had been built for the West India trade and was fitted with first class accommodation for twelve passengers situated in the poop. All the furnishings were electro-plated, seemingly a desirable feature at that time.

D Curry & Company's coastal feeder passenger and cargo ship *Melrose* (1877), seen alongside at Port Elizabeth. She was bought by Samuel Hough in 1894 and later renamed *Annie Hough*.

Two important ships joined the fleet in 1894. The first was the *Melrose*, purchased from D Currie & Company for whom she had operated the coastal feeder service from Durban, via East London and Port Elizabeth, to the mail ships lying at Cape Town. She was a valuable addition to the Hough fleet, retaining her original name when she joined the Liverpool to London service.

In addition to a large cargo capacity, she provided luxurious accommodation for first class passengers as well as space for deck passengers. The *Melrose* had attained fame on 29 July 1883, when she was the scene of the murder of Thomas Carey. Carey had turned Queen's evidence regarding the stabbing and killing of Lord Cavendish and Thomas Burke in May 1882 in Phoenix Park, Dublin. As a result five men were publicly executed. For his protection Carey and his family were secretly taken to South Africa aboard the *Kinfauns Castle* where, on arrival at Cape Town, they were transferred to the *Melrose*. Patrick O'Donnell had vowed vengeance and had also shipped on the *Kinfauns Castle*, made friends with Carey who obviously didn't know him, even shared a cabin with Carey on the *Melrose*, and on 29 July 1883 shot him dead. O'Donnell was returned to London and later hanged.

Fisher Renwick's steamer *Springhill* (1885) lying in the timber basin at Saltport near Runcorn before the Manchester Ship Canal was opened in January 1894; the company already ran a regular cargo service to London.

The commissioning of the *Melrose* in the Hough fleet early in 1894 allowed the *Edith Hough* to move to a new Manchester to London service with a single call at Southampton. This new service followed the opening of the Manchester Ship Canal on 1 January and was jointly operated with F H Powell & Company and intended to secure for both companies a berth at Manchester, in competition principally with Fisher, Renwick & Company (Chapter 4). The cabin fare was 25/- single. Typical of the advertisements for the new service was, *Manchester Courier and Lancashire General Advertiser*, Saturday 7 April 1894:

> Manchester to Southampton and London, direct sailings every Wednesday. *Edith Hough* Manchester to London April 11th, *Swan* London to Manchester April 11th. Receiving goods at No. 3 Dock Pomona, and Liverpool and Manchester Quay, Regent's Dock, London, up to 3 pm on day of sailing. Apply…

The *Baidar* was wrecked 29 November 1897 on Banjaard Bank, Brouwershaven, Holland, on passage from Rotterdam to Dunkirk in ballast. All the passengers and crew were safely landed. By 2 December it was reported that the hull was leaking and in a bad condition and that the boilers and engines had shifted. On 7 December the Liverpool Salvage Association reported:

> …that the vessel's bottom is set up in No. 2 hold, cross bunkers and engine room, lifting the engines and boilers about 3 inches. The riveting of the hull seems more or less strained, but so far as can tell, no floors are broken. The vessel is lying on the highest part of Noordland Bank, and will only have around 1 foot of water around her at ordinary spring tide. Offers are being invited to float the ship; no cure, no pay.

The following February the hull and the remaining cargo were sold by auction; the hull realised 4,956 Dutch guilders, and the materials 3,897 guilders.

The *Maggie Hough* (1884) was bought in 1898 for the London service and offered accommodation for 12 passengers. She is seen here at Dartmouth.

The *Melrose* was renamed *Annie Hough* in 1897. The following year her ownership was transferred to a new single ship holding company, the Annie Hough Steamship Company Limited.

The steamer *Nonpareil* was bought in 1898 and renamed *Maggie Hough*. She was a large iron-hulled steamer 267 feet long by 35 feet breadth and 17 feet deep. She had been built for Scrutton, Sons & Company in 1884 by T & W Smith at North Shields and was equipped with compound steam machinery and a single screw. Like the *El Dorado* before her, the *Nonpareil* was designed for Scrutton's West Indian trade and she carried first class accommodation for twelve passengers.

In 1899, during a major seamen's strike, Samuel Hough Limited agreed to pay their firemen and seamen 32s 8d per week. Hough had always looked after his employees and this was a generous offer that was welcomed by the men. It also allowed the ships to continue sailing whereas others were still strikebound.

The *Edith Hough* was lost on 2 February 1899 when she grounded and sank at Mostaganem Harbour, Oran, Algeria. She had been on passage from Swansea to Mostaganem with a cargo of coal. The wreck was later refloated and taken to Genoa to be broken up. A report from Algiers dated 3 February described the incident:

> At 04.00 the English steamer *Edith Hough* dragged her anchor and ran aground by the jetty. She was refloated, but it was found that she had sprung a leak on one side, and that her propeller was broken. The vessel is now firmly moored, but the sea is rough and it is feared she may be swept from her moorings by a heavy sea.

She sank later that day with water to bridge height, and broken in several places. Later in the week she was declared a total loss while attempts to take off some of the cargo were eventually stopped by the salvage company that had bought the wreck. The wreck was raised and taken to Genoa, where she arrived on 11 August, to be beached and demolished.

All went well with the Manchester to London service until, as reported in the *Liverpool Mercury*, Saturday 2 December 1899:

> The steamship *Annie Hough*, late *Melrose*, upon which the notorious Irish informer was shot at Cape Town, was sunk in the Ship Canal yesterday. It appears that the ship, en route from Manchester to London with a valuable general cargo, struck the canal bank with her port bow at Moore, between Warrington and Runcorn, and received damage below the water line. She commenced to leak badly, and water rapidly gathered in the fore hold, and the captain determined to reach the pontoon dock at Ellesmere Port, if possible. On arriving at the port, however, the pontoon was not available and the ship was berthed alongside Stewart's Wharf, where she sank, and grounded in 20 feet of water, the water in the hold being on a level with the water in the canal. A portion of the cargo was landed on the quayside, but a large quantity is ruined by water and the loss will be very heavy. The owners, Messrs Samuel Hough & Co., of Liverpool, were last night taking steps to repair the damage and raise the ship. The waterway is clear for traffic.

From 1900, the *Annie Hough* was deployed on a new initiative, sailing from Liverpool every Saturday for Plymouth and Falmouth, returning from Falmouth every Monday with an option to call again at Plymouth. The service was jointly marketed by F H Powell & Company and Samuel Hough Limited. This removed the pressure from the big London passenger steamers which still called at Southampton but no longer always needed to call at Falmouth and Plymouth. The Manchester service was then in the hands of Powell's steamer *Truthful* and Hough's *Maggie Warrington*, with departures from Manchester every Tuesday and every Friday from London. Intermediate calls were made at Falmouth, Plymouth, Southampton and Portsmouth as required. The *Annie Hough* and *Maggie Warrington* swapped duties for the summer months. Both the *Point Clear* and the *South Coast* were working for F H Powell & Company from Manchester to Bristol in the early 1900s, this trade not being shared with Samuel Hough Limited.

M Langlands & Sons also suffered from accidents due to coastal navigation in all weathers: the *Princess Irene* (1891) lies on Brimstone Rocks, Linney Head, Pembrokeshire, where she ran ashore in fog in August 1906.

An agreement was also put in place with M Langlands & Sons regarding that company's calls at south coast and Bristol Channel ports. The Langlands steamer sailed clockwise round Britain every fortnight and between Bristol and Newcastle-upon-Tyne and that company agreed not to call at London provided it could share other traffic. The agreement went beyond this, such that Samuel Hough became the port agent for Langlands at the south coast ports advertising the service under the Hough brand. Like Hough and like Powell, Langlands also suffered from accidents due to the hazards of coastal navigation in all weathers (see Robins and Tucker, 2015).

Samuel Hough died at the age of 70 on Monday 11 August 1902. Not only had he become an important shipowner but he also became a Justice of the Peace, and a member of Liverpool City Council. He was also an active member of the Liberal Party. Following his death his executor and son, Richard G Hough, assumed ownership of the four ships: *Mary Hough*, *Maggie Warrington*, *El Dorado* and *Maggie Hough*. The fifth member of the fleet, the *Annie Hough*, formerly *Melrose*, was sold to Bermond et Cie of Bordeaux, France and renamed *Emyrne*. The *El Dorado* was also sold the following year. The ownership of the *Maggie Warrington* was transferred to the Annie Hough Steamship Company Limited in 1902.

Samuel Hough Limited was incorporated in 1904. The new company continued to trade much as before the death of Samuel Hough, with Richard G Hough becoming the new senior partner. A number of new business links took place in the 1900s including a formal sharing agreement with F H Powell & Company. Also in 1904 a new partnership between F H Powell & Company and Samuel Hough Limited effectively came to own all the cargo steamers, which were then 50% owned by F H Powell & Company and 50% by Samuel Hough Limited. This left only the main passenger units under the sole ownership of each of the parent companies. For example, the new steamer *Cornish Coast*, which had been ordered by Powell, was delivered to the new joint ownership company in the autumn of 1904. In 1907, Samuel Hough Limited bought the new steamer *Sussex Coast* from F H Powell & Company and sold her back in 1908. The *Dorset Coast* was launched in May 1908 and the then registered under the ownership of F H Powell & Company and Samuel Hough Limited. In September 1910 the newly built *Graceful*, ordered by F H Powell & Company, was delivered to the joint venture and shortly afterwards was renamed *Devon Coast*. A month later the new steamer *Norfolk Coast*, also ordered by F H Powell & Company and launched as *Hopeful*, was registered under the ownership of F H Powell & Company and Samuel Hough Limited. In September 1911 the same change of ownership happened to Powell's new steamer *Hampshire Coast*.

In addition, the banner London, Bristol and South Coast Steamers, which had been used by F H Powell & Company, had the wording Powell & Hough Lines added to it in advertising. The trading name Powell and Hough Lines had been used for the Manchester to London service since it started in 1894 and closer links between the two companies had been fostered during the 1890s leading to an agreement to pool all the cargo carrying resources in 1904. It was also agreed that the London service would be pooled, with each company offering two passenger and cargo ships to maintain a twice weekly service between the ports. Indeed the links between the two companies became so strong that it was inevitable that some sort of merger would ultimately occur.

Various agreements were in place between the coastal liner operators, such as, for example, that with M Langlands & Sons. Competition for trade with William Sloan & Company Limited and the Clyde Shipping Company Limited, both operating along the west and south coast routes from Glasgow, was also moderated satisfactorily for all concerned.

The Clyde Shipping Company was a major competitor in the south coast ports to London trade: their steamer *Cloch* (1883) is seen at Penzance.

A brief listing in the shipping casualties lists in *Lloyd's List*, 29 June 1904, read: St John's, Newfoundland 'The steamer *Mary Hough* ashore at Brandies near Cape Wray, feared badly damaged'. The *Mary Hough* had been on a voyage from Port aux Basques to Port St George while on charter to Bowring Brothers. She went ashore on 27 June during a dense fog and within a day the fore hold was completely flooded and the following day the after part of the ship also flooded. Attempts to float the ship off the rocks took place in July but were given up as the *Mary Hough* slowly fell apart on the rocks. In early August a salvage percentage was awarded as gear continued to wash ashore from the now submerged wreck.

On 26 April 1904, the steamer *Delta* was bought from Thomas Wilson, Sons & Company of Hull and renamed *Annie Hough*. She had been built in 1900 to the order of Bailey & Leetham Limited also of Hull, which itself had been acquired by Thomas Wilson, Sons and Company in July 1903. The *Delta* was launched complete in all respects, masts rigging, lifesaving gear, the lot, as was the custom of her builder J Scott & Company of Kinghorn, Fife. She was a medium-sized cargo steamer some 225 feet long by 34 feet breadth and 15 feet deep. She was equipped with a triple expansion steam engine with cylinders 17 inch, 27 inch, 45 inch diameter with a 33 inch stroke, which provided her with a service speed of 9 knots.

The *Annie Hough* (1900) was bought in 1904. She is flying the company house flag, red with white initials SH, at the mainmast.

The new London steamer *Samuel Hough* was launched at Grangemouth on 20 April 1905. The event was reported in the *Falkirk Herald*, Saturday 22 April 1905:

> The Grangemouth & Greenock Dockyard Company launched on Thursday from their Grangemouth yard a handsomely modelled steamer which they have built to the order of Messrs Samuel Hough Ltd., of Liverpool. Her dimensions are 275 feet by 36 feet, by 20 feet, and she is built to the highest class of Lloyd's, with poop, bridge and forecastle, and 'tween decks. She is intended for regular passenger and general goods trade between Liverpool and London, and is fitted out in the most modern manner for the comfort of her passengers. She has accommodation for 80 to 100 of first class passengers in large state rooms, and there is a handsome dining saloon and large entrance hall. Special attention has been given to the ventilation and lighting of the cabins. Beds and lavatories are on the folding principle, and everything has been done to render her a popular and favourite vessel with passengers. She is fitted with electric light throughout, steam steering gear, steam windlass, eight winches, patent compasses, and all modern appliances. Machinery for a high rate of speed is being supplied by Messrs David Rowan & Co. of Glasgow, and the vessel is expected to take her place on the run by Whitsunday. As she left the ways she was named *Samuel Hough* by Miss Hough, Liverpool, daughter of the senior partner of the firm. After the launch, the company adjourned to the model room, where the usual toasts were proposed and responded to. The owners were represented by Mr Richard Hough of Liverpool, and there was also present Miss Hough and Mr and Mrs Harvey of the builders…

The *Samuel Hough* was equipped with triple expansion steam machinery driving a single propeller to maintain a service speed of 12 knots. The London service was advertised with only the two newer and bigger passenger ships highlighted out of the four ship roster in the summer of 1905:

> Delightful sea trips between Liverpool and London and the South of England every Wednesday and Saturday. ss *Samuel Hough*, 2,500 tons, ss *Powerful*, 2,100 tons. Fares 50/- single, 84/- return, including victualling. For further particulars apply to F H Powell & Company, 21 Water Street, Liverpool, Samuel Hough Limited 25 Water Street, Liverpool.

The *Samuel Hough* (1905) depicted in a series of company postcards:

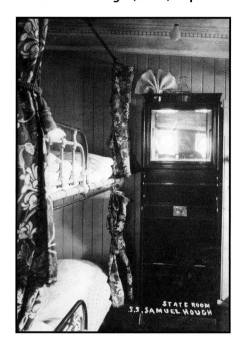

Far left: A typical state room.
Top left: The *Samuel Hough* 'passenger steamer Liverpool – London'.
Bottom left: The upper deck.
Above: The dining saloon.

The *Maggie Hough* was sold in 1910 to Turkish owners. She was sunk in the Great War by a torpedo fired from a Russian submarine.

The ultimate in design of the London to Liverpool passenger and cargo ship in either the Hough or Powell fleets was the *Dorothy Hough*.

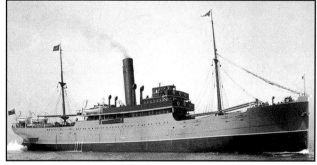

The *Dorothy Hough* (1911), the ultimate in design for the London service, seen in the grey livery worn in her first couple of years of service.

Another view of the *Dorothy Hough* (1911). Both pictures were almost certainly taken while on sea trials before acceptance from the shipbuilder.

The *Falkirk Herald*, Saturday 6 May 1911, reported on the launch of the *Dorothy Hough*, clearly using their article on the launch of the *Samuel Hough* six years previously as a template:

> The Greenock and Grangemouth Dockyard Company, Limited, launched on Saturday [29 April], from their Grangemouth yard, a handsomely modelled steamer which they have built to the order of Messrs Samuel Hough Limited, of Liverpool. …and the vessel is expected to take her place for a special run to London for the Coronation and Naval Review at Spithead. As she left the ways she was named *Dorothy Hough* by Mrs Richard Hough, wife of the senior partner of the firm…

A more detailed description of the ship was given at the time of her trials, *Falkirk Herald*, Saturday 10 June 1911:

> On Wednesday the fine passenger steamer *Dorothy Hough*, built by the Grangemouth and Greenock Dockyard Company at the Grangemouth yard was taken on a trial trip on the Forth. The *Dorothy Hough* is a handsome vessel, built to the order of Messrs Samuel Hough Limited, of Liverpool, for regular cargo and passenger service between Liverpool and London, and has accommodation for 100 passengers. She is built to the highest class at Lloyd's and Board of Trade passenger certificate, having forecastle for the accommodation

of the crew, bridge amidships, with continuous shelter decks over some of the accommodation of first class passengers, while first class state rooms are arranged on both sides of the bridge and in deck houses on the top of the bridge deck and in upper deck houses on top of the shelter deck. The main saloon is at the forward end of the bridge deck, and is fitted up in mahogany. The connection with the saloon is large and commodious, and is arranged with the most modern and up-to-date serving appliances, including a lift from the galley. A handsome stairway leads from aft the saloon to the bridge to the bridge deck entrance hall, which is finished in oak. This saloon is fitted up as a deck lounge, and has a piano.

The vessel is lighted throughout with electricity, and is fitted up with winding steam windlass, steam steering gear, and steam winches, with double derricks and large hatches. The dimensions of the vessel are 283 ft. by 36 ft. by 20 ft. 3 ins., and it carries a total deadweight of 2,700 tons on 18 feet beam [sic]. The engines, supplied by Messrs J G Kincaid & Co., Ltd., Greenock, are triple expansion, having cylinders 21 in., 25 in., and 27 in, and 39 in. stroke, two large boilers working at a pressure of 180 lbs., and has all the latest appliances for economic and efficient working. At the trial trip the machinery worked smoothly and without a hitch, and to the satisfaction of all concerned, a mean speed of 13.35 knots being attained. The construction of the vessel has been superintended by Mr J J Rowse, superintending engineer of Messrs Samuel Hough, Ltd., Liverpool.

She actually had berths for just 40 passengers in single and twin state rooms. However, at peak times up to 25 sofa beds were used in the saloon and smoke room and other additional temporary beds could be used bringing the total number of passengers up to about 70 rather than the 100 stated in the *Falkirk Herald*.

In 1911, the *Maggie Warrington* was renamed *Mary Hough*. However, in 1912 she was sold to Stone & Rolfe, Llanelli and renamed *Gwladmena*. On 2 January 1918, the *Gwladmena* was lying in the deep water anchorage to the south of Lerwick awaiting a berth to discharge the coal she had brought up from Methil in the Firth of Forth. Just before dawn the Danish ship *Flora* rammed and sank the anchored *Gwladmena*.

A national coal strike began at the end of February 1912 and ended when Government intervened with a minimum wage law in early April. The strike badly affected the Powell and Hough service between Liverpool and London as an advertisement in the *Portsmouth Evening News*, 14 March 1912, explained:

> Powell and Hough Lines, direct communication between Liverpool and London calling at Falmouth, Plymouth, Southampton and Portsmouth. Shippers and consignees are respectfully informed that, owing to the coal strike, we are compelled to reduce the sailings to and from above named ports, and that rates are advanced 2/6d per ton on all cargo until further notice. The altered service is subject to weather and other circumstances permitting. The earliest possible steps will be taken to restore the service as soon as business in the coal trade is resumed. For further particulars apply Powell and Hough, 116 High Street, Portsmouth.

In 1912, the *Annie Hough* was transferred to the Annie Hough Steamship Company Limited with Richard G Hough as the senior partner.

On 5 September 1913 the *Liverpool Journal of Commerce* reported:

> We understand a fusion of interests is being arranged between the coasting firms, the Powell Line, the Bacon Line and the Hough Line, and from 1st October these businesses will be carried on as Powell, Bacon & Hough Limited with headquarters at Liverpool and branches at London, Bristol, Manchester, Plymouth, Swansea and Cardiff. The Powell Line have a fleet of nine steamers from 600 to 1,100 tons each, the Hough Line three steamers of 1,100 to 1,800 tons, and the Bacon company four of from 500 to 900 tons. The Hough Line maintains several services between Liverpool and London.

Under the leadership of Alfred H Read, with Richard Hough at his side, the first task of the newly-formed company was to rationalise the fleet in order to provide the best services with the best ships. Routes served were the core Liverpool to London passenger and cargo service with intermediate calls at south coast ports, the similar service to London from Manchester, services between Liverpool and Bristol Channel ports and Bristol Channel ports with those on the South Coast, as well as the longstanding cattle run between Liverpool and Wexford, and services to Preston. The prestigious Liverpool to London service was operated by four modern passenger and cargo steamers and although jointly marketed by the owners until the merger, the ships vied with each other to pick up the passenger trade, an expensive task in the leaner winter months. It was inevitable that the twice weekly departure would be cut and steamers sold. Within weeks of the merger it was announced that the *Samuel Hough* had been sold to Burns, Philp & Company Limited of Sydney, New South Wales and renamed *Marsina*.

Samuel Hough's grandson, Stafford Frank Hough, born November 1889 in Liverpool, joined Samuel Hough Limited in 1904 and went to sea with the company. In 1907 he came ashore to work in the office at Liverpool. Stafford Hough went back to sea as a Sub Lieutenant in the Royal Naval Reserve during the Great War. When he was demobilised in 1919 he was appointed manager of the Falmouth Branch of what by then had become Coast Lines Limited. As such he was the last Hough to be employed in that company.

From: *Management Response in British Coastal Shipping Companies to Railway Competition*

by John Armstrong

At the top end of the market were customers who wanted fast, reliable, scheduled collection and delivery. They moved high-value goods, such as manufactures, and were willing to pay a premium (in coastal shipping terms) to have them delivered quickly and on schedule. Lever's soap, Bovril meat extract, cigars, pianos and books all travelled by this method. They used large, well-appointed steamers incorporating the latest technology, owned by companies such as Tyne-Tees, Aberdeen Steam, Powell, Bacon, and Hough. In addition, they usually owned or leased a dedicated berth at the ports they served to minimise delays in docking and moving cargo. These ships usually carried passengers and livestock as well as cargo, and so eschewed dirty, dangerous and malodorous goods, such as coal, dynamite and kips. They carried mixed cargoes and usually required no minimum quantity, thus making them ideal for small but frequent deliveries of low-bulk goods.

...the Powell Line, operating between Liverpool and London and calling at Bristol, Plymouth and Southampton, merged with the Bacon Line, also offering similar services out of Liverpool. In 1913 the merged firm also absorbed the Hough Line. These manoeuvres were minuscule compared to what was to occur after 1917 when the Powell, Bacon and Hough Line was absorbed by the Royal Mail Steam Packet Group and changed its name to Coast Lines. Between 1917 and 1920 Coast Lines absorbed thirteen separate coastal and Irish Channel firms, and engulfed another seven during the 1920s. By the onset of the Great Depression the British coastal liner trade was close to being a monopoly. How effective were these strategies? It is much easier to answer in the aggregate. On this level it may be argued that since coastal shipping still played an important part in British internal transport in 1914, the policies must have worked. The volume of transport provided by coasters expanded, and they were the most important carriers of long-distance and high-bulk cargoes; in total, they probably provided about the same ton-mileage as railways. The registered tonnage of entries and clearances of ships with cargo in the coastal trade grew steadily before 1913, and the network of coastal liners was dense and comprehensive. In aggregate terms, coastal shipping firms retained their positions.

Yet there is always the counterfactual. If coastal shipping firms had pursued alternative strategies, would they have done even better, perhaps increasing their shares of traffic or driving some railway companies out of business? The latter seems highly unlikely. By the late nineteenth century the railways were financial giants, beside which even the largest coastal liner firms were financial pygmies. If the coasters had waged war against the railways, the latter had the financial muscle to survive a period of intense price and service competition which could only have led to the withdrawal of the coastal company. In any case, such a scenario would not have pitted the coastal firms against the railways, but one coastal firm against an individual railway, let us say Cory versus the North Eastern Railway for the carriage of coal from the northeast to London. Again, the disparity is huge. When it went public in 1897, Cory was capitalised at £2 million; the North Eastern Railway at the same date had a capitalisation of over £60 million. The conclusion is that the coastal firms were irritants as far as goods were concerned but had no impact on the large and lucrative passenger traffic. The railways tolerated them while they were not too much of a problem and were mainly carrying low-value, bulky commodities. But if a coastal firm had tried seriously to impinge on the traffic of a particular railway, the latter would have retaliated, likely with great success. The railways had the formal institutions to facilitate cooperation and might have closed ranks in the face of a severe coastal threat. The coaster and railway coexisted in the late nineteenth century because it was in the interests of both not to upset this delicate balance.

Chapter 13

POWELL, BACON & HOUGH LINES LIMITED

The incorporation of Powell, Bacon & Hough Lines took place on 1 October 1913. It was created by the merger of the interests of F H Powell & Company, which included John Bacon Limited since its acquisition by Powell in October 1912, and those of Samuel Hough Limited. Ships registered under the joint names F H Powell & Company and Samuel Hough Limited were transferred into the new company and the former partnership was dissolved. Powell, Bacon & Hough Lines started by acquiring eighteen ships from its three namesake forebears, including four steam lighters from the former fleet of John Bacon Limited. All ships that did not comply with the adopted 'Coast' nomenclature, apart from the Milford Haven steam lighters, *Edith*, *Harfat*, *Pennar* and *Enniscorthy*, were appropriately renamed. It acquired from F H Powell & Company:

Powerful	1913-1919	renamed *Eastern Coast* 1913
Faithful	1913-1919	renamed *Monmouth Coast* 1913
Sussex Coast/Truthful	1913-1916	renamed *Wirral Coast* 1913
Graceful	1913-1917	renamed *Somerset Coast* 1913
Hopeful	1913-1915	renamed *Western Coast* 1913

The *Powerful* (1903) was renamed *Eastern Coast* by Powell, Bacon & Hough Lines Limited. As the *Eastern Coast*, wearing the red chevron on a white band, she is seen getting ready to sail from Liverpool on 16 May 1914.

[R A Shook]

F H Powell & Company's *Faithful* (1906) became the *Monmouth Coast* under the ownership of Powell, Bacon & Hough Lines Limited. She is seen here in the River Avon below Bristol.

The *Wirral Coast* (1907) was commissioned as the *Sussex Coast*, renamed *Truthful* in 1908 and given her new 'Coast' name in 1913 by Powell, Bacon & Hough Lines Limited.

From John Bacon Limited, wholly owned by F H Powell & Company since October 1912:

Edith	1913-1916	
Prestonian/Sir George Bacon	1913-1917	renamed *Gower Coast* 1913
Pennar	1913-1948	
Enniscorthy	1913-1916	
Harfat	1913-1939	
Sir Roger Bacon	1913-1933	renamed *Pembroke Coast* 1913
Sir Edward Bacon	1913-1914	
Sir Walter Bacon	1913-1936	renamed *Gloucester Coast* 1913

The *Sir Roger Bacon* (1912) became the *Pembroke Coast*, as seen here, in 1913, when she passed to Powell, Bacon & Hough Lines Limited. She is wearing the short-lived broad white band and red chevron on her funnel.

And from Samuel Hough Limited:

Annie Hough	1913-1919	renamed *Lancashire Coast* in 1914
Dorothy Hough	1913-1936	renamed *Southern Coast* in 1913

And from the joint ownership of F H Powell & Company and Samuel Hough Limited:

Cornish Coast	1913-1915
Dorset Coast	1913-1915
Graceful/Devon Coast	1913-1934
Hopeful/Norfolk Coast	1913-1918
Hampshire Coast	1913-1915 and 1915 -1937

The Liverpool to London service had been reduced in autumn 1912 to one sailing a week (Chapter 6). The weekly sailing was maintained by the *Dorothy Hough* and *Powerful*, now renamed *Southern Coast* and *Eastern Coast* respectively within the new company nomenclature. The *Masterful* had been sold by F H Powell & Company in 1912 to Chilean owners and the *Samuel Hough* went for service in Australian waters early in 1913.

All the other ships in the Powell fleet came into the ownership of Powell, Bacon & Hough Lines Limited, as did the five ships under the joint ownership of F H Powell & Company and Samuel Hough Limited. In the Bacon fleet, the livestock carrier *John Bacon*, and the sister ships *Lady Bacon* and *Lord Bacon* were sold during the planning process leading up to the merger. Both the ships wholly owned by Samuel Hough Limited, the *Dorothy Hough* and the *Annie Hough* became part of the new merged fleet. The Mersey sailing flat, *Invincible*, owned by John Bacon Limited, was not transferred into Powell, Bacon & Hough Lines Limited but remained in the ownership of John Bacon Limited. She was managed from a different address from that of Powell, Bacon & Hough Lines Limited by Robert Mountfied, who was a board member of the new company.

The new structure reflected a determined focus on the coasting trades at the expense of the charter and tramp trades. For example at the time of the merger the cargo steamer *Sir George Bacon* had been working between Manchester and Ghent while *Sir Edward Bacon* was running from South Wales with coal and tinplate for the Continent, services which would eventually be phased out.

The first casualty for the newly formed company was a fireman, lost overboard in the Thames on 12 October 1913 from the *Devon Coast*.

The new merged company had two steamers on order at the time of its incorporation and quickly acquired two more. The new steamers were the machinery aft, bridge amidships cargo steamer *Suffolk Coast* which was launched at the yard of W Harkess & Son Limited at Middlesbrough on 28 October 1913, and the *Northern Coast* which was launched on 13 December 1913 by Sir Raylton Dixon & Company Limited, also at Middlesbrough. The *Northern Coast* was a traditional three island ship, with accommodation for twelve passengers on the upper deck amidships, and was designed for use on the Liverpool and Manchester to Bristol and London services. She had two hatches forward and one aft, each served by a pair of five and eight ton derricks. Her triple expansion steam engine drove a single propeller to provide a service speed of 10½ knots.

The *Northern Coast* (1914) complete with the red chevron funnel colours.

87

Both the new steamers were painted in an experimental new livery. The traditional Powell funnel, and later that of Coast Lines Limited also, was black with a white chevron. The **Suffolk Coast** and the **Northern Coast** had a black funnel with a red chevron in a broad white band. A number of other ships in the fleet adopted the new funnel colours but it was found that the broad white band discoloured badly from coal smoke and the original colours were reinstated after the Great War. The experimental livery never quite looked right compared to the more straightforward black funnel with a white chevron.

The *Somerset Coast* (1911) was commissioned as F H Powell & Company's *Graceful* for the London passenger service. Seen in the Avon, she is wearing the red chevron and white band of Powell, Bacon & Hough Lines Limited on the funnel.

The steamer **Stonehenge** also joined the merged fleet in autumn 1913. She had been built in 1876 as the *Fenton* for Milnes & Chaytor for use in the North Sea collier trade. The *Fenton* was equipped with an old style compound steam engine. She passed through various ownerships until she was acquired by Henry W Page of Glasgow in 1911 and he later gave her the name *Stonehenge*. Powell, Bacon & Hough Lines Limited bought her as a stop-gap in order to service the last of the South Wales collier work to the Continent; she was not renamed as she was not intended as a long-term fleet member and was sold for further service in 1916.

The *Fenton* (1876), seen before her acquisition by Powell, Bacon & Hough Lines Limited and later renamed *Stonehenge*.

[David Whiteside collection]

Finally, the very first motor ship entered the fleet. This was the petrol engine driven barge **West Flandria** which had been built in Rotterdam for service in Belgium in 1904. She was brought round to Milford late in 1913 under her own power where she took up duties as tender to the company's steamers which called on Wednesdays from Liverpool and Tuesdays from Bristol. The small steam tender *Cleddau* was then sold. The petrol engine provided 30 brake horsepower enabling the **West Flandria** speeds up to 7 knots. Great care had to be taken with the early marine petrol engines because of the low flash point of the fuel and many of the engines were converted to burn paraffin following a number of catastrophic accidents with petrol. Nevertheless, the great advantage was that the engine could be turned on ready for immediate use without having to wait for the boilers to produce steam, and it could be turned off when finished with, without having to damp down the furnace, so providing considerable economic advantages and savings in manpower.

Although only a barge, the **West Flandria** is notable in the fleets of Powell, Bacon & Hough Lines Limited, and its successor Coast Lines Limited, as being their very first motor ship. It has often been said that the Irish Sea ferry *Ulster Monarch* was the first motor ship in the Coast Lines group and that the **Fife Coast** completed in 1934 was the first motor driven cargo ship. Neither is true and the accolade needs to be pinned firmly onto the little **West Flandria**, even though she only served in the fleet for three years before being sold.

The duties of the Milford barges working essentially on the River Cleddau are explained in advertisements placed in the *Haverfordwest and Milford Haven Telegraph*, for example during 1914 and 1915:

> The Steam Barge **Enniscorthy** and the Steam Barges **Harfat** and **Pennar**, are intended to ply on Milford Haven in connection with the above steamers [from Liverpool on Wednesdays and Bristol on Tuesdays], carrying goods to and from Pembroke Dock, Haverfordwest, and the adjacent towns, and will deliver to such towns first, as may be deemed most expedient. A few Passengers carried by arrangement. All empties on which no freight is charged are carried at Owner's risk.

On 28 July 1914, Britain declared war on Germany. This was in response to the German invasion of Belgium and Luxembourg and the German move towards France, which halted at what became the Western Front. An advertisement in the *Liverpool Echo*, Saturday 8 August 1914, announced the curtailment of the London services at Plymouth:

> London, Bristol and South Coast Steamers (Powell, Bacon & Hough Lines Ltd.) This company gives notice that, in consequence of the European crisis, the passenger and goods service between Liverpool and London has been suspended until further noticed; the service between Liverpool and Wexford, Liverpool and Bristol Channel ports, will be carried on as usual. Service between Liverpool, Falmouth and Plymouth, the sailings will be curtailed. For particulars of sailings and alterations apply to Powell, Bacon & Hough Lines Ltd., Tower Building.

The Manchester-based service was closed shortly afterwards. The curtailment was necessary until such time as war insurance could be arranged and permission granted from the authorities to navigate the English Channel and Thames approaches. The Bristol Channel services, however, were unaffected for a while but they too were stopped, as was also the Liverpool to Wexford and Bristol route soon after war was declared. The *Norfolk Coast* was requisitioned as a Stores Carrier on 11 September 1914, was found unsuited to the job and returned to her owners on 26 October the same year.

Britain's coasts were battered by severe storms at the beginning of February 1915. One of several casualties was the *Hampshire Coast*, which stranded at Shoreham as reported the following day in *Lloyd's List*, 9 February 1915:

> The Liverpool steamer *Hampshire Coast*, Liverpool for Shoreham; general cargo, ashore on main, just west Shoreham harbour. Vessel lying well; not making water; no prospect of vessel getting off for several days; tides lessening; crew remain on board.

The *Hampshire Coast*, Captain Cannel, stranded on a shingle beach 150 yards east of Shoreham Old Coastguard Station at 4.45 am on 8 February. The following day there was a strong south westerly gale accompanied by heavy rain and the vessel was driven further up the beach. Serious straining of the hull was reported and the crew abandoned the wreck. Captain Cannel revisited the wreck at low water to find her sitting three feet in sand, listing 12 degrees to starboard, seawards, broadside on to the beach. He estimated she had been driven 100 feet further up the beach since the previous day. On 10 February a contract was arranged with the Western Marine Salvage Company; their steamer *Lady of the Isles*, with pumps and heavy haulage gear, set off for Shoreham.

By 11 February, the weather had eased. The *Hampshire Coast* now listed 18 degrees seaward with 2 feet 4 inches of water in hold No. 2, No. 1 tank and No. 3 tank. The salvage vessel arrived in the afternoon and preparations were made to discharge the cargo. Work was suspended on 15 February due to a south easterly gale which prevented the salvage team from laying out anchors. At high water on the morning of 16 February there was a heavy sea running in on the beach, causing considerable movement in the vessel and driving her 12 feet further up the beach and 10 feet astern. She still maintained the position of broadside on to the beach, thus exposing her whole length to the force of the sea. On the seawards side (starboard), the shell plating was set in further, and there were a greater number of broken and loose rivets. On 14 February, during a heavy gale, the *Hampshire Coast* drove up another 40 feet, almost to the top of the high water mark, and there was no possibility of getting her off until the whole cargo had been discharged. It was also feared that the vessel was badly damaged in the bottom as she was making a considerable quantity of water. In the afternoon at low water it was reported that the deck on both sides of No. 1 hatch was buckled and set up, and on the port side (shore side) vertical buckling had developed in the shell plating abaft No. 2 hatch.

Discharge of the cargo resumed on 17 February but was stopped by the weather the next day. Upon opening out the main hold cargo on 20 February, the hold pillars were seen to be bent and broken away from their deck fastenings. Considerable leakage had occurred through damaged decks in the vicinity of the main deck winches, causing extensive damage to cargo loaded at Gravesend. Eventually on 11 August, six months after she had stranded, the *Hampshire Coast* was refloated on the morning's tide and towed into Shoreham harbour as a constructive total loss and the register was closed. She was bought by J Esplen of Liverpool, repaired and sold back to Powell, Bacon & Hough Lines. She was back in service by the end of the year.

'The policy of piracy and pillage' a torpedo strikes the unsuspecting *Western Coast* (1913) off Beachy Head.

[*Drawn by Charles Dixon for* The Graphic*]*

On 24 February 1915, the **Western Coast**, formerly the *Hopeful*, was torpedoed and sunk in the English Channel 8 miles south east of Beachy Head by the German submarine U8. The steamer had been on a voyage from London to Plymouth and Liverpool with general cargo. A report in the *Liverpool Daily Post*, 26 February 1915, stated:

> Captain Ratcliffe, of Liverpool, who was in command of the **Western Coast** at the time of the disaster, was landed with his crew at Portsmouth yesterday morning… The crew numbers nineteen all told, and they have lost everything except what they stand up in…

> Interviewed by our representative, Captain Ratcliffe gave a graphic story of the sinking of his ship. The **Western Coast** was a cargo and passenger steamer belonging to Powell, Bacon, Hough & Co., Liverpool, and traded regularly between that port and London with general cargo. In view of the German blockade menace, we took the precaution before leaving London to get the boats ready for any emergency that might arise, and they were swung outwards onto the davits and lashed ready for immediate launching. All went well until 3.40 on Wednesday afternoon, when we were about nine miles south of Beachy Head. We were going at full speed at the time, and suddenly, without the slightest warning, we felt a violent explosion. I immediately gave orders for the lashings to be cut, and the boats to be launched, and in a very short time the whole of the crew and myself had left the **Western Coast**, which disappeared below the surface in about seven minutes…

> We were picked up by the London steamer *Osceola*, bound for Portsmouth, which was following in our wake, and were landed here this morning….

The ship was struck abreast No. 2 hatch on the port side. Captain Theodore Atkinson of the Glasgow registered *Osceola* was later awarded a silver cup by the Board of Trade for rescuing the nineteen crew members and the pilot that were aboard the two lifeboats from the **Western Coast**. The loss of the **Western Coast** was just one of seven British vessels sunk in the first week of what Prime Minister Asquith called 'Germany's policy of piracy and pillage'.

The company was able to restart its services between Manchester and the Bristol Channel on 27 April 1915. A statement from Powell, Bacon & Hough Lines Limited read 'owing to the general increase in working expenses and the recent advances made by the Manchester Ship Canal Company on tolls, labour, etc., we are reluctantly compelled to raise rates 15% on sea freight'.

The *Western Coast* (1913) sinking in front of her attacker, and inset: the crew being taken on board the London steamer *Osceola* (1903).

[*Drawn by Charles Dixon for* The Graphic*]*

Chapter 14

CREATION OF COAST LINES LIMITED

Powell, Bacon & Hough Lines Limited was fortunate in being granted licences to build two new ships during 1914. These were launched the following year, the *Welsh Coast* by Charles Hill & Sons at Bristol on 11 March, and the *Wexford Coast* by J Fullerton & Sons at Paisley on 31 May 1915. Both ships were single screw, machinery aft cargo steamers, the *Welsh Coast* was equipped with a modern triple expansion steam engine to give her a service speed of 10½ knots, and the *Wexford Coast* was equipped with the now outdated, but simple to build and maintain, compound steam engine, and fit for 10 knots.

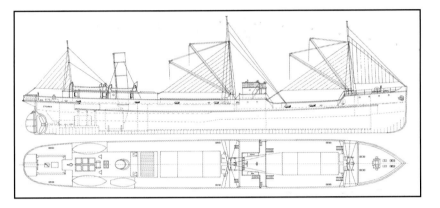

Charles Hill & Sons, Bristol: outline plans for the *Welsh Coast* (1915).

Charles Waine described the *Welsh Coast* in his book *Coastal and Short Sea Liners*:

> Twin derricks per mast are fitted, but in other respects she was similar to the raised quarter deck coasters built for the bulk trades, though her stowage rate of 49 cubic feet per ton was better than most vessels of that design. For Powell, Bacon & Hough she was well suited to their transhipment trade between the major ports of parcels of cargo arriving or leaving on ocean liners. Her triple expansion engine was provided by George Clarke of Sunderland and had cylinders of 18 inches, 29½ inches and 48½ inches in diameter with a stroke of 33 inches using steam at 180 lbs to give a service speed of about 10½ knots. Unusually the engineers were housed in the bridge accommodation with no one aft. No doubt this was appreciated as they were away from the steam steering gear and its attendant noises every time the helmsman touched the wheel. Two apprentices as well as a donkeyman and carpenter were provided for. The addition of a 'tween deck in the aft hold was proposed and a plan drawn up, to make her more suitable for general cargo, but there is no definite evidence that it was ever fitted.

Two second-hand cargo steamers were purchased to bolster the fleet and replace war losses. These were the *Hinderton* from Mann, MacNeal & Company, of Glasgow, which was renamed *Kentish Coast*, and the *Rosslyn* which came from Murray, McNab & Company, also of Glasgow, and which was renamed *Irish Coast*. They were standard three island cargo steamers; the *Kentish Coast* was equipped with a triple expansion steam engine and had a service speed of 9½ knots, while the *Irish Coast* had a compound steam engine which provided a service speed of 10½ knots. Although the *Kentish Coast* remained in the fleet for a long time, latterly under the ownership of Coast Lines Limited, the *Irish Coast*, with her old fashioned machinery, was sold for further service in 1916.

The *Kentish Coast* (1908) was acquired during the Great War. She is seen in the River Avon below Bristol.

[David Whiteside collection]

The steamer **Cornish Coast** was sunk in the Mersey following collision with the **Jeanette Woermann**, as reported in the *Liverpool Echo*, Wednesday 3 March 1915:

It is feared that five lives have been lost in the Mersey today. The Liverpool coasting steamer **Cornish Coast** (500 tons, Powell, Bacon & Hough Lines), proceeded up the river at about ten o'clock this morning, came into collision with the steamer **Jeanette Woermann** (2,046 tons, Woermann Line, Hamburg), with the result that the former was sunk.

Five men are missing, including the captain, an Egremont man and a Seacombe man... The missing men are Captain Brown, of Egremont. John Sullivan, cook and steward. F T Lawrence, Chief Engineer, Seacombe. Mr Perez, Second Engineer. Jose A Leitos, fireman. Eight men of the **Cornish Coast** were landed at the Prince's Stage...

One of the men giving an account of the collision said: We were part of the crew of the three masted vessel **Cornish Coast**, belonging to Messrs Powell & Hough, Liverpool and London. We had come from Rochester and were going to Birkenhead with a cargo of cement. Everything went well with us, the weather being fairly bright, until we had almost reached a point opposite the entrance to Birkenhead Dock. There was a vessel lying at anchor in the river, and I hardly know what happened next, everything occurring so suddenly. All I can remember is that we somehow fouled the chain, and afterwards there was a great bump. Our vessel got clear somewhat, and ran up river to get into safety.

It became evident that she was badly damaged, we got ready to leave and jump from deck, if required. There was little time to pick and choose what to do, as the vessel began to sink rapidly by the stern. She disappeared in a few minutes below the water. I only know of us six being saved. We cannot tell what became of the rest of the crew, but we believe that several – five or six – lost their lives... Had it not been for a tug belonging to the Alexandra Towing Company coming alongside, we would probably all have lost our lives...

A passenger on one of the Woodside ferry steamers told our representative that everything happened so quickly that there was no time for anything to be done. The **Cornish Coast**, he said, appeared to be swept on the strong incoming tide right across the bows of the **Jeanette Woermann**. The steamer fouled the Hamburg boat's chain and sustained severe damage. She then cleared and was swept southwards... The **Jeanette Woermann**, which formerly belonged to the Woermann Line, of Hamburg, was captured as a war prize. She sustained only slight damage, a plate on her bow being dented...

The wreck lay directly between the Alfred and Morpeth river entrances, some 350 yards below Woodside Landing Stage. An attempt was made to raise it on 26 March 1915, but the lifting wires broke through her, so the operation was abandoned. Wreck disposal work using explosives commenced on 21 April 1915 and continued until 9 June 1915, when the wreck was cleared to a satisfactory navigable depth.

The *Cornish Coast* (1904) was commissioned by F H Powell & Company. She is seen here at low tide at Birkenhead after sinking, following a collision on 3 March 1915.

[Booths, New Brighton]

On 17 April 1915, the *Gloucester Coast*, one-time *Sir Walter Bacon*, was requisitioned as an Expeditionary Force Transport. She was released in October 1916 and converted for use as an Ammunition Carrier. She was discharged back to her owners in December 1919 following service in Russian waters. The *Devon Coast*, former *Graceful*, also served in the latter part of the war as an Ammunition Carrier.

In mid-May 1915, it was announced that Powell, Bacon & Hough Lines Limited along with the Furness group had purchased a large number of shares in the British & Irish Steam Packet Company Limited (see McRonald, The *Irish Boats Volume 1* for company history). B&I was in operational difficulties, having sold the *Lady Martin* and *Lady Roberts* in July 1914 and the *Lady Hudson-Kinahan* in October 1914. However, it did manage to build one new passenger steamer, the *Lady Wimborne*, in 1915, but it was no longer able to sustain its weekly Dublin to London passenger and cargo service – war or no war. B&I, at that time, traded principally between Dublin and London as a competitor to the Liverpool to London steamers traditionally operated by the Powell and the Hough interests. Hazel P Smyth in her book The B&I Line generously reported on the sale of the three passenger ships *Lady Martin*, *Lady Roberts* and *Lady Hudson-Kinahan* before the war with no mention of lack of working capital:

The British & Irish Steam Packet Company's passenger and cargo steamer *Lady Martin* (1888) was one of three ships sold prior to Alfred Read and Christopher Furness buying into the company.

The British & Irish Steam Packet Company joined the Coast Line Group immediately it was formed in 1917. However, the Powell-Bacon-Hough interest had already begun to influence the B&I before the war. This probably explains why the crack ships had been sold out; they had been operating on the London and South of England routes and constituted a wasteful opposition to the others' operations.

B & I did manage to build one new passenger and cargo steamer, the *Lady Wimborne* (1915), in lieu of ships that had been sold out of the fleet.

Alfred H Read and Frederick W Lewis were elected to the Board of B&I in 1915, their job to safeguard the investment of both Powell, Bacon & Hough Lines Limited and Furness Withy & Company Limited. It was to be a further two years before British and Irish would be wholly owned by Coast Lines, when Furness Withy & Company wanted to dispose of its interests in the coasting trades. Furness also sold its Kirkcaldy, Fife & London Steam Shipping Company Limited in 1918 to what had become Coast Lines Limited, and Coast Lines Limited also bought the Furness owned London, Welsh Steamship Company Limited in 1924.

The authorised capital of the British & Irish Steam Packet Company Limited was £120,000 in £50 shares and the amount issued was £110,000 in 2,200 shares, fully paid. The joint investment between Alfred Read and the Furness group of companies in B&I was confirmed on 28 May 1915 by the Press Association's Dublin correspondent who reported:

...that an offer has been made by Sir Stephen Furness, of London and Manchester, and Mr Alfred H Read of Liverpool, to purchase the shares of the British and Irish Steam Packet Company, Ltd., and a provisional agreement for purchase has been entered into. The British and Irish company will continue under its old title and management in Dublin.

It is interesting that Powell, Bacon & Hough Lines Limited provided B&I with a soft loan during 1916. This suggests that either an agreement for the Powell company to acquire B&I was already in place or, more likely, that some kind of service agreement had been agreed upon by the two companies. Whichever was the case it made the prospects of a Powell take-over of B&I much stronger.

The ordinary business of the company continued despite the war, as illustrated by the following claim for damages reported in the *Liverpool Daily Post*, Friday 26 May 1916:

> In the Admiralty Division yesterday, the President (Sir Samuel Evans), sitting with Trinity masters, disposed of an action brought by Powell, Bacon & Hough Lines, Ltd., as owners of the steamship *Eastern Coast*, against Messrs. William, Company and Son Ltd., as owners of the dumb barge *Treagh*. Plaintiffs claimed damages arising from the barge getting jammed between the *Eastern Coast* and the dock wall as the steamer was being taken into the lock of the Shadwell New Basin, London, on 27 April 1915.
>
> The President said that the barge was dropped by a tug against the rules of good navigation and against the express orders of the dock master, and she afterwards placed herself and the *Eastern Coast* in a position of danger. Those on the steamer were in consequence unable to avoid the barge, which became jammed, and caused the damage complained of. Judgement would be for the plaintiff, with costs, the damages to be assessed.

The Bristol services were in the hands of the steamers *Somerset Coast*, *Welsh Coast* and *Wirral Coast* for much of 1916. The brand 'Coast Line – fast coastwise services' had been adopted in advertising, it being realised that the full title of the company needed a short and punchy alternative. Liverpool departures were every Tuesday and Saturday, returning also on Tuesdays and Saturdays, and Manchester sailings were on Mondays and Fridays, returning on Tuesdays and Saturdays. Sailings from Bristol to Milford, Haverfordwest and Pembroke were suspended, as was the service from Liverpool to Wexford and Bristol.

The *Suffolk Coast* was captured at sea by U17 on 7 November 1916 and sunk. The *Suffolk Coast* had been on passage from Glasgow to Fécamp with general cargo. Her crew was cast adrift in the ship's boats and later picked up and landed safely. The *Suffolk Coast* was scuttled with explosive charges at a point in the English Channel 14 nautical miles east south east of Cape Barfleur, Seine-Maritime.

In December 1916, Powell, Bacon & Hough Lines Limited accepted the big three island cargo steamer *Western Coast* from her builders the Dublin Dockyard Company. She had a length of 240 feet and a beam of 36 feet and her depth was 18 feet. She was equipped with triple expansion steam machinery and was good for 10½ knots. W Harkess & Son Limited delivered another machinery aft cargo steamer, with bridge amidships, the following spring. Her triple expansion steam machinery sustained a service speed of 10 knots. She was christened *Suffolk Coast* at her launch on 22 March 1917. Recycling names of ships that had been sunk by enemy action was recommended by the Shipping Controller in order to add a sense of confusion. However, in the case of the two *Suffolk Coast*s, which had radically different profiles, little confusion was likely even when viewed from a U Boat periscope.

In January 1917 the steamer *Gower Coast* was sold to the Ford Shipping Company Limited (Messrs Mann, MacNeal & Company) of Glasgow.

On 4 April 1917, the *Somerset Coast*, formerly the *Graceful* when she was in the Powell fleet, with general cargo, grounded on the Blackwater Bank, off Wexford Bay. She floated off with the rising tide, apparently undamaged. She was on passage from Liverpool to Bristol under Captain D Davies.

A few weeks later, on a voyage from Bristol to Liverpool, the *Somerset Coast* collided with the *Sound Fisher* on 22 April in a position about 1½ miles south west by west of the Bardsey Light. The *Sound Fisher* was on passage from her home port of Barrow to Rouen with pig iron. The *Somerset Coast* foundered, but the crew of fourteen was safely landed at Milford. The *Sound Fisher* had her port anchor and hawse-pipe damaged and the poop and forecastle decks were also damaged. She made a little water in the forepeak but was able to proceed on her voyage.

In May 1917 the wartime Shipping Controller, Sir Joseph Maclay, appointed Alfred H Read, to be Director of Home Trade Shipping. Read was also then a member of the Mersey Docks & Harbour Board. Until then coastal shipping had not been controlled in the same manner as deep sea shipping. Nevertheless, the *Norfolk Coast*, *Gloucester Coast* and *Devon Coast* had earlier been requisitioned as auxiliaries, albeit the *Norfolk Coast* only for a period of six weeks.

The *Norfolk Coast* (1910) acted as an auxiliary for a six month period and was later sunk by a torpedo fired by a U boat on 18 June 1918.

In February 1917 Alfred Read agreed to take the company into the ownership of the Royal Mail group of companies under the Chairmanship of Sir Owen Phillips. Alfred Read was retained as the Managing Director. The *Journal of Commerce*, 26 February 1917, reported:

Messrs Elder Dempster & Co., and associated companies have acquired the business of the Coast Line (Powell, Bacon & Hough Lines Ltd.). The Coast Line is one of the oldest and largest shipping companies in the kingdom and maintains regular services for both passengers and cargo on the west and south coasts, particularly between Liverpool and London calling en route at all the chief English Channel ports, where the line has its own branch offices; also maintaining services between Liverpool and South Wales. The fleet consists of some of the finest steamers trading round the British coast. Apparently no change is to be made in the service.

That Elder Dempster was chosen to liaise with 'the Coast Line', reflected the long standing relationship between that company and F H Powell & Company, latterly also with Powell, Bacon & Hough Lines. The African service into Liverpool relied on Powell for transhipment of imports, many of them being tropical hardwoods in long stands, to the south of England and in particular to London. In June 1917 Owen Philipps, Chairman of Royal Mail, stated at a public meeting in Bristol that 'We have also acquired an interest in Coast Lines Limited, which business is likely to prove a useful auxiliary as providing connections with our own ocean services'. He did not appreciate that Alfred Read had other ideas and saw his new parent company as a source of funds from which he could acquire other coasting companies and grow his own interests.

In mid-May 1917, it was announced the Powell, Bacon & Hough Lines Limited had purchased a large number of shares in the British & Irish Steam Packet Company Limited. The shares were mostly those owned by Stephen Furness that had been bought when Alfred Read joined the board of B&I almost exactly two years previously. Alfred Read now assumed the role of Managing Director of B&I as well as Powell, Bacon & Hough Lines Limited. In July the remaining shares in B&I were bought, so it was now a wholly owned subsidiary, of Powell, Bacon & Hough Lines Limited. The so called Coast Line then rebranded itself as Coast Lines Limited during the early summer and started to use its new company title from July onwards; the ships were registered under the new brand on 12 June. The acquisition of the British & Irish Steam Packet Company Limited was to be the first of many take-overs, the next would be the purchase of the City of Cork Steam Packet Company Limited, which was completed in July 1918, a company like B&I that also had operated a service to London via south coast ports prior to the war, but from Cork not from Dublin.

The *Norfolk Coast*, formerly the *Hopeful*, setting out from London for Dublin on 15 November 1917, with general cargo, was in collision with the steamship *Belvedere*. The accident happened in Long Reach and the *Norfolk Coast* had her port quarter damaged and several plates sprung. Both ships were able to proceed following inspection and minor repairs.

The *Western Coast* was lost on 17 November 1917. The *Western Coast*, Captain Tennent, was torpedoed and sunk by *U40* some 10 miles west south west of the Eddystone Light off Plymouth. She had been on passage from Portsmouth to Barry in ballast. Seventeen men died in the sinking.

On 18 June 1918, the **Norfolk Coast**, Captain H Thomas, was sunk by torpedo fired by U30. The **Norfolk Coast** had been on passage from Rouen to the Tyne in ballast and was in a North Sea convoy travelling northwards. At a point 23 miles east by south of Flamborough Head, at 6.23 pm, the torpedo struck directly under the bridge immediately killing eight men and badly injuring another. With the vessel sinking immediately, seven survivors were picked up out of the sea by a patrol vessel and later landed at Middlesbrough and the Tyne.

The **Suffolk Coast** was requisitioned in August 1918 and converted into the heavily armed and disguised 'Q' ship HMS **Suffolk Coast**. Her conversion was made under the supervision of Lieutenant Commander Harold Auten. The ship received a 4 inch gun mounted on a lift in No. 1 hatch forward which could be brought rapidly to upper deck level once a U boat was lulled within range. Part of the sham was a panic crew that would rush to the lifeboats and prepare the boats for launching, so distracting attention from the gun crews while they took up their stations. The **Suffolk Coast** was also intended to be used commercially as a collier and was intentionally kept in a dirty state and seemingly poorly maintained as part of her disguise. Canvas deck houses, ventilators and funnels were available coupled with a variety of names painted on the bow and different ensigns at the stern. However, the White Ensign had to be shown immediately prior to engagement. While many of the Q ships were lost, the **Suffolk Coast** was commissioned too late to be of service. Harold Auten in his book on Q ships tells the story after he visited the **Suffolk Coast** when she was lying at Leith, and her being requisitioned at his suggestion:

> I was commanded by my Admiral to prepare the plans of the necessary alterations. This I did in twenty four hours, assisted by the constructive department of the dockyard. Three days later the **Suffolk Coast** arrived [at Queenstown]. Then we got to work and for nine weeks laboured incessantly in turning the **Suffolk Coast** from a peaceable collier into a 'Mystery Ship'. On November 10th we sailed from Queenstown to test her guns. Owing to bad weather she had to put into Milford Haven on the following day, only to be greeted by the hoarse-throated hooters of all the ships in the neighbourhood – it was the Armistice.

> And that is why the **Suffolk Coast** is a disappointed ship. She had been told that she was to become a ship-of-war, and then, within 24 hours of her being ready to 'do her bit', the Hun threw up the sponge… On the day following we left for Plymouth… Out of Plymouth we proceeded to test our guns, which seemed rather farcical under the circumstances, but it had to be done. Then we were told that we were to become a show ship and tour round the ports of England, telling people how it had been done.

THE MYSTERY SHIP

H.M.S. SUFFOLK COAST.
She looks like a tramp steamer, but in reality is a vessel of entirely novel type, and has sunk many U-boats.

The 'Mystery Ship HMS **Suffolk Coast**'– a postcard advertising her post-war role as a touring 'show ship'.

The Q ship **Suffolk Coast** (1917) lying alongside a former German U boat in St Katherine's Dock, London, at the start of her tour as a show boat.

The **Suffolk Coast** was returned to her owners in July 1919, as was the **Wexford Coast** which had also been requisitioned the year before for similar duties but was never converted. The big cargo steamer **Carrigan Head**, owned by the Ulster Steamship Company Limited of Belfast, also served as a Q Ship, and she served under various names to confuse the enemy including that of **Suffolk Coast**! In all, Powell, Bacon and Hough Lines Limited and Coast Lines Limited lost four ships in the war to enemy action and three others to collisions. The companies had managed several ships for the Ministry of Transport at various times during the war, but none was lost to enemy action. Coast Lines Limited was now left alone to pursue its peaceful civilian business under the expert guidance of its Managing Director Alfred Read.

The British & Irish Steam Packet Company Limited was quickly acquired by Alfred Read in 1917, followed in 1918 by the City of Cork Steam Packet Company Limited, M Langlands & Sons and Stocks Turnbull & Company Limited, and in 1919 by the Belfast Steamship Company Limited. G & J Burns Limited was acquired in 1920, as was G Bazeley & Sons Limited at Penzance and its three ships. Burns & Laird Lines Limited was formed in 1922 soon after the purchase of the Laird Lines Limited.

Coast Lines Limited flourished in the 1920s despite the downturn in the Irish trade during 'the troubles' and the subsequent partitioning of Ireland. Meanwhile the parent Royal Mail Line Group, under Lord Kylsant, was encountering increasing financial difficulties. A number of measures were taken within Coast Lines to isolate it from the inevitable collapse of the parent, ironically aided by the intransigence of Lord Kylsant to refinance the company in 1922. The inevitable fall of both Lord Kylsant and Royal Mail occurred in 1931, by which time Coast Lines and its associate companies had become sufficiently independent to ride out the storm, and ultimately in 1936 able to buy themselves out of the Royal Mail Group altogether.

H L Stocks & Company Limited was an early acquisition by Coast Lines and with it came three ships, one, the *New Abbotshall* (1912) which was renamed *Durham Coast*; seen here high and dry at Wallasey after a collision in the river on 24 June 1924.

Coast Lines Limited went from strength to strength, being the dominant major independent coastal sea carrier in steadfast competition with the railway owned fleets. The company realised the value of offering a door-to-door goods and parcel service and developed road haulage and delivery/collection interests by purchase of existing companies. The first was the acquisition of the Liverpool Cartage Company Limited, with its stables at Grafton Street, later adapted for lorries on the ground floor, stables on the first floor and hay loft on the second floor.

The Stables at Grafton Street, Liverpool, home of the Liverpool Cartage Company which was acquired in 1913.

Coast Lines Limited acquired the Tyne-Tees Steam Shipping Company Limited in 1943 and Tyne-Tees bought the Aberdeen Steam Navigation Company Limited in 1945. Coast Lines bought William Sloan & Company Limited in 1958, and the North of Scotland, Orkney and Shetland Shipping Company Limited in 1961, both companies suffering financing problems. The group's ships were then mostly general cargo coasters, a few of which still offered a handful of passenger berths in season, along with a selection of conventional passenger ferries with cargo facilities on the Irish Sea and Orkney and Shetland services.

Burns & Laird Lines *Royal Ulsterman* (1936) against a backdrop of Federal, Blue Funnel and Harrison Line ships at Glasgow.

[Nick Robins]

Not quite the last cargo ship to be built for Coast Lines, the motor ship *Cheshire Coast* (1954) was a complete contrast to the early steamships.

[Nick Robins]

Time was moving on, and already purpose built vehicle ferries were operating between Preston and Larne, while the directors of Coast Lines plodded on, oblivious of either the roll-on roll-off innovation or the introduction of the container. The decline in the cattle-on-the-hoof imports from Ireland in favour of the refrigerated carcass trade did little for the fortunes of the company either.

The Tyne-Tees Steam Shipping Company Limited became a founder member of North Sea Ferries Limited in 1965 along with the General Steam Navigation Company Limited. GSNC had been a part of the P&O group since 1920 but had retained its own identity and independent management. The success of North Sea Ferries led P&O to acquire a higher 50% stake in the new company in 1971 by successfully bidding, for just £5.6 million, for all of the ailing Coast Lines companies, including Tyne-Tees with its share of North Sea Ferries. This move also gave P&O the valuable Coast Lines' road haulage and delivery companies.

Coast Lines was merged with GSNC and the pair was almost immediately subsumed into the European & Air Transport Division of the newly restructured P&O. The Coast Lines management responsibilities were removed and the ships transferred to corporate duties or sold; an undignified end to a once mighty company. The ro-ro revolution was gathering pace, but it was a revolution that the tradition and conservatism of the Coast Lines board was unable to address. The black funnel with its white chevron was seen no more.

APPENDIX

FLEET LISTS

All Powell, Bacon and Hough ships registered at Liverpool unless stated otherwise

1)   Powell and associate companies

F H Powell & Company including Cram & Powell, Rowe & Powell, John Ellis, Ferdinand Honey & Alfred Read, Watchful Steamship Company, Point Clear Steamship Company and other part owners.

Sailing ships:

Name	Powell Service	Gross tons	Comments
Swift	1829–1841	104	Built by John Bools Good, Bridport, 1822 for Clyde and Liverpool Shipping Co., Glasgow, as *Swift*; 1828 sold to John Swainston & George Cram; 1829 sold to John Swainston & George Cram & others; 1838 sold to George Cram & others, following the death of John Swainston in 1837; run down and sunk 13 February 1841 by an unidentified vessel off the Skerries, Anglesey, on passage from Bristol to Liverpool.
Hope	1828–1848	107	Built by John Bools Good, Bridport, 1822 for Clyde and Liverpool Shipping Co., Glasgow, as *Hope*; 1829 sold to John Swainston & George Cram; 1829 sold to John Swainston & George Cram & others; 1838 sold to George Cram & others, following the death of John Swainston in 1837; 1846 sold to George Cram, Frederick H Powell & others; sank 21 December 1848 off Holyhead on passage from Liverpool to Bristol, following a collision with the sailing ship *Eugenia*.
Arrow	1829–1842	99	Built at Bideford 1826 for Bristol and Liverpool Smack Co., Bristol, as *Arrow*; 1829 sold to Ferdinand Beeston & others, Bristol, & John Swainston & George Cram (Swainston & Cram) & others, Liverpool; 1838 to Ferdinand Beeston & others, Bristol, & George Cram & others, Liverpool (Cram & Co.), following the death of John Swainston in 1837; stranded 7 November 1842 near Cemlyn Bay, Anglesey, on passage from Bristol to Liverpool.
Dart	1829–1856	112	Built at Chepstow 1826 for Bristol and Liverpool Smack Co., Bristol, as *Dart*; 1829 sold to Ferdinand Beeston & others, Bristol, & John Swainston & George Cram (Swainston & Cram) & others, Liverpool; 1838 to Ferdinand Beeston & others, Bristol, & George Cram & others, Liverpool (Cram & Co.), Liverpool, following the death of John Swainston in 1837; 1854 sold to Ferdinand Beeston & others, Bristol, & Frederick H Powell & others, Liverpool (F H Powell & Co.); 1856 sold to Owen Davies, Carnarvon; 1870 sold to Andrew L Muir & William Vost, Stirling; 1873 sold to James Myles, Dundee; 1878 sold to James Martin, Dundee; 1886 sold to George Lawrie, Dundee; 1890 sold to William Kinnear, Dundee; 1891 sold to James Milne, Aberdeen; 1896 sold to James Souter, Arbroath; 1898 sold to James Souter & William Balfour, Arbroath; 1902 sold to William Balfour, Arbroath; wrecked 16 September 1907 on Plough Seat, Holy Island, Northumberland, on passage from Sunderland.

Name	Powell Service	Gross Tons	Comments
Carlisle	1831-1835	81	Built at Liverpool 1824 for William Dowson, Liverpool & others, Carlisle, as *Carlisle*; 1831 sold to John Swainston & George Cram; 1831 sold to John Swainston & George Cram & others; wrecked 21 November 1835 at Parton, near Whitehaven, on passage from Liverpool.
Lady Peel	1832	80	Built by Robert Lubbock, Yarmouth, 1827 for Sir Robert J Harvey, Thorpe, Norfolk as *Lady Peel*; 1832 sold to James Clark; 1832 sold to John Swainston & George Cram; 1832 sold to John Swainston, George Cram & others; stranded 10 October 1832 on Flat Holm, Bristol Channel, in fog, on passage from Liverpool to Bristol.
Adonis	1833-1838	80	Built by Peter Scurlock, Nayland, Pembrokeshire, 1832 for Thomas Scurlock, Joseph Scurlock & Peter Scurlock, Nayland, & Benjamin Scurlock, Pembroke as *Adonis*; 1833 sold to John Swainston & George Cram; 1833 sold to John Swainston, George Cram & others; sailed from Newport 9 March 1838 and presumed lost at sea.
Confidence	1833-1839	135	Built at Dartmouth 1827 for John Gibbs, Plymouth, as *Confidence*; 1833 sold to John Swainston & George Cram & others; 1838 to executors of John Swainston, & George Cram & others, following the death of John Swainston in 1837; sailed from Bristol 4 January 1839, for Liverpool. Empty lifeboat found 14 February in St. Bride's Bay, Pembrokeshire, after gales.
Ann	1833-1847	137	Built at Chester 1815 for John Lewis, Barmouth, & others as *Ann*; 1833 sold to John Swainston & George Cram; 1833 sold to John Swainston & George Cram & others; 1838 to executors of John Swainston, George Cram & others, following the death of John Swainston in 1837; 1839 sold to George Cram & others; 1839 sold to George Cram; 1840 lengthened by 8 feet; 1847 sold to Edward Bridges, Lynn; 1848 sold to Edward Bridges & Samuel Catbarth, Lynn; stranded in gale 7 January 1854 on Herd Sand at mouth of River Tyne, on passage from King's Lynn to the Tyne.
Greyhound	1833-1856	108	Built at Bridport 1820 for M. Grey, Londonderry, as *Greyhound*; 1825 sold to James McCrea, Londonderry; 1833 sold to John Swainston & George Cram; 1833 sold to John Swainston & George Cram & others; 1838 to executors of John Swainston & George Cram & others, following the death of John Swainston in 1837; 1840 sold to George Cram & others; 1853 sold to George Cram, Frederick H Powell, Richard Rowe & others; 1856 sold to James Corrin, George Goldsmith & John Corris, Douglas, Isle of Man; 1856 sold to James Corrin, George Goldsmith, John Corris & Richard D Edwards, Douglas, Isle of Man; 1859 sold to John Corris, James Corrin & George Goldsmith, Douglas, Isle of Man; sank 2 February 1862 off Corsewall Point, after collision with schooner *Earl*, on passage from Troon to Douglas.
Manchester	1834-1859	150	Built by John Storey, Monkwearmouth, Co. Durham, 1826 for Thomas Hampson, snr, Thomas Hampson, jnr., Ambrose Lace & others, Liverpool, as *Manchester*; 1829 sold to Thomas Hampson, snr, Thomas Hampson, jnr, Ambrose Lace, William F Vale & others, Liverpool; 1834 sold to John Swainston & George Cram; 1834 sold to John Swainston & George Cram & others; 1837 to executors of John Swainston, George Cram & others, following the death of John Swainston; 1840 sold to George Cram & others; 1852 sold to Frederick H Powell & others; 1854 sold to George Cram, Frederick H Powell & others; 1855 sold to Frederick H Powell & others; 1859 sold to John Meaze, Dublin; sank at entrance to Strangford Lough, 5 February 1861, on passage from Whitehaven to Dublin.

Name	Powell Service	Gross Tons	Comments
Jane	1835-1851	94	Built by William Hutchings, Bideford, 1830 for William Tardrew, Monkleigh, Devon as *Jane*; 1835 sold to John Swainston & George Cram; 1835 sold to John Swainston & George Cram & others; 1838 to executors of John Swainston, George Cram & others, following the death of John Swainston in 1837; 1840 sold to George Cram & others; abandoned 31 July 1851 off the Skerries, after striking the Platters, on passage from Bristol to Liverpool.
Arethusa	1837-1853	98	Built by Robert Lubbock, Yarmouth, 1830 for Samuel Paget & William Simms, both Yarmouth, & George Luffingham, Wapping, as *Arethusa*; 1837 sold to John Swainston & George Cram; 1837 sold to John Swainston & George Cram & others; 1837 to executors of John Swainston, George Cram & others, following the death of John Swainston; 1840 sold to George Cram & others; 1853 sold to William Hewett, Belfast; 1855 sold to James Charley, James McKinley & John Robinson, Belfast; 1866 owned by William Templeton, Island Magee, Co. Antrim; stranded 19 March 1872 at Rathlin Island, on passage from Glasgow to Londonderry.
Monkton	1839-1845	112	Built by Thomas Stevens, Quaco, New Brunswick, Canada, 1839 for John Steadman, Monkton, New Brunswick as *Monkton*; 1839 sold to Frederick H Powell & others; 1845 sold to Wilson Forster & John Ingham, Liverpool; 1846 sold to Archibald H Rennie, John McEwen & Archibald Rennie, Inverness; 1851 sold to Archibald H Rennie & James Gordon (Rennie & Gordon), Inverness; 1853 sold to James Gordon, Inverness, following the death of Archibald H Rennie; 1855 sold to James Rosse, Inverness; 1872 sold to Thomas Maddison, Blyth, Northumberland; 1873 sold overseas
Latimer	1841-1846	119	Built by Thomas Gibbs, Holyhead, 1839 for Thomas Gibbs & Ann C Owen, Holyhead as *Latimer*; 1839 sold to Charles R Simpson, Liverpool & Ann C Owen, Holyhead; 1840 sold to Charles R Simpson; 1841 sold to Frederick H Powell & others; 1846 sold to Stephen Campbell & Richard Burton, Newport, Monmouthshire, & Thomas Ellis, jnr., Tredegar; 1851 sold to Stephen Campbell & George William Jones, Newport, Monmouthshire, & Thomas Ellis, jnr, Tredegar; 1851 sold to Stephen Campbell, Newport, Monmouthshire, & Thomas Ellis, jnr, Tredegar; 1852 sold to Stephen Campbell, Newport, Monmouthshire; 1854 sold to David Jenkins, Carnarvon; 1856 sold to Daniel King, London; 1856 sold to Daniel King, Moses Hasor, William Cringle, Samuel Bullard & Samuel Bullard, London; 1859 lengthened by 19 feet; 1861 sold to Daniel King, Moses Hasor, Samuel Bullard, William E McKenzie, London; 1861 sold to Daniel King, Moses Hasor, Samuel Bullard, William E McKenzie & Thomas Colton, London; wrecked on Dagoe Island, prior to 10 September 1864, on passage from Newcastle to Kronstadt, St Petersburg.
Pearl	1841-1856	141	Built by Fellowes and Pounds, Yarmouth, 1826 for William Barter & George Holland, Yarmouth, David Dunnell, Southtown, & Samuel Lillistone, Beccles, (Dunnell & Co.) as *Pearl*; 1831 sold to William Barter, George Holland, David Dunnell, Samuel Lillistone (per executors) & Robert Crickmer, Beccles; 1837 sold to George Cram; 1837 sold to George Cram & others; 1841 sold to Cram, Smith & Co.; 1856 sold to William Ross, Workington; 1856 sold to John Cademy, Clay, Norfolk; 1856 sold to John Cademy & Joseph Haycock, Wells, Norfolk; 1867 sold to John Cademy; 1876 scrapped.

Name	Powell Service	Gross tons	Comments
Ann Powell	1847–1861	105	Built by John Dawson & Co., Liverpool, 1847 for Frederick H Powell & others as **Ann Powell**; sank 14 February 1861 after striking the Scarweathers, Bristol Channel, on passage to Bristol.
Herefordshire	1852–1858	97	Built at Hereford 1824 for Ferdinand Beeston, Bristol, as **Herefordshire**; 1831 lengthened by 9 feet; 1852 sold to Cram, Powell & Co.; wrecked 25 January 1858 at Cemlyn Bay, Anglesey, on passage from Liverpool to Bristol.

Steam ships:

Name	Powell Service	Gross tons	Comments
Amelia	1853–1857	300	Built by George Cram, Chester, 1853 for G Cram & F H Powell, Liverpool; transferred 1855 to F H Powell & Co.; wrecked 29 March 1857 at St Gowan's Head, Pembrokeshire on passage Bristol to Liverpool.
Augusta	1862–1877	278	Built by J M Hyde & Co., Bristol, 1856 as **Augusta** for Robert and Charles Castle, Frederick Powell and others, Bristol; sold 1862 to F H Powell & Co., Bristol; 1872 engines compounded; sold 1877 to Edward M de Bussche, London, then to James J Wallace, London; sold 1878 to Thomas Hannay, Glasgow and James Anderson, Middlesbrough, then to Timothy Bost, Glasgow; wrecked 14 February 1879 on Tory Island, Donegal on voyage under tow from Sligo to Glasgow.
Athlete	1863–1876	356	Built by J & M Hyde & Co., Bristol, 1855 for F Rowe & F H Powell, Bristol; transferred 1857 to F C Rowe & F H Powell, Bristol; lengthened 1860; transferred 1861 to R C Rowe; transferred 1863 to F H Powell & Co.; sold 1876 to Alexander McD B Fraser, Robert P Houston and others, Liverpool; sold 1881 to William C Allingham & Co., Waterford; sold 1882 to James J Wallace, London; lost at sea 20 May 1882 on passage Bilbao to Bristol.
William France	1862	403	Built by J W Hoby & Co., Renfrew, 1856 as **William France** for William France, Leeds and others; sold 1862 to F H Powell & Co. and others; sank 5 December 1862 off the Nore following collision with French steamer **Albert**, on passage Liverpool to London.
Marley Hill	1863–1874	462	Built by Palmer Bros. & Co., Jarrow, 1854 as **Marley Hill** for General Iron Screw Collier Co., London; sold to F H Powell & Co. 1863; wrecked 1 January 1874 on Whitehaven beach on passage Liverpool to Whitehaven.
Clyde	1863–1867	403	Built by Smith & Rodger, Govan, 1851 as **Clyde** for the Carron Co, Grangemouth; 1860 lengthened by 14 feet; sold 1863 to F H Powell & Company; sold 1867 to Thomas R Oswald, Sunderland; sold 1870 to Robert Hough and others, Sunderland; foundered off Hirtshals, Jutland, 4 January 1870, on passage Egelholm to Hartlepool.

Name	Powell Service	Gross tons	Comments
Northumberland	1864-1874	446	Built by Palmer Bros. & Co., Jarrow, 1853 as *Northumberland* for General Iron Screw Collier Co., London; sold to F H Powell & Company 1864; sold 1876 to Charles Chrystal Duncan and others, Middlesbrough; 1895 engine removed and rigged as schooner; sold 1899 to Eusebius Derwent, Middlesbrough; sold 1910 to Edward Dawson, Middlesbrough; sold 1917 to Brito-Franco Shipping Co, Middlesbrough; grounded 29 October 1917 on Orford Ness, Suffolk on voyage under tow from Fécamp to Newcastle, refloated 25 November and drifted away.
Mersey	1867-1876	608	Built by T R Oswald, Pallion, Co. Durham; 1873 new engines; sold 1876 Alfred Hine, Maryport; wrecked 11 August 1876 on Grassholm Island, Pembrokeshire, on passage Barrow to Antwerp.
Sheldrake	1868	482	Built by Gourlay Bros. & Co., Dundee; sold 1868 to Edward Paul and Hugh Smyth, Liverpool; 1871 engines compounded; sold 1872 to Charles Bingham, Llanelli; sold 1875 to Thomas Hamilton, Glasgow; new engines 1876; sank 12 December 1879 after striking a rock near Stevenet, France, on passage Bilbao to Glasgow.
Edith Owen	1868-1879	497	Built by Marshall Brothers, Willington Quay, Newcastle 1864 as *Edith Owen* for James Laing, Sunderland; sold 1865 to Robert Ford, London; sold 1868 to F H Powell & Co. (London); 1870 new engines and 1875 engines compounded; wrecked 27 January 1879 off Carmel Head, Anglesey, on passage Bristol to Liverpool.
Faithful	1871-1899	816	Built by Dobie & Co., Govan; sold 1899 to J J Sitges Frères & V Salinas, Alicante, and renamed *Africa*; transferred 1902 to J J Sitges Frères, Alicante, and renamed *Sitges Hermanos*; sold 1913 to Linea de Vapores Tintoré, Barcelona, and renamed *Torreblanca*; sold 1917 to Compañía Trasmediterranea, Barcelona; sold 1920 to Naviera Hispano-Oriental; sold 1922 to Moustafa Hadji Houssein, Istanbul, and renamed *Cosovo*; sold 1923 to Kalkavanzade Mehmet Riza Kaptan ve Kirzade Sevki, Istanbul, and renamed *Soulh*; sold 1924 to Kalkavanzade Mehmet Riza Kaptan ve Kirzade Sevki, Istanbul; sold 1925 to Kalkavanzade Mehmet Riza ve Mahmudu Ismail Vapur Sti., Istanbul, and renamed *Sulh*; sold 1931 to Velizade Mustafa Faik, Istanbul, and renamed *Iktisat*; sold 1932 to Kalkavanzade Mehmet Riza ve Mahmudu Ismail Vapur Sti., Istanbul and renamed *Sulh*; scrapped 1933.
Swan	1874-1898	710	Built C Mitchell & Co., Newcastle, 1867 as *Swan* for Henry F Swan, Newcastle; sold 1868 to Arthur Cox Pring, Newcastle; sold 1874 to F H Powell & Co.; re-engined 1875; sold 1898 to Cuthbert Wilkinson and others, Sunderland; scrapped 1912.
Truthful	1877-1881	956	Built by Barrow Shipbuilding Co. Ltd., Barrow; sold 1881 to Basileo Papayanni, Liverpool; resold 1881 to Cie Hellenique de Nav à Vapeur, Syra, Greece, and renamed *Elpis*; sold 1895 to New Hellenic Steam Navigation Co., Syra; posted missing in the Black Sea having sailed from Bourgas on 15 November 1904, on passage to Varna.

Name	Powell Service	Gross Tons	Comments
Hispania	1878–1893	420	Built by Scott & Co., Greenock, 1870 as *Hispania* for Mories, Munro & Co., Glasgow; sold 1872 to William Tomlinson, Glasgow; sold 1873 to Biscayan Steamship Co., Liverpool; sold 1876 to Rainey Knox & Co., Liverpool; sold 1878 to F H Powell & Co., Liverpool; sold 1893 to Tyne Dock Engineering Co., South Shields; sold 1894 to J Grieves & Co., South Shields; sold 1896 to Hispania Steam Shipping Co. Ltd., South Shields; sunk in collision with *City of Berlin* near the Outer Elbe Light Vessel, 31 August 1902, on passage Fraserburgh to Hamburg with fish.
Asia	1879–1883	662	Built by J & R Swan, Dumbarton, 1872 as *Asia* for Mories, Munro & Co., Glasgow; sold 1873 to David Wallace, Glasgow; sold 1878 to William Wear, Glasgow; sold 1879 to F H Powell & Co.; posted missing, having sailed from Middlesbrough on 5 March 1883 for Liverpool with pig iron.
Elaine	1879–1899	544	Built by Harland & Wolff Ltd., Belfast, 1869 as *Elaine* for F Levick & Co., Newport; 1870 damaged by fire at La Rochelle, repaired and lengthened by 32 feet; sold 1873 to Yeves y Cia., Bilbao, and renamed *Yeves*; sold 1875 to Thomas Homer, Sydenham, Kent, renamed *Elaine* and re-engined; sold 1879 to John Lordan, London; resold 1879 to F H Powell & Co.; sold 1899 to Cuthbert Wilkinson and others, Sunderland; sold 1913 to George MacNeal, Glasgow; resold 1913 to Rayford Shipping Co, Glasgow and renamed *Tyneford*; sold 1916 to Tyneford & Co. Ltd., Glasgow; sank 3 August 1917 off Cromer, on passage Tréport to Newcastle.
Ethel Caine/ Cheerful	1881–1885	1,014	Built by Osbourne, Graham & Co., Sunderland, 1874 as *Ethel Caine* for Nathanial Caine jr., Liverpool; sold to F H Powell & Co. 1881; 1883 renamed *Cheerful*; sunk in collision with HMS *Hecla* near the Longships Light on 21 July 1885, on passage London to Liverpool with passengers and general cargo.
Graceful	1893–1902	1,372	Built by Raylton, Dixon & Co., Middlesbrough, 1886 as *African* for Union Steamship Co., Southampton; sold 1893 to F H Powell & Co. and renamed *Graceful*; sold 1902 to A/S Ostlandske Lloyd, Kristiania (Oslo), and renamed *Sovereign*; sold 1906 to A/S Ganger Rolf, Kristiania; sold 1912 to Det Bergenske D/S, Bergen, and renamed *Zeta*; scrapped 1931.
Hopeful	1897–1903	1,219	Built by Ailsa Shipbuilding Co., Troon, 1888 as *Lady Ailsa* for J & A Wyllie, London; sold 1890 to James Knott (Prince Steam Shipping Co.,) and renamed *Belgian Prince*; sold 1897 to F H Powell & Co. and renamed *Hopeful*; sunk 13 February 1903 in collision with the steamer *Raloo* off the Longships Light, on passage Liverpool to Plymouth and London.
South Coast/ Mindful	1897–1909	421	Built by Murdoch & Murray, Port Glasgow, 1879 as *Mary Monica* for J Grant Smith, Ayr; sold 1882 to James J Carroll, Dublin; sold 1897 to F H Powell & Co. and renamed *South Coast*; 1907 renamed *Mindful*; sold 1909 to Romeo de Angelis, Civitavecchia, and renamed *Candido de Angelis*; sold 1917 to Soc Anglo-Romana Trasporti Marittimi e Fluviale, Civitavecchia; wrecked 22 May 1917 near Cape Spada, Crete.

Name	Powell Service	Gross Tons	Comments
Truthful	1898–1906	1,212	Built by Palmers Shipbuilding & Iron Co. Ltd., Jarrow, 1877 as **Morgan Richards** for Henry Morgan Liverpool; sold 1890 to R Nicholson & Sons, Liverpool; 1892 new engines; sold 1898 to F H Powell & Co. and renamed **Truthful**; sold 1906 to Cia. Pesca y Nav, Valparaiso, and renamed **Concepcion**; sold 1910 to R Campbell, Valparaiso, and renamed **Tito**; renamed 1913 **Tarapaca**; sold 1914 to Alberto Haverbeck, Valdivia, and renamed **Teja**; wrecked 24 April 1923 off Punta de Lobos, south of Iquique, on passage Tocopilla to Lobos.
West Coast	1898–1901	480	Built by D & W Henderson & Co. Ltd., Meadowside, Glasgow, as **Kampokus** 1883 for A Slorach & Son, Cork; sold 1894 to Charles Sugrue, Cork; sold 1895 to Arnati & Harrison (J T Harrison), London, renamed **Val de Travers**; sold 1898 to F H Powell & Co. and renamed **West Coast**; sank 23 August 1901 in Crosby Channel following collision with Isle of Man Steam Packet Co. steamer **Ben-my-Chree** at the start of a passage Liverpool to London, register closed; 1902 wreck raised and repaired and sold to Nova Scotia Steel & Coal Co., Pictou, and renamed **Wasis**; transferred 1905 to Wasis Steamship Co., Pictou; sold 1915 to Spartan Steamship Co., London, and renamed **Sparta**; sunk by mine 28 October 1916 off Southwold, on passage Hull to Le Havre with coke.
Azalea	1899–1903	496	Built by Sunderland Shipbuilding Co. Ltd, Sunderland, 1886 as **Azalea** for C F Leach, London; sold 1890 to London, Antwerp & Continental Navigation Co., London; sold 1899 to F H Powell & Co. and Samuel Hough Ltd.; 1902 to F H Powell & Co. and R G Hough (executor); sunk in Crosby channel in collision with hopper barge **No. 21** December 1903 at start of passage Liverpool to Exmouth, Newhaven and London.
Voltaic	1900–1902	580	Built by MacNab & Co., Greenock, as **Voltaic** 1867 for Belfast Steamship Co., Belfast; 1882 new engines; sold 1896 to Samuel Higginbottom, Belfast and resold to Charles McIver, Belfast; sold 1897 to Fishguard & Rosslare Railways & Harbours Co. Ltd.; sold 1900 to F H Powell & Co.; sold 1902 to V Tolstopjat, Kerch, Russia, and renamed **Prince Oldenbourgsky**; wrecked October 1903 in the Black Sea on passage Batoum to Kerch.
Creaden/ North Coast	1900–1906	521	Built by J T Eltringham, South Shields, 1883 as **Creaden** for Waterford Steamship Co., Ltd., Waterford; sold 1900 to F H Powell & Co.; 1904 renamed **North Coast**; sold 1906 to Lloyd Comercial Mar del Plata, Argentina, and renamed **General Pueyrredon**; sold 1918 to S Solari, Buenos Aires; sold 1919 to T Larrieu & Co., Buenos Aires; sold 1920 to Cie Normande de Nav. à Vapeur, Le Havre, and renamed **Peronne**; stranded 6 January 1924 near St Valery sur Somme, France, on passage Le Havre to St Valery, refloated and scrapped.
Watchful	1900–1906	353	Built by Campbeltown Shipbuilding Co., Campbeltown, 1882 as **Orpheus** for F Johnston, Liverpool; sold 1886 to South Wales & Liverpool Steamship Co.; sank following collision 28 June 1900 off Rock Ferry, register closed. Raised and repaired 1900 and sold to Watchful Steamship Co. Ltd. and renamed **Watchful**; sold 1906 to G Couper, Wick; sold 1923 to Bretby Shipping Co., Wick; hulked 1927.

Name	Powell Service	Gross tons	Comments
Faithful/ Thoughtful/ Suffolk Coast	1900-1911	783	Built by Dundee Shipbuilders Co., Dundee; 1906 renamed ***Thoughtful***; 1908 renamed ***Suffolk Coast***; sold 1911 to J & P Hutchison, Glasgow and renamed ***Astra***; sold 1913 to A/S Astra, Porsgruna, Norway, no change of name; sold 1919 to D/S A/S Storborg, Haugesund, Norway no change of name; sold 1923 to Ferdinand H Smith, Goole, and renamed ***Elvington***; resold 1923 to Thomas G Irving, Sunderland; sold 1932 to Monroe Brothers, Liverpool; 1934 renamed ***Kyle Bute***; transferred 1936 to Kyle Steam Shipping Co., Liverpool; scrapped 1955.
Hanbury/ East Coast	1901-1906	489	Built by Blyth Shipbuilding Co. Ltd., Blyth, 1895 as ***Hanbury*** for E Stock & Son; sold 1901 to F H Powell & Co.; 1904 renamed ***East Coast***; sold 1906 to Cie. Maritime des Chargeurs Réunis, Le Havre and renamed ***Le Gabon***; foundered in tow off Mauritania on 1 August 1925, on passage Dakar to Marseilles.
Point Clear/ Hopeful	1902-1909	507	Built by Ritson & Co., Maryport, 1901 as ***Point Clear*** for Kilgour & Baker, Glasgow; sold 1902 to Point Clear Steamship Co. Ltd., (F H Powell & Co.); renamed ***Hopeful*** 1904; sold 1909 to Goole & Hull Steam Towing Co. Ltd., Goole, and renamed ***Dicky***; sold 1941 to Culliford Shipping Co., London; sold 1948 to K McLagan, Northwood, and renamed ***Hestor***; sold 1950 to B & M Lines, Liverpool; scrapped 1952.
River Tay/ West Coast	1903-1908	467	Built by Ardrossan Drydock and Shipbuilding Co. Ltd., Ardrossan, 1902 as ***River Tay*** for Steamship River Tay Co., Liverpool; 1903 controlled under mortgage by F H Powell & Co.; 1904 renamed ***West Coast***; sold 1908 to North Coast Steamship Co., Liverpool; sold 1910 to Lloyd Comercial Mar del Plata, Argentina, and renamed ***Cabo Corrientes***; sold 1917 to Dampskibsselskab 'Excelsior', Copenhagen, and renamed ***Niels***; sold 1917 to Thomas Just, Copenhagen; sold 1919 to Dampskibsselskab Aktieselskab Transport, Copenhagen; sold 1921 to P Bondo Petersen, Rudkøbing, Denmark; sold 1927 to C. Schmidt, Rendsburg, Germany, and renamed ***Hoffnung***; sold 1932 to O/Y Laiva Toivo, Helsingfors, Finland and renamed ***Toivo***; sold 1934 to William G James, Cardigan, and renamed ***Castlegreen***; sold 1936 to Ernst Bergmann, Tallinn; Estonia, and renamed ***Kaida***;1940 taken over by Ministry of Shipping and managed by Neill & Hannah, Leith; struck Owers Shoal 22 December 1945 on passage from London to Southampton, beached at Middleton-on-Sea, near Bognor Regis, refloated and scrapped.
Powerful	1903-1913	1,612	Built by Swan Hunter & Wigham Richardson Ltd., Newcastle; 1913 to Powell, Bacon & Hough Lines Ltd., and renamed ***Eastern Coast***; 1917 owner renamed Coast Lines Ltd; sold 1919 to British Hispano Line, Cardiff and renamed ***Perez***; sold 1920 to Harken Steamship Co., Swansea and renamed ***Eaton Grove***; sold 1923 to John Alan MacDonald, Glasgow; resold 1923 to Vaccaro Bros & Co., La Ceiba, Honduras, and renamed ***Alegria***; sold 1924 to Standard Fruit & Steamship Corporation, La Ceiba, Honduras; sold 1936 to J S Webster & Sons, Kingston, Jamaica, and renamed ***Allister***; sunk by torpedo 29 May 1942 off Grand Cayman Island, on passage Kingston to Tampa.
Mindful	1904-1906	361	Built by Murdoch & Murray, Port Glasgow, 1893 as ***Maggie Barr*** for R B Ballantyne & Co.; sold 1898 to William Postlethwaite, Millom; sold 1904 to Watchful Steamship Co. (F H Powell & Co.) and renamed ***Mindful***; sold 1906 to J Kennedy & Sons, Glasgow, and renamed ***Welshman***; scrapped 1935.

Name	Powell Service	Gross Tons	Comments
Cornish Coast	1904-1913	676	Built by W Harkess & Son Ltd., Middlesbrough; 1904 to F H Powell & Co. and Samuel Hough Ltd.; 1913 to Powell, Bacon & Hough Lines Ltd.; sunk 3 March 1915 in Mersey following collision with steamship *Jeanette Woermann*, on passage Rochester to Birkenhead.
Devon Coast	1905-1908	668	Built by W Harkess & Son Ltd., Middlesbrough; sunk 4 November 1908 in collision with *Jeanie* off Newhaven, on passage Swanscombe, Lower Thames, to Liverpool with cement.
Masterful	1905-1912	1,794	Built by W Harkess & Son Ltd., Middlesbrough; sold 1912 to Braun & Blanchard, Valparaiso, and renamed *Valdivia*; sold 1918 to French owners; sunk by torpedo off Gibraltar, 2 May 1918 on delivery voyage Buenos Aires to Sète (southern France).
Faithful	1906-1913	874	Built by W Harkess & Son Ltd., Middlesbrough; 1913 to Powell, Bacon & Hough Lines Ltd., renamed *Monmouth Coast*; 1917 owner renamed Coast Lines Ltd.; sold 1919 to Richard P Care, Cardiff; resold 1919 to Camber Shipping Co., Cardiff; resold 1919 to Miller Steamship Co. Ltd., Hull; sold 1922 by Admiralty Marshal to Sociedade Geral de Comércio, Indústria e Transportes Ltda., Lisbon and renamed *Silva-Gouveia*; wrecked 23 December 1927 at Playa do Rostro Peton Pardas, Spain, 5 miles from Cape Toriñana, on passage from Hamburg to Oporto.
Sussex Coast/ Truthful	1907-1913	640	Built by W Harkess & Son Ltd., Middlesbrough, as *Sussex Coast* for F H Powell & Co.; 1907 briefly owned by Samuel Hough; 1908 renamed *Truthful* and later transferred to Watchful Steamship Company; 1913 to Powell, Bacon & Hough Lines Ltd., renamed *Wirral Coast*; sold 1916 to Limerick Steamship Co, Limerick and renamed *Claddagh*; sold 1918 to City of Cork Steam Packet Co. Ltd.; sold 1924 to Ellerman's Wilson Line Ltd. and renamed *Nero*; briefly owned by General Steam Navigation Co. Ltd., London, during 1927 and sold back to Ellerman's Wilson Line Ltd.; sold 1927 to Ada Cristina Piazza in D'Arrigo, Catania, Italy, and renamed *Cristina*; sold 1929 to E Patanè, Trieste, and renamed *Gagliardo*; sold 1931 to Ivo Vacchi Suzzi, Trieste, and renamed *Imola*; sold 1933 to Dante Pompei, Ancona and renamed *Marchigiano*; sold 1935 to Societa Italiana ATIL, Genoa; sank in Red Sea 13 March 1936 following explosion on board, on passage Genoa to Assab with petrol in drums.
Dorset Coast	1908-1913	672	Built by W Harkess & Son Ltd., Middlesbrough, as *Dorset Coast* for F H Powell & Co.; sold 1908 to F H Powell & Co. and Samuel Hough Ltd.; 1913 to Powell, Bacon & Hough Lines Ltd.; sold 1915 to Thomas Steven & Co., Edinburgh and renamed *Arbonne*; sunk by torpedo 26 February 1916 near the Kentish Knock lightship, Lower Thames estuary, on passage Le Havre to Newcastle.
Graceful/ Devon Coast	1909-1913	782	Built by W Harkess & Son Ltd., Middlesbrough, 1909 as *Graceful* for British & Continental Steamship Co. (Alfred H Read - manager); sold 1910 to F H Powell & Co., resold to F H Powell & Co. and Samuel Hough Ltd., 1910 renamed *Devon Coast*; 1913 to Powell, Bacon & Hough Lines Ltd.; 1917 owner renamed Coast Lines; sold 1934 to Brook Shipping Co., London and renamed *Devonbrook*; sold 1937 to Companhia de Navegação Norte Sul, Rio de Janeiro, and renamed *Sao Pedro*; sold 1943 to Companhia Commércio e Navegação, Rio de Janeiro; scrapped 1952.

Name	Powell Service	Gross Tons	Comments
Hopeful/ Devon Coast	1910	792	Built by W Harkess & Son Ltd., Middlesbrough, 1910 as *Hopeful* for British & Continental Steamship Co. (Alfred H Read - Manager); sold 1910 to F H Powell & Co. and renamed *Devon Coast*; sold 1910 to Union Steamship Co. of New Zealand Ltd., Dunedin and renamed *Kowhai*; scrapped 1950.
Hopeful/ Norfolk Coast	1910-1913	782	Built by W Harkess & Son Ltd., Middlesbrough, launched as *Hopeful* and completed as *Norfolk Coast*; sold 1910 to F H Powell & Co. and Samuel Hough Ltd; 1913 to Powell, Bacon & Hough Lines Ltd.; 1917 owner renamed Coast Lines Ltd.; sunk by torpedo 18 June 1918 south east of Flamborough Head, on passage Rouen to Newcastle.
Hampshire Coast	1911-1913	787	Built by W Harkess & Son Ltd., Middlesbrough, as *Hampshire Coast* for F H Powell & Co. and then sold to F H Powell & Co. and Samuel Hough Ltd; 1913 to Powell, Bacon & Hough Lines Ltd.; wrecked 8 February 1915 at Shoreham, on passage Liverpool to London, register closed. 1915 wreck sold to J Esplen, Liverpool, refloated and repaired and sold to Powell, Bacon & Hough Lines Ltd.; 1917 owner renamed Coast Lines Ltd.; sold 1936 to Monroe Brothers, Liverpool and renamed *Kylebay*; sold 1937 to Walton Steamship Co., Newcastle; scrapped 1950.
Graceful	1911-1913	1,149	Built by Sir Raylton Dixon & Co., Middlesbrough; 1913 to Powell, Bacon & Hough Lines Ltd., renamed *Somerset Coast*; sank 21 April 1917 after collision with steam ship *Sound Fisher* off Bardsey Island, on passage Bristol to Liverpool.
Hopeful	1913	1,166	Built by W Harkess & Son Ltd., Middlesbrough; 1913 to Powell, Bacon & Hough Lines Ltd., renamed *Western Coast*; sunk by torpedo 24 February 1915 off Beachy Head, on passage London to Liverpool.

2)   Bacon and associate companies

John Edward Redmond

Name	JER Service	Gross Tons	Comments
Town of Wexford	1837-1852	297	Wooden-hulled paddle steamer built by Archer & Leared, Wexford, for J E Redmond; 1838 lengthened by 26 feet; wrecked 4 January 1852 at Trefadoc, Holyhead Bay.
Brigand	1840-1842	513	Iron-hulled paddle steamer built by Grantham Page & Co., Liverpool, for J E Redmond; wrecked 12 October 1842 on Bishop's Rock, Scilly, on passage Liverpool to Falmouth, Plymouth, London and St Petersburg.

Name	JER Service	Gross tons	Comments
Troubadour	1841-1860	616	Iron-hulled paddle steamer built by Thomas Vernon & Co., Liverpool, for J E Redmond; 1858 lengthened by 36 feet; sold 1860 to William A Redmond and resold to Wexford Steam Ship Co. Ltd.; sold 1867 to Malcomson Brothers, Waterford; scrapped 1870.
Erin	1845-1851	250	Wooden-hulled paddle steamer built by William Simons & Co., Greenock, as *Erin* for Dublin & Glasgow Steam Packet Co.; sold 1834 to Saint George Steam Packet Co., sold 1845 to J E Redmond, scrapped 1851.
Glendower	1850-1855	468	Iron-hulled paddle steamer built by John S Spencer, Swansea, for J E Redmond; wrecked 29 July 1855 three miles south of South Stack, Holyhead Island, on passage Hayle to Liverpool.

Wexford Steam Ship Company Limited

Name	WSSC Service	Gross tons	Comments
Troubadour	1860-1867	615	Iron-hulled paddle steamer built by Thomas Vernon & Co., Liverpool, 1841 for J E Redmond; 1858 lengthened by 36 feet; sold 1860 to William A Redmond and resold to Wexford Steam Ship Co. Ltd.; sold 1867 to Malcomson Brothers, Waterford; scrapped 1870.
Vivandiere	1861-1862	245	Built by William Simons & Co., Renfrew, 1856 as *Vivandiere* for Kidston & Whyte, Glasgow; sold 1860 to Blackwood & Gordon, Glasgow; sold 1860 to Clyde Shipping Co., Glasgow; sold 1861 to Wexford Steam Ship Co.; sold 1862 to William A Redmond, resold to J A Dunkerley, Hull, and resold to Mathias et Cie., Le Havre; sold 1862 to W S Burger aan Zon, Rotterdam, and renamed *Amicitia*; sold 1873 to Brodrene Ameln, Bergen, and renamed *Norma*; foundered 15 April 1879 after collision with ice near Riga, on passage Bergen to Riga.

Joseph d'Aguilar Samuda & John Bacon and John Bacon & Joseph d'Aguilar Samuda (both companies' ships registered at London), Fitzsimons, Applebee & Company, John Bacon, Joseph Wright and John Bacon Ltd.

Name	Service	Gross tons	Comments
Emerald	1852-1860	340	Wooden-hulled paddle steamer built by John Banckham, Gravesend, 1834 as *Emerald* for Gravesend & Milton Steam Packet Co.; sold 1835 to Commercial Steam Packet Co., London; sold 1843 to William Coates and others, London; reacquired 1846 by Commercial Steam Packet Co. under default of mortgage; sold 1847 to Jonathan Hopkinson and others, Pembury, Kent; sold 1852 to John Grantham, William Applebee and others; sold 1856 to John Grantham, John Bacon and others; sold 1860 to William and Thomas Jolliffe, Liverpool, resold to James Lever, Manchester and resold to William Newett, Liverpool; sold 1861 to Nicholas H Delamere, Liverpool and resold to Thomas B Callenan and John Smurthwaite, Sunderland, converted to sailing ship; lost at sea 18 June 1865.

Name	Service	Gross tons	Comments
Iron Prince	1853	181	Built by James Hodgson, Liverpool, 1844 as *Iron Prince* for James Hodgson & Co., Liverpool; sold 1848 to William Neill; sold 1853 to John Grantham, William D Applebee and others, lengthened by 7 feet and sent to work for Australian owners; scrapped 1866.
Blarney	1854-1855	252	Built by Robert Leckie & Co., Cork, 1846 as *Blarney* for Cork Steam Ship Co.; lengthened 1849 by 16 feet; sold 1854 to Fitzsimons, Applebee & Co.; 1855 sent to Constantinople to be sold; wrecked 9 November 1864 near Varna in Black Sea.
Isabella Croll	1854-1866	525	Built by Palmer Bros & Co., Jarrow, 1854 as *Isabella Croll* for Alexander A Croll, London; sold 1854 to McLarty & Co., John Grantham and John Bacon, Liverpool; sold 1866 to United Kingdom Screw Collier Co. Ltd., Dublin; sold 1869 to John C Robertson, Grangemouth and renamed *Harvard*; wrecked 6 April 1870 on Cromwell's Rock, Waterford, on passage Spain to Glasgow.
Antelope	1855-1857	1,008	Built by James Hodgson, Liverpool, 1846 as *Antelope* for McTear & Hadfield and others; sold 1849 to Richard Rostron, Manchester and converted to sailing ship; sold 1852 to Edward Thompson and others; lengthened by 43 feet and re-engined, sold to Edward Thompson & others, Manchester; sold 1855 to Frederick Lyon & John Bacon & Co., Liverpool; sold 1857 to Zachariah Charles Pearson & James Coleman, Hull; sold 1858 to John O Lever, for Galway Line; sold 1864 to John Pile, West Hartlepool, resold to A N W Ludders, Hamburg and renamed *Coral Queen*; sold 1864 to West Hartlepool Steam Navigation Co., West Hartlepool; sold 1865 to Pile, Spence & Co. Ltd., West Hartlepool; sold 1866 to Christopher M Webster, Pallion Hall, for charter to West Hartlepool Steam Navigation Co., West Hartlepool and re-engined; sank 18 February 1890 off Spurn Head after collision with Dutch ship *Brinio*, on passage Gothenburg to West Hartlepool.
Annie Vernon	1856-1868	519	Built by Thomas Vernon & Son, Liverpool, 1856 as *Annie Vernon* for John Bacon & Company; sold 1868 to Daniel Jones, Briton Ferry, resold to George S Stowe, Cardiff; sold 1872 to London & Yorkshire Steam Shipping Co., London; sold 1874 to John W Blakeney & Co., Hull; 1875, sank after collision at Huelva, raised and repaired at Cadiz, sold to James Henry Morgan, Limehouse, resold to Henry Clasper, Sunderland; sold 1880 to William C Allingham, Waterford; sold 1883 to Edwin Jenkins, Cardiff; foundered 19 November 1885 off Godrevy Head, Cornwall, on passage Cardiff to Plymouth.
Sovereign	1856-1870	439	Built by Thomas Vernon & Son, Liverpool, 1856 as *Sovereign* for John Bacon & Co.; wrecked 2 April 1870 near Dulas Bay, Anglesey, on passage Liverpool to Bristol.

Name	Service	Gross Tons	Comments
Montagu	1856-1891	420	Built by C Mitchell & Co., Low Walker, Newcastle, 1855 as *Montagu* for Aire & Calder Navigation Steam Shipping Co., Goole; sold 1856 to John Grantham, William Applebee and others; 1860 ownership retitled John Bacon & Co.; re-engined 1863; 1887 to Joseph Wright (executor); 1890 length reduced by 11 feet; sold 1891 to Thomas F Ward, Middlesbrough and converted to lighter; foundered 2 February 1899 off Cromer, on passage from Newcastle to Lowestoft under tow.
Gipsy	1857-1873	33	Built at Whiteinch, Glasgow; scrapped 1873.
James Kennedy	1857-1873	535	Built by Thomas Vernon & Son, Liverpool; lengthened 1871 by 25 feet; abandoned at sea 30 November 1873 and stranded at Petten, to the south of Nieuwe Diep, on passage Rotterdam to Shields.
Helena	1863-1865	189	Built by George Cram, Chester, 1854 as *Helena* for James Haddock, Liverpool; sold 1855 to Frank Sandon Thomas and others, London; sold 1857 to Richard Clay, London; sold 1860 to East of England Screw Coasting Co., Hull; sold 1861 to Robert McCracken and others, Newry; sold 1863 to John Bacon, sold 1865 to James Graham, Londonderry; sold 1866 to John Meek, Liverpool, sold 1869 to owners in Coruña.
Artizan	1864-1872	544	Built by Stothert Slaughter & Co., Bristol, 1857 as *Artizan* for George K Stothert, Bristol; 1859 lengthened by 25 feet; 1861 John Bacon became part owner; abandoned sinking on 5 January 1872 off Cape Finisterre, on passage Huelva to Liverpool.
Jane Bacon	1865-1897	505	Built by Bowdler, Chaffer & Co., Seacombe, registered owner John Bacon; 1870 lengthened by 21 feet; re-engined 1879; transferred 1887 to Joseph Wright (executor); transferred 1890 to John Bacon Ltd.; sunk in Crosby Channel 23 December 1897 following collision with steamship *Lombardy*, on passage Bristol to Liverpool.
Swansea	1865-1867	309	Built by Bowdler, Chaffer & Co., Seacombe; sank 21 December 1897 in Crosby Channel after collision with the Belfast Steamship Co.'s steamer *Magnetic*, on passage Liverpool to Swansea.
Agnes Jack	1865-1883	574	Built by Bowdler, Chaffer & Co., Seacombe; lengthened 1877 by 26 feet; wrecked 27 January 1883 at Oxwich Point, Gower, on passage Cagliari to Llanelli.
Bristol	1867	576	Built by Bowdler, Chaffer & Co., Seacombe; foundered 30 November 1867 off Start Point, Devon, on passage Middlesbrough to Briton Ferry.
Llewellyn	1868-1871	179	Built by Thomas Charlton, Grimsby; lengthened 1870 by 18 feet; sold 1871 to Antrim County Iron Ore Co. Ltd., Belfast; 1872 to Antrim Iron Ore Co. Ltd., Belfast; sold 1875 to William Hinde, Belfast; 1885 re-engined; sold 1890 to Maria E Shaw, Knock, Co Down; stranded 19 October 1904 on Ballykeel Point, Kilkeel, Co Down, on passage Whitehaven to Warrenpoint, refloated and scrapped.

Name	Service	Gross tons	Comments
John	1870-1872	7	Yacht built by Laurence Hill & Co., Port Glasgow for John Bacon; sold 1872 to C S Johnstone, Newry, ultimate fate unknown.
Louisa	1870-1878	773	Built by Samuda Brothers, Poplar, London, for John Bacon and Joseph d'Aguilar Samuda; sold 1878 to George Kelson, London; sold 1886 to T M Madland, Bodø, Norway; wrecked off Norwegian coast on 30 March 1892, on passage Burntisland to Brettesnes.
Sunlight	1870-1913	388	Built by Laurence Hill & Co., Port Glasgow, 1868 as *Sunlight* for Laurence Hill, Port Glasgow, sold 1870 to John Bacon; 1883 re-engined; 1887 to Joseph Wright (executor); 1889 to John Bacon Ltd.; sold 1913 to Paul Dauguet, St Malo and renamed *Menhir*; sold 1916 to D E Sterghiopoulos, Marseilles; missing on passage Piraeus to Mersina in January 1920.
Heptarchy	1871-1903	780	Built by Samuda Brothers, Poplar, London, 1871 as *Heptarchy* for Joseph d'Aguilar Samuda and John Bacon; sold 1872 to John Bacon; 1887 to Joseph Wright (executor); 1890 to John Bacon Ltd.; damaged in collision with German sailing ship *Roland* in Carmarthen Bay 11 December 1903, on passage Newport to Waterford, towed to Swansea, broken up the following year.
Pharos	1872-1873	319	Iron paddle steamer built by William Fairbairn & Son, Millwall, 1846 as *Pharos* for Commissioners of the Northern Light Houses; sold 1861 to John T Rennie and others, Aberdeen; sold 1866 to Aberdeen, Newcastle & Hull Steam Company Ltd., Aberdeen; sold 1870 to John C Couper, Craigiebuckler; sold 1872 to John Bacon; sold 1873 to North Lonsdale Steamship Co., Barrow; sold 1876 to Thomas Williamson, Barrow; scrapped 1877.
Plantagenet	1872-1880	726	Built by Samuda Brothers, Poplar, London, 1869 as *Plantagenet* for Joseph d'Aguilar Samuda; sold 1872 to John Bacon; 1873 engines compounded; 1878 re-engined; sank 14 October 1880 after striking wreck off Cabo de Palos near Cartagena on passage Newport to Barcelona.
Pembroke	1872-1896	45	Built by G & R Cross, Winsford, Cheshire; 1887 to Joseph Wright (executor); 1890 to John Bacon; wrecked 9 December 1896 at Angle Bay, Milford Haven, on passage Neyland to Angle. Wreck raised 1901 and used as hulk at Fowey.
Furness Abbey	1873-1874	178	Built by MacFadyen & Co., Port Glasgow, 1872 as *Furness Abbey* for Mories, Monro & Co., Glasgow; sold 1872 to John Gunn, Ulverston; sold 1873 to North Lonsdale Steamship Co., Barrow; sold 1873 to John Bacon; wrecked 24 April 1874 on Bishop's Rocks Pembrokeshire, on passage Swansea to Garston.
Muncaster	1874-1896	889	Built by Whitehaven Shipbuilding Co., Whitehaven; 1887 to Joseph Wright (executor); 1890 transferred to John Bacon Ltd.; sold 1896 to Baylis Haynes & Co., London; sold 1897 to Ångfartygs A/B Esperance, Helsingborg; sold 1914 to P M Venelsianos and others, Piraeus, and renamed *Achileus*; sunk by gunfire 5 August 1916, 70 miles south of Toulon.

Name	Service	Gross tons	Comments
Tudor	1876–1889	924	Built by John Key & Son, Kinghorn, 1876 as *Tudor* for John Bacon and George A Key, Kirkaldy; sold 1877 to John Bacon; 1887 to Joseph Wright (executor); wrecked 1 July 1889 on Devil's Bank off Garston, on passage Sestri Levanti, Italy, to Liverpool. Wreck sold to George R Clover, Birkenhead, raised, repaired and lengthened by 4 feet, resold to Palgrave Murphy & Co, Dublin and renamed *City of Belfast*; seized by German Government at Hamburg 1914; returned to Palgrave Murphy & Co, Dublin 1919 and sold to William McAllum, London; resold 1919 to G N Pittas & Co, Chios, Greece and renamed *Artemis*; sold 1924 to G N Pittas Brothers, Chios; 1930 renamed *Zannis Xenios*; wrecked 22 October 1930 on Stringolo Point, Seskli Island in the Aegean Sea, on passage Piraeus to Cyprus.
Cleddau	1879–1913	89	Built by Milford Haven Ship Building and Engineering Co., Pembroke Dock; registered owner John Bacon; 1887 to Joseph Wright (executor); 1890 to John Bacon Ltd.; sold 1913 to George Hooton, Liverpool; sold 1916 to Grain Elevating & Automatic Weighing Co. Ltd., Liverpool; 1921 converted to dumb barge; sold 1950 to Michael Halligan, Birkenhead, scrapped 1971.
Stuart	1880–1882	1,380	Built by William Pickersgill & Sons, Sunderland, registered owner John Bacon; sold 1882 to R Couppa, Piraeus and renamed *Adelphi Couppa*; sold 1891 to Nicolo Couppa, Piraeus; sold 1894 to Constantin G Malandrachi, Argostoli, Greece; 1897 renamed *Sofhia Maladrachi*; sold 1898 to Heinrich Heht, Kiel and renamed *Emil*; wrecked 1 April 1898 near Giardini, Sicily, on passage from Kustendje to Marseilles with grain.
Brunswick	1881–1888	1,389	Built by William Pickersgill & Sons, Sunderland, registered owner John Bacon; 1887 to Joseph Wright (executor); sold 1888 to Christopher Furness, West Hartlepool and resold to Guthe, Murdoch & Co., West Hartlepool; sold 1890 to J Wood & Co. West Hartlepool; sold 1892 to Crosby, Magee & Co., West Hartlepool; wrecked 23 October 1895 on breakwater at Bilbao, on passage Bilbao to Stockton-on-Tees with iron ore.
Plantagenet	1883–1897	696	Built by William Allsup & Sons, Preston, registered owner John Bacon; 1887 to Joseph Wright (executor); 1890 to John Bacon Ltd.; wrecked 20 March 1897 near the Lizard at Black Head, on passage St Valery to Runcorn with flints.
Slaney	1884–1885	602	Built by William Allsup & Sons, Preston, registered owner John Bacon; wrecked 14 January 1885 on Wexford Bar, on passage Liverpool to Wexford with passengers and general cargo.
Stuart	1884–1888	641	Built by William Allsup & Sons, Preston, registered owner John Bacon; 1887 to Joseph Wright (executor); sold 1888 to Dampfs AG 'Albis', Hamburg and renamed *Borgfelde*; wrecked 17 July 1888 on Hillswick Ness, St Magnus Bay, Shetland, on passage Liverpool to Danzig via Lerwick with fish and general.
Vigilant	1884–1906	438	Built by T & W Toward & Co., Newcastle, registered owner John Bacon; 1887 to Joseph Wright (executor); 1890 to John Bacon Ltd.; wrecked 25 July 1906 south of Roches Douvres, off Guernsey, on passage Cardiff to St Brieuc with coal.
Eden Vale	1889–1904	488	Built by S McKnight & Co., Ayr, registered owner Joseph Wright (executor); 1890 to John Bacon Ltd.; sold 1904 to M D de Vasconcellos, Manaus and renamed *Constantino Nery*; damaged by grounding 18 October 1905 at Amarração, later arrived at Manaus; scrapped.

Name	Service	Gross tons	Comments
Talbot	1890–1912	547	Built by S McKnight & Co., Ayr; sunk 7 September 1912 in collision with steamship **Kent** in the Queen's Channel, off Liverpool, on passage Cardiff to Birkenhead.
Salerno	1892–1897	1,274	Built by Osbourne, Graham & Co., Sunderland, 1882 as **Salerno** for RW & T Jones, Newport; sold 1882 to Scrutton, Sons & Co., London; sold 1886 to Salerno Steamship Co., London; sold 1892 to John Bacon Ltd.; sold 1897 to A Bröstrom & Son, Gothenburg, and renamed **Hogland**; sold 1901 to Ångfartygs A/B Göteborg-Manchester, Gothenburg; sold 1911 to A/S Norlands, Tonsberg, Norway and renamed **Norlands**; wrecked 2 May 1918 near Godrevy Lighthouse, near St Ives Head, on passage Swansea to Rouen with coal.
Tudor	1892–1910	1,113	Built by Irvine & Co., West Hartlepool; sold 1910 to Svorono & di Pollone, Italy, and renamed **Shura**; captured by Turkish cruiser **Hamidieh** and sunk 29 October 1914 by gunfire at Yalta.
Edith	1893–1913	116	Built by John Thompson, Northwich, Cheshire, 1880 as **Edith** for Cheshire Amalgamated Salt Works Ltd., Winsford; sold 1889 to Salt Union Ltd., London; sold 1893 to John Bacon Ltd.; 1913 to Powell, Bacon & Hough Lines Ltd.; sold 1916 to H & C Grayson Ltd., Liverpool and resold to Kymo Shipping Co. Ltd., Liverpool; sold 1921 to Wadsworth Lighterage & Coaling Co. Ltd., Liverpool; scrapped 1930.
Stuart	1894–1910	1,212	Built by Irvine & Co., West Hartlepool; sold 1910 to Joseph Constant, London and resold to F Puglisi, Italy, and renamed **Giustizia**; sold 1916 to Vito Cassisa, Trapani, Italy; captured 3 December 1916 by U Boat and sunk by explosive charges off the Scilly Isles, on passage Lisbon to Glasgow.
Carew	1894–1900	133	Built by McAndrew, Cowan & Potts, Sunderland; sold 1900 to Manchester, Liverpool & North Wales Steam Ship Co. Ltd., Liverpool; sold 1911 to Irish Industrial Minerals Ltd., Liverpool; sold 1912 to Trasporti Marittimi Costieri, Genoa and renamed **Carlo Givone**; sold 1913 to F Paoletti, Genoa and renamed **Terzo**; sold 1916 to S Pellegrino, Bengasi; sold 1919 to Francesco Fabiano, Port Said; sold 1922 to Costa Xydia & Son Alexandria; sold 1924 to Apostolis Vrahamis, Constantinople and renamed **Elif**, foundered 10 September 1927 near Zonguldak, Turkey, on passage Zonguldak to Constantinople.
Kelvinside	1894–1898	209	Built by Scott & Sons, Bowling, 1893 as **Hare** for Charles Pile, London; sold 1894 to Kelvin Steamship Co. Ltd., Glasgow and renamed **Kelvinside**; sold 1894 to John Bacon Ltd.; sold 1898 to John E Crisp, Lowestoft; acquired 1906 by General Steam Navigation Co. Ltd., London; sold 1923 to Capt. Alexander Dempsey, Wigton; foundered 4 August 1932 off Mull of Galloway.
Invincible	1894–1913	57	Sailing flat built by Richard G Cross, Winsford, Cheshire, 1881 as **Invincible** for Cheshire Amalgamated Salt Works Co. Ltd., Winsford; sold 1889 to Salt Union Ltd., London; sold 1894 to John Bacon Ltd.; scrapped 1923.

Name	Service	Gross Tons	Comments
Tivyside	1895-1900	108	Built by London & Glasgow Engineering & Iron Shipbuilding Co. Ltd., Glasgow, 1869 as *Tivyside* for Cardigan Steam Navigation Co. Ltd.; sold 1887 to Thomas Jenkins, Carmarthen; sold 1895 to John Bacon Ltd.; lengthened 1896 by 15 feet; wrecked 15 June 1900 at Overton Cliffs, Port Eynon, on passage Carmarthen to Bristol.
Brunswick	1898-1900	716	Built by Murdoch & Murray, Port Glasgow; wrecked 24 December 1900 on Hook Sands, off Clevedon, on passage Liverpool to Bristol.
Prestonian / Sir George Bacon	1900-1913	804	Built by Dundee Shipbuilders Co. Ltd., Dundee, 1899 as *Prestonian* for Henry Tyrer & Co., Preston; sold 1900 to John Bacon Ltd.; 1913 renamed *Sir George Bacon*; 1913 to Powell, Bacon & Hough Lines Ltd. and renamed *Gower Coast*; sold 1917 to Ford Shipping Co. Ltd., Glasgow; sunk by mine 4 April 1917 off Tréport, on passage Newcastle to Tréport.
Taurus	1901-1909	56	Built by Henry Scarr, Beverley as *Taurus* 1890; sold 1898 to Matthew Jackson, Louth and resold to Robert S Dower, Horsforth, Leeds; sold 1901 to John Bacon Ltd.; sold 1909 to William G Vivian and others, Swansea; sold 1925 to Walter G Easton, Swansea; sold 1927 to Nicholas Zarettis, Aberavon; scrapped 1929.
Wexford	1901-1912	564	Built by S McKnight & Co. Ltd., Ayr; sold 1912 to Western Australian Government and renamed *Eucla*; partly demolished 1926, hull scuttled off Fremantle 1932.
The Lady Belle	1904-1912	341	Built by J Fullerton & Co., Paisley, 1900 as *The Lady Belle* for G Farren, Caernarvon; sold 1901 to Clanrye Steamship Co. Ltd., Newry; sold 1904 to John Bacon Ltd.; sold 1912 to the Lady Belle Steamship Co. Ltd., Cardiff; sold 1915 to Care & Young Steamship Co. Ltd., Cardiff; sold 1916 to Cheviot Coasters Ltd., Newcastle; sold 1919 to John Murphy, Waterford; sold 1922 to A Maloney & Sons Ltd., Dungarvan; sold 1943 to S & S Steamship Co. Ltd., Waterford; scrapped 1949.
Pennar	1907-1913	130	Built by W J Yarwood & Sons, Northwich, Cheshire; 1913 to Powell, Bacon & Hough Lines Ltd.; 1917 owner renamed Coast Lines Ltd.; sold 1948 to James Massey, London; re-engined 1950; sold 1951 to S J Hadlow, Sittingbourne; stripped and gutted 1954.
John Bacon	1910-1913	589	Built by Murdoch & Murray, Port Glasgow; sold 1913 to J Kuman, Wolochin & Co., Odessa, and renamed *Merkury*; sunk by mine 20 June 1916 off Odessa, on passage Otchakov to Odessa.
Lady Bacon	1911-1913	335	Built by George Brown & Co., Greenock; sold 1913 to Joseph Monks & Co. Ltd., Liverpool and renamed Lady *Elsena*; captured by U Boat and sunk by gunfire 22 November 1917 off Strumble Head, Pembrokeshire, on passage Waterford to Manchester with grain.
Enniscorthy	1908-1913	42	Built by W J Yarwood & Sons Ltd., Northwich, Cheshire; 1913 to Powell, Bacon & Hough Lines Ltd.; sold 1916 to United Grain Elevators Ltd., Liverpool; scrapped 1935.

Name	Service	Gross tons	Comments
Lord Bacon	1911–1913	335	Built by George Brown & Co., Greenock; sold 1913 to James Henry Monks (Preston) Ltd. and renamed **Elizabetta**; 1924 transferred to John S Monks Ltd., Liverpool; renamed **Riverville** 1934; scrapped 1952.
Harfat	1911–1913	128	Built by W J Yarwood & Sons Ltd., Northwich, Cheshire; 1913 to Powell, Bacon & Hough Lines Ltd.; 1917 owner renamed Coast Lines Ltd.; sold 1939 to Tay Sand Co. Ltd., Dundee; foundered 15 January 1952 off Dundee on passage from River Tay to Dundee.
Sir Roger Bacon	1912–1913	809	Built by J Fullerton & Co., Paisley, 1912 as **Clydeholm** for J B Couper, Glasgow and completed as **Sir Roger Bacon** for John Bacon Ltd.; 1913 to Powell, Bacon & Hough Lines Ltd. and renamed **Pembroke Coast**; 1917 owner renamed Coast Lines Ltd.; transferred 1930 to City of Cork Steam Packet Co. Ltd., Cork; 1931 renamed **Blarney**; sold 1933 to Wexford Steamships Co. Ltd., Wexford, and renamed **Wexfordian**; wrecked 29 February 1936 on Dogger Bank, off Wexford coast.
Sir Edward Bacon	1912–1913	483	Built by Irvine Shipbuilding & Engineering Co. Ltd., Irvine, 1899 as **Birker Force** for W S Kennaugh & Co., Whitehaven; sold 1912 to John Bacon Ltd. and renamed **Sir Edward Bacon**; 1913 to Powell, Bacon & Hough Lines Ltd.; sold 1914 to J Bennetts & Co., Penzance and renamed **Pivoc**; sold 1919 to Holman Coal & Shipping Co. Ltd., Penzance; beached and abandoned on 22 January 1922 near Rouen after striking a submerged object, on passage Rouen to Swansea.
Sir Walter Bacon	1913	919	Built by George Brown & Co., Greenock; 1913 to Powell, Bacon & Hough Lines Ltd. and renamed **Gloucester Coast**; 1917 owner renamed Coast Lines Ltd.; sold 1936 to Bristol Steam Navigation Co. Ltd. and renamed **Alecto**; sank 2 May 1937 off North Hinder Lightship, Ostend, after collision with Yugoslavian steamer **Plavnik**, on passage Swansea to Rotterdam.

3) Hough and associate companies

Thomas McClune & Frederick Augustus Tamplin, Frederick Augustus Tamplin & Company and Pennington & Company, Pennington & Hough, Samuel Hough & Company, S Hough, R G Hough (executor), Annie Hough Steamship Company Limited and Samuel Hough Limited

Name	Hough Service	Gross tons	Comments
Loire	1854-1858	469	Built by Thomas Vernon & Son, Liverpool, 1854 as *Loire* for Thomas Vernon & Sons, McClune & Tamplin, and McLarty & Co., Liverpool; sold 1855 to McClune & Tamplin and others; sold 1857 to Frederick A Tamplin and others; wrecked 27 January 1858 on East Hoyle Bank, Wirral, on passage Liverpool to London.
Empress Eugenie	1855-1861	582	Built by Rennie, Johnson & Rankin, Liverpool, 1855 as *Princess Eugenie* for McClune & Tamplin and others; sold 1857 to Frederick A Tamplin and others; foundered 25 January 1861 30 miles north of Great Orme, Llandudno, on passage Liverpool to London.
Genova	1858-1868	484	Built by Alexander Denny, Dumbarton, 1850 as *Genova* for Anglo-Italian Steam Navigation Co., Glasgow; sold 1856 to Archibald Sword and others, Glasgow; sold 1858 to Frederick A Tamplin and others, including Samuel Hough from 1860 onwards; sold 1864 to Charles B Harrington and others (including Samuel Hough); wrecked 16 January 1868 at St Michael's.
Rose	1859-1861	565	Built by George Lunnel & Co., Bristol, 1842 as *Rose* for Bristol General Steam Navigation Co., Bristol; sold 1855 to John Tulloch, Dumbarton, resold to John Robinson, Stockton-on-Tees, and resold again to James N Holmes, Bristol; sold 1856 to James N Holmes and Frederick A Tamplin, Bristol; sold 1858 to Peter Leicester, London; sold 1859 to Frederick A Tamplin, Liverpool; sold 1861 to John Smurthwaite, Sunderland and converted to sailing ship; lost at sea 27 November 1862.
Young England	1860-1862	39	Built at Willington Quay, Newcastle, 1860 as wooden tender *Young England* for Frederick A Tamplin, Liverpool; sold 1862 to Michael S Crealock, Aberystwyth; wrecked 30 September 1862 off Aberystwyth Bar.
Liverpool	1862-1863	621	Built by Marshall Brothers, Willington Quay, Newcastle, 1862 as *Liverpool* for Frederick A Tamplin and Caleb D Watson; sank 6 January 1863 off Point Lynas, Anglesey, following collision with barque *La Plata*, on passage London to Liverpool.

Name	Hough Service	Gross tons	Comments
East Anglian	1863-1868	395	Built by J W Hoby & Co., Renfrew, 1854 as *East Anglian* for Philip Smith, Lynn; sold 1855 to Philip Smith and others; sold 1857 to John Johnson, London; lengthened 1860 by 30 feet; sold 1863 to Frederick A Tamplin and others, Liverpool; sold 1864 to William Pennington and Samuel Hough; sold 1867 to Samuel Hough; foundered 14 January 1868 south west of Lundy Island, on passage Porthcawl to Plymouth.
Edith	1865-1878	615	Built by Thomas R Oswald & Co., Pallion, Co. Durham, 1861 as *Edith* for Christopher Webster and others, including Samuel Hough from 1865 onwards; sold 1877 to Samuel Hough; sold 1878 to Thomas R Oswald, Southampton and resold to Theodore Edwards, Liverpool; sold 1880 to Charles H Pile, London; sold 1881 to Edith Steamship Co. Ltd., Cardiff; sank 26 August 1883 off Brest following collision with steamship *Dordogne*, on passage Swansea to Charente.
West of England	1866-1878	609	Built by Bowdler, Chaffer & Co., Seacombe, 1866 as *West of England* for Pennington & Hough, Liverpool; sold 1867 to Samuel Hough & Co., Liverpool; sold 1878 to R Irvine & Co., West Hartlepool; foundered 15 September 1880 about 130 miles west of Pointe du Raz, Brittany, on passage *Villa Real* to Liverpool.
South of England	1875-1876	815	Built by R Irvine & Co., West Hartlepool; wrecked 2 July 1876 on Hats and Barrels Rocks, Milford Haven.
Mary Hough	1876-1904	869	Built by Löbnitz Coulborn & Co., Renfrew, 1876 for Samuel Hough and to Samuel Hough & Co.; 1877; re-engined 1891; 1902 to R G Hough (executor), Liverpool; 1904 transferred to Samuel Hough Ltd., Liverpool; wrecked 27 June 1904 at Brandies, near Cape Ray, Newfoundland, on passage from Port aux Basques to Port St George, Newfoundland, with general cargo.
Edith Hough	1878-1899	759	Built by Bowdler, Chaffer & Co., Seacombe, 1869 as *Zakynthos* for W Glynn & Sons, Liverpool; sold 1878 to Samuel Hough and renamed *Edith Hough*; re-engined 1884; grounded and sank 2 February 1899 at Oran, Algeria, on passage Swansea to Oran.
Maggie Warrington/ Mary Hough	1878-1912	896	Built by R Irvine & Co., West Hartlepool, 1878 as *Maggie Warrington* for Samuel Hough and sold to Samuel Hough & Co.; 1902 to R G Hough (executor) and then to Annie Hough Steamship Co. Ltd., Liverpool; 1911 renamed *Mary Hough*; sold 1912 to T Stone & Co., Liverpool and renamed *Gwladmena*; sunk 2 January 1918 in collision with the steamer *Flora* in Brae Wick Bay, Shetland, on passage from Methil, Fife, to Lerwick with coal.
Baidar	1888-1897	1,003	Built by Humphrys & Pearson, Hull, 1871 as *Baidar* for W N Smith & Co., Hull; sold 1881 to John W Smith and others, Hull; sold 1884 to Davis, Gillies and others, Hull; sold 1888 to Samuel Hough, Liverpool; wrecked 29 November 1897 on the Banjaard Rock, Brouwershaven, on passage Rotterdam to Dunkirk in ballast.

Name	Hough Service	Gross Tons	Comments
El Dorado	1893-1903	1,290	Built by T & W Smith, North Shields, 1882 as *El Dorado* for Scrutton Sons & Co., El Dorado Steamship Co. Ltd., London; sold 1893 to Samuel Hough; 1902 to R G Hough (executor); sold 1903 to Paul Hopf, London; wrecked 31 August 1902 off Fort George, Hudson's Bay, on passage Liverpool to James Bay with coal and general cargo.
Melrose/ Annie Hough	1894-1902	839	Built by Robert Steele & Co., Greenock, 1877 as *Melrose* for Donald Currie & Co. (launched as *Maritzburg*); sold 1894 to S Hough; 1897 renamed *Annie Hough*; 1898 transferred to Annie Hough Steamship Co. Ltd.; 1902 sold to Bermond, (Hector-Hee) et Cie., Bordeaux, 1903 and renamed *Emyrne*, then transferred to Bermond et Cie.; sold 1906 to Moinard & Rouxel, Diego Suarez, Madagascar; wrecked 12 May 1911 on Diego Island, north east of Diego Suarez, on passage under tow from Diego Suarez to Majunga with cargo of salt.
Maggie Hough	1898-1910	1,545	Built by T & W Smith, North Shields, 1884 as *Nonpareil* for Scrutton, Sons & Co., (Nonpareil Steamship Co. Ltd.), London; sold to Samuel Hough 1898 and renamed *Maggie Hough*; 1902 transferred to R G Hough (executor); 1904 to Samuel Hough Ltd.; sold 1910 to Turkish buyers; sold 1911 to I Stark, Trieste and renamed *Carmen Sylva*; sold 1911 to Bank of Mytilini, Istanbul, and renamed *Polis Mitylini*; sold 1913 to M Gumucgdjian, Istanbul, and renamed *Zonguldak*; sunk by torpedo 10 August 1915 off Zonguldak, on passage Zonguldak to Istanbul with coal.
Annie Hough	1904-1913	1,110	Built by John Scott & Co., Kinghorn, Fife, 1900 as *Delta* for Bailey & Leetham, Hull; acquired 1903 by Thos. Wilson Sons & Co. Ltd., Hull; sold 1904 to Samuel Hough Ltd. and renamed *Annie Hough*; 1912 transferred to Annie Hough Steamship Co. Ltd.; 1913 to Powell, Bacon & Hough Lines Ltd.; 1914 renamed *Lancashire Coast*; 1917 owner renamed Coast Lines Ltd.; sold 1919 to Roberts, Brining & Co., Liverpool and renamed *Arwyco*; sold 1927 to Trafford Steamship Co. Ltd., London; sold 1929 to General Navigation Co. (of Canada) Ltd., Vancouver; sold 1935 to Lisardo Garcia, Porto Cortes, Honduras, resold to Alfredo Garcia and renamed *Corisco*; sold 1941 to A Garcia & Compania Ltda., Havana, Cuba and renamed *Corinto*; scrapped 1950.
Samuel Hough	1905-1913	1,832	Built by Grangemouth & Greenock Dockyard Co., Grangemouth; sold 1913 to Burns Philp & Co. Ltd., Sydney and renamed *Marsina*; sold 1932 to J Patrick & Co. Ltd., Sydney and renamed *Craigend*; sold 1937 to Wah Shang Steamship Co. Ltd., Shanghai, and resold to Yih Zeu Fong, Shanghai, and renamed *Haiping*; foundered off Double Island Point, Queensland, 15 March 1937, on passage Sydney, New South Wales, to Rabaul and Shanghai with coal.
Dorothy Hough	1911-1913	1,872	Built by Grangemouth & Greenock Dockyard Co. Ltd., Grangemouth; 1913 to Powell, Bacon & Hough Lines Ltd. and renamed *Southern Coast*; 1917 owner renamed Coast Lines Ltd.; sold 1936 to Falkland Islands Co. Ltd., London and renamed *Lafonia*; sunk 26 March 1943 in collision with steamship *Como*, near Coquet Island, Northumberland, on passage London to Greenock.

See F H Powell & Co. list for: *Cornish Coast, Sussex Coast, Dorset Coast, Graceful, Hopeful* and *Hampshire Coast.*

4)	Powell, Bacon & Hough Lines Ltd.

Acquired from F H Powell & Company in 1913 (see above):

Powerful	1913-1919	renamed *Eastern Coast* 1913
*Cornish Coast**	1913-1915	
Faithful	1913-1919	renamed *Monmouth Coast* 1913
Sussex Coast/Truthful	1913-1916	renamed *Wirral Coast* 1913
*Dorset Coast**	1913-1916	
*Graceful/Devon Coast**	1913-1934	
*Hopeful/Norfolk Coast**	1913-1918	
*Hampshire Coast**	1913-1915 and 1915-1937	
Graceful	1913-1917	renamed *Somerset Coast* 1913
Hopeful	1913-1915	renamed *Western Coast* 1913

*Registered owner previously F H Powell & Company and Samuel Hough Limited

Acquired from John Bacon Ltd in 1913 (see above):

Edith	1913-1916	
Prestonian/Sir George Bacon	1913-1917	renamed *Gower Coast* 1913
Pennar	1913-1948	
Enniscorthy	1913-1916	
Harfat	1913-1939	
Sir Roger Bacon	1913-1939	renamed *Pembroke Coast* 1913
Sir Edward Bacon	1913-1916	
Sir Walter Bacon	1913-1936	renamed *Gloucester Coast* 1913

Acquired from Samuel Hough Ltd. in 1913 (see above):

| *Annie Hough* | 1913-1919 | renamed *Lancashire Coast* in 1914 |
| *Dorothy Hough* | 1913-1936 | renamed *Southern Coast* in 1913 |

120

Name	P, B & H/CL Service	Gross tons	Comments
West Flandria	1913-1916	97	Built at Willebroek, Belgium, 1904 as Belgian-owned barge **West Flandria**, equipped with petrol engine; sold 1913 to Powell, Bacon & Hough Lines Ltd.; sold 1916 to the Board of Trade, later Ministry of Shipping.
Stonehenge	1913-1916	732	Built by S P Austin & Hunter, Sunderland, 1876 as **Fenton** for Milnes & Chaytor, London; sold 1891 to Earl of Durham; sold 1896 to Lambton Collieries Ltd.; sold 1902 to Isaac W Laing and then Isaac W Laing and Francis D Laing; 1904 ownership reverted to Isaac W Laing on death of partner; sold 1911 to Kempock Steamship Co. Ltd., Glasgow, and resold to Henry W Page, Liverpool; 1913 renamed **Stonehenge**; sold 1913 to Powell, Bacon & Hough Lines Ltd.; sold 1916 to Harold Harrison & Edward T Lindley, London and resold to Stonehenge Steamship Co. Ltd., London; sold 1917 to John Harrison Ltd., London (H Harrison Shipping Ltd.); sold 1922 to John Harrison Ltd., London and resold to MacNab, Rougier & Co. (Italy) Ltd., London; sold 1923 to Ganlobis Ltd., London and resold to A Giuffrida di C. Catania, Italy, and renamed **Adone**; wrecked 6 March 1932 near Pozzallo, on passage Crotone to Licata.
Suffolk Coast	1913-1916	780	Built by W Harkess & Son Ltd., Middlesbrough; captured and scuttled by German U Boat, 7 November 1916 off Cap Barfleur, on passage from Glasgow to Fécamp.
Northern Coast	1914-1920	1,189	Built by Sir Raylton Dixon & Co. Ltd., Middlesbrough; 1917 owner renamed Coast Lines Ltd.; 1920 to British & Irish Steam Packet Co. Ltd., renamed **Lady Martin**; 1936 to British & Irish Steam Packet Co. (1936) Ltd.; sold 1938 to A/S Eestis Laevandus, Tallinn, Estonia, and renamed **Pearu**; seized in June 1940 by Russia and renamed **Vodnik**; lost 14 August 1941 near Prangli Island probably in German air attack, on passage Kronstadt to Tallin.
Irish Coast	1915-1916	603	Built by Murdoch & Murray, Port Glasgow, 1904 as **Rosslyn** for Rosslyn Steamship Co. Ltd., Glasgow; sold 1915 to Powell, Bacon & Hough Lines Ltd., and renamed **Irish Coast**; sold 1916 to Associated Portland Cement Manufacturers (1900) Ltd., London and renamed **Landport**; sold 1917 to Albert Chester, Middlesbrough; sold under mortgage 1923 to Iona Shipping Co., Ltd., Newcastle; sank 9 December 1925 following collision off Flamborough Head, on passage Newcastle to Portsmouth.
Welsh Coast	1915-1920	1,070	Built by Charles Hill & Sons, Bristol; 1917 owner renamed Coast Lines Ltd.; 1920 to City of Cork Steam Packet Co. Ltd. and renamed **Macroom**; 1922 to Coast Lines Ltd., name reverted to **Welsh Coast**; sold 1936 to Monroe Brothers Ltd., Liverpool and renamed **Kyleglen**, later transferred to Kyle Shipping Co. Ltd., Liverpool; sold 1937 to Bristol Steam Navigation Co. Ltd., Bristol, and renamed **Melito**; sold 1950 to Fairwood Shipping & Trading Co. Ltd., Swansea, and renamed **Fairwood Oak**; sold 1955 to Holderness Steamship Co. Ltd., Hull, and renamed **Holdervale**; scrapped 1957.
Wexford Coast	1915-1920	423	Built by J Fullerton & Co., Paisley; 1917 owner renamed Coast Lines Ltd.; 1920 to City of Cork Steam Packet Co. Ltd. and renamed **Blarney**; 1930 to Coast Lines Ltd., and renamed **Pentland Coast**; sold 1934 to John S Monks Ltd., Liverpool, and renamed **Coastville**; aground off Bangor, County Down 21 November 1940, on passage Bangor to Liverpool, refloated and scrapped.

Name	P, B & H/CL Service	Gross tons	Comments
Kentish Coast	1915-1928	758	Built by Dundee Shipbuilding Co. Ltd 1908 as *La Flandre* for Cie. D'Armament des Flandres, Bruges; 1915 sold to Mann, MacNeill & Steeves and renamed *Hinderton*; 1915 sold to Powell, Bacon and Hough Lines Ltd. and renamed *Kentish Coast*; 1917 owner renamed Coast Lines Ltd.; aground 18 November 1928 off Plymouth, salvaged and scrapped.
Western Coast	1916-1917	1,394	Built by Dublin Dockyard Co., Dublin; 1917 owner renamed Coast Lines Ltd.; sunk by torpedo 17 November 1917 off Eddystone Light, on passage Portsmouth to Barry Roads.
Suffolk Coast	1917-1938	870	Built by W Harkess & Son Ltd., Middlesbrough; 1917 owner renamed Coast Lines Ltd.; 1918 commissioned as Q Ship; 1919 returned to owners; sold 1938 to Kyle Shipping Co. Ltd (Monroe Brothers Ltd) Liverpool; 1939 renamed *Kylebank* and later sold to Consolidated Fisheries Ltd., Grimsby and renamed *East Anglian*; sold 1940 to George W Grace & Co. Ltd., London, and renamed *Sussex Oak*; 1951 to Grace and Chancellor Ltd., Lowestoft; sold 1954 to Holderness Steamship Co., Ltd., Hull and resold for breaking up.

REFERENCES

Armstrong, John 1997.	Management response in British coastal shipping companies to railway competition. The Northern Mariner, Vol. 7, No. 1, pp17-28.
Auten, Harold 2003.	Q Boat Adventures. Periscope Publishing Ltd., Reading
Chandler, George 1960.	Liverpool Shipping, A Short History. Phoenix House, London.
Farr, Graham E. 1967.	West Country Passenger Steamers (3rd ed.). T Stephenson & Sons, Prescot.
HMSO 1919.	British vessels lost at sea 1914-1918. HMSO, London.
Lewis, Samuel 1837.	Topographical Dictionary of Ireland. Samuel Lewis & Company, London.
McNeill, David 1971.	Irish Passenger Steamship Services, Volume 2, South of Ireland. David & Charles, Newton Abbott.
McRonald, Malcolm 2005.	The Irish Boats, Volume 1, Liverpool to Dublin. Tempus Publishing Ltd., Stroud.
McRonald, Malcolm 2006.	The Irish Boats, Volume 2, Liverpool to Cork and Waterford. Tempus Publishing Ltd., Stroud.
Moss, Michael 2004.	Read, Sir Alfred Henry (1871–1955). In: Oxford Dictionary of National Biography, Oxford University Press, Oxford.
Robins N S 2011.	Coastal Passenger Liners of the British Isles. Seaforth Publishing, Barnsley.
Robins, Nick & Tucker, Colin 2015.	Coast Lines Key Ancestors: M Langlands & Sons. Bernard McCall, Portishead.
Smyth, Hazel P 1984.	The B&I Line: A History of the British and Irish Steam Packet Company. Gill and Macmillan, Dublin.
Wayne, Charles 1999.	Coastal and Short Sea Liners. Waine Research Publications, Albrighton.

F H Powell & Company: The *Devon Coast* (1909) was launched as *Graceful* and renamed in 1910. She is seen in Latchford Locks on the Manchester Ship Canal.

The *Hampshire Coast* (1911) was typical of the big engines aft coasters developed by F H Powell & Company before the Great War.

John Bacon Limited: The *Sir Roger Bacon* (1912) became the *Pembroke Coast* in 1913 when she passed to Powell, Bacon & Hough Lines Limited and later to Coast Lines Limited.

One of the many passenger ships acquired by Coast Lines Limited was Laird Line's *Olive* (1893)   *[DP World]*

Samuel Hough Limited: *Samuel Hough* (1905), seen in the Mersey.

[from an oil painting by Nick Robins]

The *Dorothy Hough* (1911) was renamed *Southern Coast* by Powell; Bacon & Hough Lines Limited and maintained the London passenger service until she was sold in 1936.

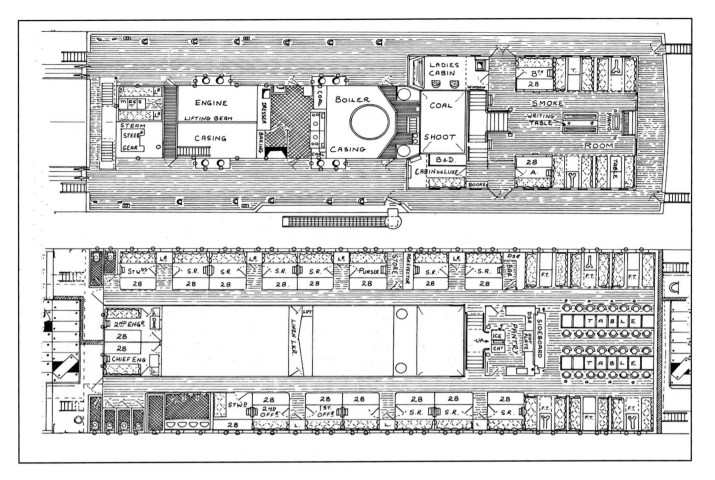

Cabin plans and public rooms aboard the *Dorothy Hough* (1911).

Powell Bacon & Hough: The *Welsh Coast* (1915) was built under licence for Powell, Bacon & Hough Lines Limited by Charles Hill & Sons of Bristol during the Great War. She is seen here in the Avon minus the white chevron on the funnel while on charter to the Bristol Steam Navigation Company Limited, whose houseflag is flying at the mainmast.

The *Wexford Coast* (1915) became the *Coastville* in 1934, as seen here, when she was sold out of Coast Lines' ownership to John S Monks Limited of Liverpool.

The *Suffolk Coast* (1917), one time Q Ship, finally working as intended as a coastal cargo steamer.